# BEFORE THE STARS

# BEFORE THE STARS

*Early Major League Hockey and*
*the St. Paul Athletic Club Team*

ROGER A. GODIN

MINNESOTA HISTORICAL SOCIETY PRESS

www.mnhs.org/mhspress

The Minnesota Historical Society Press is a member of the Association of American University Presses.

Manufactured in the United States of America

10 9 8 7 6 5 4 3 2 1

A small portion of chapter 1 and all of chapter 2 originally appeared in "On the Trail of the McNaughton (sic) Cup: The 1915–16 St. Paul Athletic Club Team," *The Hockey Research Journal* vol. V, no. 1 (Fall 2001).

The "State of Hockey" is a trademark registered and owned by the Minnesota Wild.

♾ The paper used in this publication meets the minimum requirements of the American National Standard for Information Sciences—Permanence for Printed Library Materials, ANSI Z39.48–1984.

International Standard Book Number
0–87351–476–9 (cloth)

**Library of Congress
Cataloging-in-Publication Data**

Godin, Roger A., 1938–
   Before the stars : early major league hockey and the St. Paul Athletic Club Team /
   Roger A. Godin.
      p.   cm.
   Includes bibliographical references and index.
      ISBN 0-87351-476-9 (cloth : alk. paper)
         1.   Saint Paul Athletic Club Hockey Team
              (Saint Paul, Minn.)
         2.   Hockey—Minnesota—Saint Paul—History.
         I.   Title.
GV848.S33G63 2005
797.962'09776'591—dc22                    2004013868

In memory of Frank "Moose" Goheen
and his teammates on the St. Paul Athletic Club team.
If not for them, there might not have been a "State of Hockey."

"Those were the days when everybody
took their best dates to the Hip, rode a 10-cent fare,
ate a beef dinner for a buck and saw Moose Goheen
dump enemies into the fifth row for a 75-cent ticket."

Dimensions, *a Northern States Power (NSP) newsletter, 1974*

# BEFORE THE STARS

# *Preface*

The St. Paul Athletic Club Hockey Team occupies a unique niche in the sports history of Minnesota and the nation. At a time when the National Hockey League (NHL) had not yet established an American presence, St. Paul played successfully at the highest level in the United States and achieved that success largely, but not exclusively, with players from the United States. Their opponents, with the odd exception, were teams composed of Canadians. I argue that the AC's, as I will call them, played at a major league level and were pioneers in establishing what the Minnesota Wild of the NHL have so aptly called the "State of Hockey."

The AC's, also referred to as the Saints and the Apostles, were led by the St. Paul–born, White Bear Lake–raised Frank "Moose" Goheen, a player roughly contemporary to the great Hobey Baker. A more aggressive player than Baker and nearly equal to his legendary status, Goheen was only the second player from the United States elected to the Hockey Hall of Fame in Toronto when selected after Baker in 1952. Other Minnesotans on the team over the years were Tony Conroy and his brother George, Ed Fitzgerald, Emmy Garrett, Everett McGowan, George Nichols, Vern Peterson, and Cy Weidenborner. They were joined by Nick Kahler and Clarence "Taffy" Abel, natives of Michigan's

Upper Peninsula. Goaltender Ray Bonney and defenseman Denny Breen were both born in the United States but apparently raised in Canada.

Noteworthy Canadians were George Clark, Herb Drury, Babe Elliott, Joe McCormick, Bert Mohan, Wilfred Peltier, Jeff Quesnelle, and "Duke" Wellington. Both Drury and McCormick were naturalized citizens who, with Goheen, Tony Conroy, Fitzgerald, Weidenborner, and Bonney, were members of the 1920 United States Olympic Team. At the time of the Olympics, Drury and McCormick, as well as Bonney, played for Pittsburgh. Goheen was a charter enshrinee of the United States Hockey Hall of Fame in 1973, and Tony Conroy was elected two years later.

As a team, the AC's captured the MacNaughton Cup in 1916 and shared it with the "Canadian Soo," from Sault Ste. Marie, Ontario, in 1920. The MacNaughton Cup, now competed for by members of the Western Collegiate Hockey Association, was originally established to honor the winner of the American Amateur Hockey Association (AAHA) title, a senior league located in the Upper Midwest. ("MacNaughton" is the correct spelling. Newspapers of the day tended to drop the "a" and the error continues to this day.) With the AAHA's demise in 1920, a new, truly national league was formed called the United States Amateur Hockey Association (USAHA). Teams were located in the hockey-playing areas of the United States and competed for the Fellowes Cup. In 1922 and 1923, St. Paul advanced to the national finals against two different Boston-based teams but came up short both times. The arrival of the professional NHL in the United States in 1924 meant the end of major league amateur hockey and the great run of the AC's. By 1926, professional hockey had put its roots down, and St. Paul became a member of the minor league American Hockey Association.

Despite the achievements of the St. Paul Athletic Club and its players, writers on Minnesota sports have largely chosen to relegate them to the dustbin of history. *Sports Illustrated*, certainly regarded as an icon of sports journalism, chose to ignore Frank Goheen in its listing of the fifty greatest athletes from the state. And one Twin Cities newspaper placed Goheen a distant 59th on its list of the "Top 100" most important Minnesota sports figures of the century. The other daily did not view him important enough to be one of their seven icons of state sports when they created an athletic equivalent to the famous Americans carved on Mount Rushmore in South Dakota. When reams of media copy were generated on hockey as a result of St. Paul's hosting the NHL All-Star Game in 2004, Goheen was mentioned by only one writer and viewed as unworthy, although he was considered, for the first or second All-Time Teams selected by a local panel. Considering Goheen's early election to the Hockey Hall of Fame in Toronto, his exclusion is difficult to comprehend. The public should understand that the sport's origins in Minnesota predate the period just before World War II.

It is my objective in this book to remedy this dismissal of early hockey excellence and to give the AC's, and especially Goheen, along with his teammates, their just due. My dedication says it most succinctly, but it merits repeating: the State of Hockey began with these men.

Research for the book comes largely from the daily newspapers of the time, primarily the *St. Paul Pioneer Press, St. Paul Dispatch,* and, to a lesser extent, the long-defunct *St. Paul Daily News.* By the time I started research on the project in 2001, all of the principals were long deceased, as were many of the next of kin. Of the latter, those that I contacted, while certainly interested in what I was doing, could add little to what was already known. An exception was Beverly Goheen, Frank's daughter-in-law, who allowed me access to a scrapbook maintained by the family. Bob Dill, Jr., similarly permitted me to review a scrapbook on the great MacNaughton Cup–run of the AC's in 1915–16, which had been left to him by the late hockey historian Don Clark. Others providing assistance were Don Clark's son, Tom; Steve Hardy; Paul Kitchen; Don MacEachern; Mary Jo Murray; Tom Sersha; and Ernie Fitzsimmons. Ernie, president of the Society for International Hockey Research (SIHR), of which I am a proud member, was particularly helpful in providing information on the personnel of the Boston Westminsters and the Boston Athletic Association, St. Paul's opponents in the 1922 and 1923 national finals. He was always willing to take time out from his busy day to assist. I am particularly grateful to my boss with the Minnesota Wild, executive vice president Matt Majka, who was always supportive of my efforts. Special thanks to Greg Britton, director of the Minnesota Historical Society Press, who realized that the press from the State of Hockey could use a hockey book, and to my editor, Pam McClanahan, who was always a joy to work with on this project. My work colleague Ron Ramirez was always willing to assist me with my numerous computer problems.

A word about Appendix B. I have reconstituted the rosters of the AC's and statistics from the available newspaper sources. As far as I can determine, comprehensive stats have never previously been done. I suspect the game summaries of the day may be inaccurate as far as the awarding of assists and penalties. Nonetheless, I have chosen to accept them at face value rather than attempt to recompile them by a time-consuming search of the game narratives. Penalty minutes were frequently difficult to determine, so I have elected to simply go with total penalties.

Readers may note that there is no foreword to this book. I had spoken with the late Herb Brooks about doing that honor and he had indicated he would consider the possibility once the manuscript was complete. More than any other Minnesota hockey figure, Coach Brooks was well aware of the AC's. His father had known a number of these men, and their deeds had filtered down to young Herb. His tragic death in August 2003 took away the best foreword writer this author could ever have hoped to have. There was simply no one else left to fill that void. I can only hope he would have been pleased with the effort.

During my time as director of the United States Hockey Hall of Fame, I had the privilege of meeting both Frank Goheen and Tony Conroy. I did not fully realize the impact of their contributions to hockey in the United States and Minnesota at the time. It is my fervent wish that this effort portrays their contributions, as well as those of their teammates, in a way that helps establish their proper place in the history of the sport in the State of Hockey and in the nation at large.

*Roger A. Godin*
*St. Paul, Minnesota*

# BEFORE THE STARS

# St. Paul at the Time of the AC's

The St. Paul Athletic Club's time in early major league hockey included parts of two decades that saw the tumultuous events of World War I and what the Minneapolis Star and Tribune book, *Bring Warm Clothes: Letters and Photos from Minnesota's Past*, describes as "the Jazz Age, the era of the flapper, the speakeasy and crazy fads. Industrialization increased rapidly. Lumbering petered out. Organized crime moved into the state. Women were given the right to vote" (Meier 1981, 261).

Added to that list should be the birth of modern media, with the advent of radio broadcasting, as well as the rise of the automobile and subsequent decline of the streetcar. In 1920, the halfway mark of the run of the AC's, the city of St. Paul had a population of 234,698. That population had seen manufacturing go from a value of $30 million in 1900 to $150 million in 1919. This growth continued during the 1920s, in industries such as printing and publishing, railroad car construction and repair, signs and advertising novelties, butter, bread and bakery products, clothing and fur, electrical machinery, beverages, and planing mill products.

The population found employment in these industries while largely living in single-family homes. Slightly more than 75 percent of city residents lived in these structures, while only 1.4 percent resided in apartment buildings. By 1920 most housing was served by sewer systems, but outhouses were still common. Gas lamps had given way to electric lights, and appliances such as refrigerators, irons, fans, and vacuum cleaners began to make their appearance.

Prohibition, the outlawing of the consumption of alcoholic beverages, became the law of the land in 1920 as a result of efforts initiated by Minnesota congressman Andrew Volstead. Prohibition spawned speakeasies, illegal taverns, and the fun and games that went with them. Dance halls thrived, as such dances as the Charleston and that new music from down South, jazz, took hold. The tamer elements of the population contented themselves with using the city's growing parks system and viewing silent motion pictures and spectator sports. The St. Paul Saints baseball team was competitive in the minor league American Association (AA), playing in the Junior World Series in 1920, 1922, and 1924. This series featured the winner of the AA against that of the International League. St. Paul won the 1924 event over Baltimore, five games to four.

St. Paul carries an Irish identity, though the Irish were, in fact, a distant fourth in the city's ethnic makeup—behind Germans, Scandinavians, and the descendants of early Americans from principally New England. But, as Mary Lehert Wingerd wrote in her book, *Claiming the City: Politics, Faith, and the Power of Place in St. Paul*: "What the Irish lacked in numbers they more than made up for with a political savvy that utilized ethnicity in complicated ways" (106).

One place where the Irish did not lack the numbers was on the St. Paul Athletic Club hockey team. A look at the names on the roster indicates the mark they made on the "State of Hockey."

# 1

# 1914-1915

## *Rising from the Phoenix*

"One of the strongest hockey teams in the United States for St. Paul."

*from the St. Paul Athletic Club booster slogan, November 30, 1914*

The last decade of the nineteenth century has been referred to as the "Gaslight Era" and the "Gay 90s," but in the world of ice sports in Minnesota it marked the transition from ice polo to ice hockey. Ice polo was played by teams of six or seven players who used short, curved sticks to propel a ball into a goal cage somewhat smaller than that used in present-day soccer.

The hockey of this time in North America is best described in Jeff Klein and Karl-Eric Reif's *The Hockey Compendium: NHL Facts, Stats, and Stories* (2001, 8):

Hockey was a seven-man game—the three forwards, somewhat as we still know the positions, although to a much greater extent kept in land-bound patterns; a rover, who had more latitude to freelance; the point and cover-point positions, whose responsibilities were confined almost exclusively to defense and who would evolve into the more modern defense pairings; and the goaltender, who used an ordinary narrow stick and was forbidden to drop to the ice to make saves . . . Hockey was

*Ice skating at Como Park, 1895. Ice sports were popular in Minnesota during the "Gay 90s."*

*People of all ages were interested in the new sport of hockey.*

still an "onside game"—no forward passing was allowed . . . Games were played in 30-minute halves. Rinks, some barely half the size of today's standard, often had boards less than a foot high [and] featured natural ice . . . Players, including the goaltenders, took to the ice with the skimpiest of padding—cane shinpads were still in vogue for most players, cricket-style leg pads for goalies, and even hockey gloves were only a recent introduction. And teams rarely comprised more than eight men—the seven regulars, who played the entire [game], and a substitute.

Games were officiated by one referee and two goal umpires (judges) who stood directly behind the net. When a goal was scored, the umpire would raise a white flag and collect the puck, and play would resume. Penalties could be of varying durations of one, two, three, or five minutes, without the later distinctions of minor and major.

At this time, ice polo was played extensively in the state, but twenty-one-year-old St. Paul resident Ed Murphy was not impressed. He had seen hockey in Canada, and to his mind, this was the wave of the future. While the state's first recorded game is generally regarded to be an 11–3 rout of the University of Minnesota by the Winnipeg Victorias on February 18, 1895, in Minneapolis, Murphy had, in fact, organized a St. Paul team a year earlier. While that team's games are lost to history, a tournament played at the Aurora Rink, at Dale and University, on January 24–25, 1896, is not. As part of the St. Paul Winter Carnival, two teams from St. Paul and one each from Minneapolis and Winnipeg squared off. The two St. Paul teams lost their opening round games, setting up a Winnipeg-Minneapolis final, which was won by the Canadians, 7–3.

The sport continued to develop in the Capital City, and just before the turn of the century, a new St. Paul team was formed and a trip east was planned. The intent was to play squads in New York, Philadelphia, and Washington during the 1898–99 season, but the venture was cancelled when not enough players and insufficient practice time proved to be insurmountable obstacles. By the following season, several senior teams had been formed, most notably the St. Paul Athletic Club (not to be confused with this book's subject), the St. Paul Hockey Club, and the Virginias. The St. Paul Hockey Club joined Mechanic Arts High School and two Minneapolis teams in a 1900–1901 league that would lead to the formation of the Twin Cities Hockey League (TCHL) the next year. In a meeting at St. Paul's Clarendon Hotel on January 17, 1902, five St. Paul–based teams—the previously mentioned Hockey Club and Mechanic Arts High School were joined by Central High School, the Mascots, and the Virginias—along with Minneapolis formed the Twin Cities

in the Twin Cities, Duluth, and northwestern Minnesota. Soon after the start of the league's first season, Minneapolis dropped out, and the Virginias went on to capture what would be their only league title. Over the circuit's nine-year history, the Victorias would win five Dunbar Cups from 1903 to 1907, the Mic Macs would triumph in 1908, and the Phoenix would prevail the last two years.

Following the league's first season in 1902, apparently flushed with the success of winning the Dunbar Cup, the Virginias ventured to Houghton in Michigan's Upper Peninsula to meet Portage Lake. This was two years before John "Doc" Gibson would launch the world's first professional league, the International, a venture that would last three years before succumbing to upwardly spiraling player salaries.

*1903 view of St. Paul, looking southeast from the Kittson House (now the location of the St. Paul Cathedral)*

Hockey League. Curler Robert Dunbar donated a trophy in his name to be presented to the yearly champion.

The league's composition would change over the next decade to include, among others, such St. Paul teams as the Mic Macs, the Phoenix, and the Victorias. This league would prove to be a significant player in establishing the sport in the state; at this time hockey was concentrated

Portage Lake was Houghton's team, named after the nearby lake, and would become a power in that league. The team was quite competitive in 1902 and would blitz the Virginias 11–2 and win again in St. Paul by a more modest 2–0. Tending goal in both games for the St. Paul team was Joe "Chief" Jones, who kept the first game from being even more of a blowout than it was and turned in quite a competitive performance back

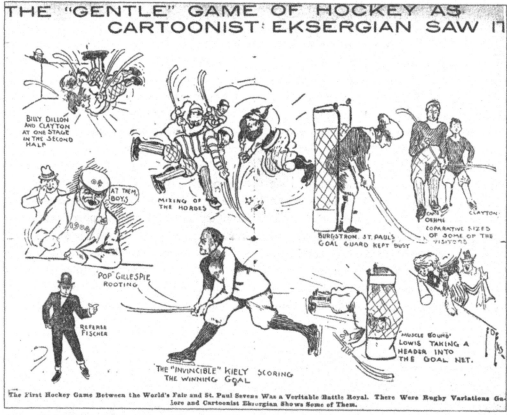

*A 1904* St. Paul Dispatch *cartoon replays St. Paul's participation in the 1904 World's Fair hockey tournament.*

home. His work impressed the visitors enough that they lured him to Michigan to play there the following year.

During the 1904 St. Louis World's Fair, popularized in the Hollywood film and Broadway play *Meet Me in St. Louis,* an All-Star team from St. Paul competed against teams from the host city and Michigan. That same year, and continuing in 1905, 1906, 1908, and 1910, the Twin Cities Hockey League champion played off against either Duluth or Two Harbors to determine a state Senior Champion. Once again, St. Paul teams dominated as the Victorias won the first three years and the Phoenix in 1910. The Duluth Northerns broke the pattern when they defeated the Mic Macs in 1908.

Among the outstanding St. Paul players who participated during this first decade were Ray Armstrong, Bert and Harry Clayton, Charles Driscoll, Ed Fitzgerald, John Foley, Joe Jones, Art Larkin, Leo Leonard, Harvey McNair, Fred Minser, Jack Ordway, Port Palmer, Vern Peterson, Walter Seeger, and Jack Taylor. Of these, Fitzgerald and Peterson would go on to the Athletic Club team, with Fitzgerald being the most notable. A premier defenseman (the position was known as point and cover point until 1920) of his time, "Fitz" would also play on the 1920 United States Olympic Team and coach the AC's in the 1920s.

With the demise of the TCHL, the sport went into decline in the state's capital. It would take the creation of a new athletic organization and the vision of two men from Duluth to bring the game back and, in fact, to raise it to major-league status in this pre-professional era.

## The Birth of Major League Hockey in Minnesota

The St. Paul Athletic Club was the brainchild of promoter Charles H. Genslinger. Something of an enigma, Genslinger came to St. Paul in late 1912 after helping establish similar clubs in Illinois, Missouri, and Pennsylvania. Such clubs provided athletic facilities that for the times offered what today's health clubs offer for the improvement of one's physical fitness. Beyond that, however, there was a social aspect that provided such amenities as dining rooms, residential rooms, and periodic special events such as dances and banquets. The clubs also sponsored team athletic competitions in various sports. In addition to the hockey team that inspired this book, there were also teams in such sports as basketball, indoor baseball, and swimming. Well into 1913, Genslinger had succeeded in convincing a group of leading citizens to form a local club, and some $55,000 had been raised to get the organization off the ground. Oscar L. Taylor was named the club's first president in November 1913, and money was subsequently raised to allow construction of a permanent clubhouse at the corner of 4th and Cedar Streets. Excavation of this site began in December 1916, and construction began the following year. In the meantime the club rented temporary quarters from the Minnesota Club, now the home of the National Hockey League (NHL) Minnesota Wild.

Professional hockey had made its North American debut in Michigan's Upper Peninsula in 1904 through the International Hockey League (which lasted until 1907), but the players described in this book were officially amateur. Records of the Athletic Club reflect reimbursement for expenses only, though it is not unreasonable to assume that these could have been embellished on a player-to-player basis. Most would have graduated from high school and were still unmarried. Among the core players for the AC's, Frank Goheen graduated from White Bear Lake High School and Tony Conroy and Ed Fitzgerald were products of St. Paul Mechanic Arts High School. Goheen and Conroy attended Valparaiso University in Indiana and the College of St. Thomas in St. Paul, respectively.

Enter Ray Johns, an Indiana native who had been transported to Duluth at an early age. Johns had played a role in both amateur hockey and baseball in the Zenith City, as Duluth was also known, starting in 1906. He had assembled the

*Frank Goheen, circa 1912*

*White Bear Lake senior team, circa 1910–13. Frank Goheen is at far right.*

Duluth Northerns, who had defeated the Mic Macs in 1908 for the state Senior title. The following year he organized the Amateur Hockey Association of Duluth and followed that by creating a similar organization for baseball. Looking for new worlds to conquer, Johns came south to St. Paul in 1913 and within a year had founded an amateur baseball organization for his new hometown. Now it was time for hockey, and the Athletic Club would be his vehicle for success, with Nick Kahler, a genuine American star from Dollar Bay, Michigan, leading the way. The *St. Paul Pioneer Press*, December 1, 1914, announced the new team:

> "One of the strongest hockey teams in the United States for St. Paul." Such was the slogan adopted at a meeting of enthusiastic boosters of the spectacular Canadian game at Eurkhard's last night ... The St. Paul team will be coached by Nick Kahler, last year's center of the speedy Duluth septet. He is regarded [as] one of the greatest players in the game, fast, daring, a crack shot and a wonder on teamwork. As a forward at Duluth last winter, he was in the limelight continually.

The article went on to name potential players. Among them were those who would form the American core of the team for the next twelve years: Ed Fitzgerald, Frank Goheen, Tony Conroy, and Cy Weidenborner. Conroy would recall an early practice of prospective players in an interview with Dick Cullum of the *Minneapolis Tribune*, October 19, 1975:

Nick Kahler ... and Ray Johns ... called a meeting of "anybody interested in hockey." I was just a kid off the Mechanic Arts High School team, but I reported. There were a lot of candidates. Moose [Goheen] came in from White Bear and the older guys gave him a bad time. I went down there and asked if I could get in on the action on Moose's side. We got to be friends. We played and roomed together through our entire careers.

St. Paul was invited to join the American Amateur Hockey Association (AAHA), but the decision was made to pursue an independent schedule, "this being the first attempt at the game here in years," as the *Pioneer Press*, December 1, 1914, reported. Kahler had arrived in St. Paul on November 30 and a week later began nightly runs, starting from the Wilder baths (near the present day Xcel Energy Center). Conroy's recollections probably come from December 13, when the player/coach ran his first on-ice workout at the outdoor Hollows rink. (The exact location of this surface is not known, but it should not be confused with the Swedes Hollow area.) Following the session, Kahler pronounced himself satisfied, but more hard work lay ahead.

Practice shifted indoors to the huge ice surface at the Hippodrome located on the state fairgrounds near Snelling and Como avenues. The Hippodrome had been built in 1906 by the Minnesota State Fair Board for livestock judging, and a natural ice surface of 270 feet by 119 feet was added in 1911. Kahler held his first workout there on December 17 after arrangements had been made with manager Gale Brooks. The facility had a seating capacity of sixty-seven hundred but was unheated—reserved and box seat holders could go to a warming room during intermissions. It would be the principal home arena for the AC's during their 1914–26 period as a major league amateur hockey team, except for the 1919–20 season.

Indoor practices continued on a nearly nightly basis, with Kahler expressing satisfaction at

various times during the week leading up to and after Christmas. Such comments as "I am more than pleased with the work of the candidates so far and feel confident that the team will be a winner" and "when I began playing with the Duluth hockey team, it didn't begin to look near as good as the St. Paul city squad looks now" were made to the *Pioneer Press* (December 20 and 22, 1914).

There was periodic press speculation about what kind of schedule manager Ray Johns was lining up for the team. Finally, on December 27, it was announced that the home opener for the AC's would be on January 5, 1915, against the Minneapolis ABC's. However, before that, Johns and Kahler took the team to Duluth for a personal homecoming game on New Year's Day. Making the trip besides Kahler would be Tony Conroy, Ed Fitzgerald, Frank Goheen, George Henderson, Le Claire, Leo McCourt, Vern Peterson, and Cy Weidenborner. All were Americans except Henderson and McCourt, who hailed from Fort William, Ontario, and Saskatoon, Saskatchewan, respectively.

The new team would be facing a veteran championship club in Duluth, one led by Joe Linder, a Houghton, Michigan, native. In 1941, *Esquire* magazine wrote of him: "Any list of the 30 best hockey players the whole world has had, would have to include the American born Linder." Tony Conroy described him to Dick Cullum in the 1975 interview as "a great one, a big, raw-boned ruffian who knew every trick." Conroy was delighted that Kahler had decided to take him to Duluth. He told Cullum: "Nick gave me a lot of encouragement. He'd say, 'nice going, kid; keep it up.' When he read the names of players who would go to Duluth for our first official game I was surprised to be on the list. He told me I had to play left wing and check Jack Mahan, a famous player. I held him scoreless. After that I was a regular" (*Minneapolis Tribune*, October 19, 1975).

Well, a regular, yes—but holding Mahan scoreless, not quite. After Kahler got the game's first goal at the twenty-minute mark, Bert Mohan quickly tied it for Duluth, which was soon followed by two Jack Mahan goals to put the locals up 3–1 at the intermission. Mahan would get two more in the second half, while his teammates added three others to welcome St. Paul into big-time competition with an 8–1 pasting. Considering the score, the *Pioneer Press*, January 2, 1915, was quite generous in its game story: "Captain Kahler's St. Paul men played a beautiful game, but lacked the teamwork in the punches. In the first half, they more than held their own, sweeping down the ice in a great burst of speed. Barkell of Duluth . . . sailed into the visitor's defense at a terrific pace, striking Weidenborner over the head and cutting a large gash open."

Back home, Kahler similarly put the best spin on things, claiming that St. Paul was the superior skating team and that Duluth's success was based on better overall conditioning (they had played an earlier game). There was a lack of teamwork, but that would improve with practice, and Weidenborner's injury had left him in a daze. As today, officials came in for their usual abuse. At one point, Kahler held up play and threatened to pull his team off the ice over some perceived injustice.

Weidenborner, known popularly as "Squel," would be sufficiently recovered from his injury to start the home opener against the septet from the Minneapolis ABC's on January 5. Prior to that game the Athletic Club's secretary, W. D. Jenkins, had sent a letter to the membership describing the coming season:

This will advise you that the St. Paul Athletic Club has taken its initial step in the development of amateur sports, through the formation of the St. Paul Athletic Club Hockey Team, which will represent the St. Paul Athletic Club, and the City of St. Paul. Games will be played not only in this city but in other large cities and with the visiting teams from other large cities here; the first game to be played with the Minneapolis City Team, January 4th [5th] in St. Paul.

Mr. Ray C. Johns is manager of the team and we trust you will give him all the encouragement and support possible. It is planned to play from six to ten games at the Hippodrome in this city. Season tickets costing $5.00 entitling the holder to two box seats for each game may be obtained from Mr. Johns at Telephone Cedar 1205 or from the Secretary at the Club office.

### The Home Debut

A large crowd, paying 25 cents for general admission and 50 cents for reserved seats (according to the *St. Paul Pioneer Press*, January 6, 1915), was on hand for the 8:15 P.M. opener. The AC's came away with their first-ever win. The St. Paul paper credited the soft ice and "the better condition of the locals and . . . superior teamwork . . . [for assisting] materially in the outcome." Kahler and Goheen scored in the first half, while Peterson, Conroy, and Fitzgerald made the final score 5–0 with goals after the break. Weidenborner got the

shutout, though that term was yet to join the lexicon of the sport.

Ray Johns had been at work developing a challenging schedule, and he succeeded in bringing in Portage Lake from Houghton, Michigan. While the glory years of Doc Gibson's entry in the International League were now past, the Upper Peninsula team was still potent. They had won the Western Section of the AAHA in 1912–13 with a strictly local lineup, which featured goaltender Carlos "Cub" Haug. Haug would fill in at goal for the AC's three years later, but on January 11 he would be beaten three times as the AC's got their first victory over a big-time opponent.

Three days earlier, Johns had signed Jimmy Owens, former Duluth right wing, and the acquisition proved quite timely. Owens got the first goal two and a half minutes into the game, on a pass from Goheen, while the latter made it 2–0 at the half on a pass from Henderson. Portage Lake closed to 2–1 early in the second half, but Kahler closed it out at 3–1 on a scramble in front of the net. It had been an impressive showing against a veteran team, and Haug gave them their due. He told the *Pioneer Press*, January 12,

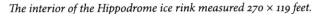

*The interior of the Hippodrome ice rink measured 270 × 119 feet.*

1915, that St. Paul's speed, coupled with the large Hippodrome ice surface, would make them competitive against any team. The Athletic Club's bulletin proudly proclaimed to the membership: "The visitors were out-played, out guessed, out skated. All our boys distinguished themselves."

The AC's would be more than competitive against the Grand Forks Flickertails on January 19, crushing the visitors 13–0. Grand Forks was a highly touted team composed principally of Canadian players, but once Kahler opened the first half scoring, the rout was on. He would add two more, while Goheen and Peterson would also contribute hat tricks. It was not all good news, as George Henderson broke his wrist and would be replaced briefly by Chester Stroud from Calumet, Michigan. Absent from the St. Paul lineup was the promising Jimmy Owens, who had left the team to pursue studies at Syracuse University.

Stroud proved to be an immediate success as he scored St. Paul's first goal against Port Arthur, Ontario, on January 25 before two thousand Hippodrome fans. When play began in the second half with the score tied at 1–1, Port Arthur's goaltender Bell was sent off for two minutes for repeatedly kneeling in front of his net, a practice not then permitted by the rules. Under those rules he had to serve his own penalty, and Nick Kahler quickly seized the moment, going around wing Le Hereaux, who was back covering, to score the winning goal.

The new team had now won four in a row, with two of the wins coming over well-established teams. The club bulletin was justifiably proud: "The third sensational victory in three weeks came to the hockey team . . . when the local players met the fast Port Arthur team . . . and defeated it by the score of 2–1 . . . The game was one of the most sensational seen here in recent years . . . A large number of members of the club were present to join in the cheering which was maintained practically every moment the puck was in play."

As quickly as Stroud had arrived, he de-parted, to be replaced by Larry Brennan from Pembroke, Ontario. Brennan arrived in time to participate in Kahler's January 28 practice. The other town from the Thunder Bay region, Fort William, was next on the schedule for the AC's. Supposedly better than their Port Arthur neighbors, they arrived after losing two games in Duluth and would leave with another loss. Ray Johns had anticipated a larger crowd for the February 1 game, as advance sales were good, but his four thousand estimate for the crowd was eight hundred short.

The crowd would see Brennan start as fast as Owens and Stroud before him, when he too scored St. Paul's first goal just before the half. Goheen quickly added another, and the locals led 2–0. In addition to inserting Brennan into the lineup, Kahler had to make other adjustments— Vern Peterson had become ill. St. Paul native John Dellinger, who had officiated some earlier games, took his place at cover point, and Ed Fitzgerald moved to point. George Henderson was still out. Dellinger quickly made his mark in the second half, with a shot following a rink-length dash that eluded Port Arthur goalie Bernie McTeigue, who would later make his way to Eveleth in the 1920s. Conroy and Kahler got two more goals, before Port Arthur ruined Weidenborner's shutout bid with three goals in the last seven minutes, to make the final score 5–3.

Brennan had made an impressive debut. The February 2, 1915, *Pioneer Press* described him as "a magnificent stick handler, a wonderful skater, and a finished back checker." Unlike his predecessors, he would finish the season with the team and be joined in the lineup by another Pembroke native, Oliver Landirault, when Duluth visited the AC's on February 8. The game was touted as "the biggest local game of the season . . . the winner [of which] will be the champion team of the Northwest," according to the *Pioneer Press* (February 7, 1915). This was a mythical concept, since St. Paul was an independent and Duluth was competing in the AAHA.

Duluth came to the capital with the same

team that had welcomed the AC's to the big time on New Year's Day. But that was then and this was now, and Johns oozed confidence, telling the *Pioneer Press* on February 8, 1915:

> We expect the largest crowd that ever witnessed a hockey game in the Northwest. Our boys feel they can win, but are not overconfident for they know the [mettle] of the men they will meet.
>
> The fans can be assured that former delays in handling the crowd will he done away with tonight. New entrances have been arranged at the rink and there will be no handicaps. The street car service will also be better.

It would be the season's best crowd, with estimates running from 4,750 to 5,000, including a small Duluth contingent. The spectators would witness a classic "barn burner," which went Duluth's way within the game's first three minutes. Duluth native Ainni Olson made it 1–0 for his hometown team, and it would end that way at the half as Weidenborner turned away all comers. After the break, Kahler evened the score when he picked up a loose puck at center ice. The *Pioneer Press* best described the action and aftermath from that point on (February 9, 1915):

> A lunge, a beautiful exhibition of squirming and stick handling and the St. Paul captain dashed through the Zenith City defense. Sweeping past the visitors' goal at breakneck speed, he took one wild peg. It was true as a die, and St. Paul had knotted the score.
>
> For the next five minutes the battle was truly a desperate affair ... The pace was terrific, but the invaders' veteran aggregation failed to come through in the pinch.

It was Kahler who came through in the pinch midway through the second half when, trailing Goheen, he picked up his pass and went

in to score as the Duluth defense was drawn to Goheen. The *St. Paul Dispatch* (February 9, 1915) observed that "it seemed as if the roof of the massive structure [Hippodrome] would be forced high into the air, so deafening was the demonstration." The 2–1 lead held, for the AC's sixth victory, and as events played out, it would be the season's high-water mark.

The game had been intense and marked by penalties—so intense that when Duluth cover point Nick Bogan was sent off the ice, he swung at the timekeeper. Subdued by two policemen, he was—amazingly—not thrown out of the game.

Ray Johns was ecstatic. The following day, February 9, 1915, he told the *Dispatch:*

> Show me a better hockey town in the United States ... When it is considered that hockey has been dead here for so long, it is truly remarkable. I don't believe that a bigger crowd ever gathered to see an amateur hockey game in the United States, unless it was in New York, but surely last night's crowd was the biggest that ever saw a game in the Western part of the United States.

Crowd control had been improved with more entrances to the building, and an announcer was outside, presumably with a megaphone, advising as to the most convenient entryway. When the game was over, the large doors at the east and west ends of the building were opened to allow for a speeder and safer exit.

### Is Hobey Baker Coming to Town?

The wake of the victory over Duluth produced hopes for even better things in the future. The February 10, 1915, *Pioneer Press* reported that Hobey Baker, the Princeton wonder, then skating for the St. Nicholas club in the AAHL, might be coming to St. Paul: "This interesting bit of information was made public by Captain Nick Kahler of the St. Paul septet last night. Kahler says he has been reliably informed that Baker has accepted a position with a local bonding company and that he will arrive here in the summer."

Interesting it might have been, and the fact that Baker was working on Wall Street would appear to give the report some credence, but it never happened. Baker was the first player from the United States selected by the Toronto-based Hockey Hall of Fame, and Frank Goheen of the AC's would be the second, causing one to contemplate what might have happened if they had become teammates. Baker was only 5 feet 9 inches tall and weighed 160 pounds. He was a superb finesse player. He was, in effect, the "American Gretzky" before there was a Gretzky. Goheen was 6 feet tall, weighed 220 pounds, and played a far more physical game. Baker was rarely penalized, and Goheen received more than his share. The two of them together would have been as awesome a combination as were Gretzky and Mark Messier of the Edmonton Oiler teams of the 1980s.

Ray Johns was off to Cleveland to attend amateur baseball meetings, but before he left he announced a two-game series with the Aberdeens of Ottawa for February 15 and 16. The strong Aberdeens were on a western tour, and their lineup included George Boucher, who would become an early NHL star and also find his way into the Toronto Hall of Fame. The series would prove costly in terms of injuries, but it started well enough when Kahler gave St. Paul the early lead, only to have the Ottawa seven take a 2–1 lead at the half. After Hillman made it 3–1 for the visitors, play was delayed for three minutes when Vern Peterson of the AC's received a bloody nose. He was able to continue to play, but not so fortunate was Goheen, who left the game with a broken collarbone when he fell after being checked near his own goal. The injury would not only end Goheen's season but would seriously affect how the schedule would play out. Under the rules of the day, the Aberdeens dropped one player when Goheen left the game,

but that didn't stop them from getting another goal and a 4–1 win.

The twenty-three hundred fans had seen a talented team with "much heavier players than the St. Paul midgets and quite as fast," as the *Pioneer Press* on February 16, 1915, put it. They would see more of the same the next night, when Boucher got three of his squad's six goals and the Ottawa team took the second game 6–2. St. Paul had trailed only 2–0 at the half, but it was 4–0 before Kahler got the first tally for the AC's, at 12 minutes and 52 seconds into the second session. It mattered little, as the Aberdeens scored twice more, although Kahler got another just before the end. Weidenborner had played well in goal, and if not for him the final might have been worse. Landirault had taken Goheen's place on left wing. Press reports to the contrary, the loss had been one sided, but Ray Johns would always see the glass half full. He told the *Pioneer Press* on February 17, 1915: "I am well pleased with the showing the boys made, especially in tonight's game. There is nothing to be ashamed of. Indeed not. The teamwork was much better than that displayed Monday night and the goal guarding of little Weidenborner was marvelous. We are going to Duluth with blood in our eyes next Monday, and we will give the outfit at the Head of the Lakes the hardest battle they have ever had."

Kahler conducted evening workouts leading up to the team's departure for Duluth on the Sunday prior to the February 22 game. While the loss of Goheen for the second Ottawa game was significant, Landirault was thought to be able to hold his own. Kahler added Canadians Roddie Smith, a right wing, and cover point Joe Simpson to the roster.

The game was sold out, and this included 125 tickets provided for St. Paul. Fans who purchased them boarded special cars provided by the Great Northern and Northern Pacific Railroads on Monday afternoon for the five-and-a-half-hour trip north. The game would be only the second away contest for the AC's, and like most other ice surfaces, the Duluth Curling Club was considerably smaller than the Hippodrome. This would be cited as a reason for the team's worst showing of the year, but the loss of both Kahler and Peterson early on would be of greater impact. Within the game's first six minutes, Duluth scored three times before Landirault countered to make it 3–1. Shortly thereafter, Kahler was tripped and slid into the side of the rink, injuring his ankle. Carried off the rink, he was soon followed by Peterson, who wound up with the left side of his face torn and his nose reinjured. If this was intimidation, 1915-style, it worked. Duluth scored three more times, to lead 6–1 at the half. They added five more in the second half, for an 11–1 rout. Amazingly, Joe Linder was held scoreless but picked up six minutes in penalties.

Ray Johns thought there should have been more penalties and put the blame on Duluth for providing only one official. It was at that time the practice to provide a second official, called a "judge of play," actually an assistant referee. Despite Johns's protest, referee F. Crassweller was left to handle things alone. Johns vowed never to return to Duluth, but he was back there the following December playing a second-level team as the AC's took Duluth's place in the AAHA.

On March 1, the Athletic Club Bulletin picked up on Johns's distaste over the Duluth game in a brief piece called "Our Boys at Duluth": "All honor to members of the St. Paul Athletic club hockey team! They went to Duluth to play hockey, and play hockey they did, despite the efforts of their opponents to turn the game into an Indian massacre. Our boys played a clean game straight through and their defeat, because they refused to stoop to the tactics of the Duluth bruisers, was the most honorable kind of a victory."

With five players now out with injuries—Goheen, Henderson, Kahler, Peterson, and Smith—Johns was forced to turn down games with Canadian teams, effectively ending the season. The plight of the injured was graphically illustrated when the *Pioneer Press* ran a picture on March 7, 1915, of Kahler on crutches and Henderson with his left arm in a sling.

The medical expenses of the injured were such that it was decided to stage a benefit match on their behalf on March 8. The remnants of the AC's, Brennan, Conroy, Fitzgerald, and Weidenborner, would be joined by "Brownie" Romans, who had played at St. Paul Central, and two other local players. They would be opposed by a collection of former college players called the University Club. Normally such a team would have been no match for the AC's, but on this night they lost 3–2. Brennan and Conroy scored for St. Paul. The loss and the late rash of injuries put a damper on what had been a promising start, but the *Pioneer Press*, in a season-end profile on Ray Johns, prophetically concluded: "There's another winter coming, however, before many moons, and Duluth (as well as others I would add) hockey-ists would be well to keep it in mind" (April 4, 1915).

# 2

# 1915-1916

## Taking Home the MacNaughton Cup

"St. Paul won the cup fair and square and by real hockey ability."

The Evening News, *Sault Ste. Marie, March 4, 1916*

The place to play major league hockey in the United States in the first two decades of the twentieth century was either the American Amateur Hockey League (AAHL) in the East, with Cleveland and Pittsburgh in the lower Midwest, or the previously mentioned AAHA in the upper Midwest. While the AC's were playing their independent schedule in 1914–15, three teams from Michigan's Upper Peninsula—Calumet, Portage Lake, and Sault Ste. Marie—were competing in the AAHA along with Duluth. The teams played for the MacNaughton Cup, a trophy with a two-thousand-dollar prize donated by mining executive James MacNaughton. At this time in Canada, teams from the professional National Hockey Association and Pacific Coast Hockey Association were competing for the Stanley Cup, whose origins go back to 1893. When Duluth with Joe Linder and company dropped out of the competition for 1915–16, Ray Johns quickly volunteered the St. Paul Athletic Club as their replacement.

The AC's were admitted to the AAHA on December 13, 1915, in a league meeting at Marquette, Michigan. The twelve-game regular season would get under way on January 10, 1916, in St. Paul. But first came the task of organiz-

ing the team for the new season and playing two exhibition games. Nick Kahler would he back, along with the Minnesota base of Conroy, Fitzgerald, Goheen, and Weidenborner. Weidenborner would not be "the man" in goal this year. Ray Bonney would assume that role. Bonney was born in Phoenix, New York, near Syracuse, but developed as a player in Canada. Canadians Bill Adams of Fort William, Ontario, and Bert Mohan of Midland, Ontario, who had been with Duluth the prior year, would start the season with the team. The addition of these key imports, as well as those who would join as the season wore on, gave St. Paul an opportunity to be competitive in their first year in the league.

Kahler held his first practice outdoors at Lake Como on December 12 before moving indoors to the giant Hippodrome ice surface the following evening. Captain Kahler was hopeful that St. Paul native Homer Sweeney, who had captained Yale's team and was actually mentioned in the same breath with Hobey Baker, might make the team. But Sweeney would play only one exhibition game before his job took him away from St. Paul. Other candidates who would not make the team were holdover George Henderson and Bob Flanagan of Fort William, Ontario.

*An early 1900s postcard view of the entrance to Como Park*

Johns had scheduled an exhibition game against Duluth in St. Paul for December 27 and was optimistic that another could be played against either a Winnipeg or a Fort William team before the regular season began. Kahler handled the team for the Duluth game before a crowd of fifteen hundred. The locals won easily 7–2 on goals by Conroy (two), Adams, Fitzgerald, Goheen, Henderson, and the captain himself. A local newspaper cautioned its readers not to be too optimistic this early: "Considering the short time for practice the team work of [the] St. Paul seven was excellent, although Capt. Nick Kahler and his crew have [a] considerable . . . task before them to be in trim by the time the league season opens."

As events unfolded, it would not be Kahler who would have to be the primary molder of the team. Johns had been in touch with Hugh "Dad" Gawley, the Canadian coach, who had most recently been living in the Port Arthur/Fort William, Ontario, area. Gawley was a veteran player and coach but had been retired for two years. Now he would face a new challenge as Johns tapped him to lead St. Paul. Gawley had arrived in time to see the Duluth game, but rover

Bert Mohan was still en route. Within a day or two of the exhibition game, the Athletic Club hosted the team at a turkey dinner, and soon after Gawley instituted twice-daily practices.

Mohan arrived in St. Paul on January 4, but two other expected players, Am Whalen and Alex Wellington from Port Arthur, would not be there for the opener. The team played an intrasquad game on January 5 as part of "Women's Suffragist Night," and "Dad" continued his intense workouts. He was of the opinion, on taking over, that the team had individual stars but that teamwork was lacking. Over the two-week period leading up to the first game, Gawley made progress in that direction. He decided to put Mohan at center and let Kahler be the rover. Bonney, who had split the Duluth game with Weidenborner, would open in goal. Adams and Fitzgerald would be at point and cover point (defensemen). Conroy and Goheen would be at right and left wing, respectively.

The Hippodrome had ample seating, but only two thousand fans were on hand for the curtain raiser of the January 10–11 series with Portage Lake. Somewhat belatedly, on January 8, the chairman of the Athletic Committee, C. K.

*Ed Fitzgerald, premier defenseman and later manager-coach of the St. Paul Athletic Club team*

Blandin, had put out a form letter to the membership urging the sale of box seats on the north side of the rink:

> Last winter the St. Paul Athletic Club Hockey team was a great success and put St. Paul on the "hockey map." The team this year gives even greater promise . . . and will furnish many evenings of exciting sport with the best teams in the country . . . [I]t devolves upon the Athletic Club to sell the boxes. There are forty of them. Ten are already sold. Each box contains six seats and there are at least eight games. The price is $25.00 per box for the season, or 40 cents per seat per game. If you cannot use one entire box, divide it with a friend, but lend your support to this game, which is growing in popularity and building up fame for the Athletic Club.

Despite this appeal and more direct streetcar service to the rink, below-zero weather kept the expected capacity crowd down. The boxes on the north side of the rink were taken by members of the Athletic Club. St. Paul's opponent,

Portage Lake, was described by the *St. Paul Daily News* (January 9, 1916):

> Monette . . . is one of the best goal guards. Trathen, Cullman and Hogan, the three defense men, have played together for years and excel in teamwork. Briden . . . comes from Salisbury, Ont., and is said to be one of the best forwards in Canadian amateur circles. Bailey is a Port Arthur graduate and [Sicotte] ranks as one of the most skillful right wings on this side of the boundary line. Coughlin and Coutu are fast skaters and clever stickhandlers.

Briden, Coughlin, and Coutu would ultimately find their way into the soon-to-be-established NHL, (Billy) Coutu most notably with the Montreal Canadiens of the 1920s. In *The Trail of the Stanley Cup* (1966), Charles Coleman would describe Coutu as "one of the roughest defense men."

During the first half, the lighting system failed and play was held up for about four minutes. Once action resumed, Mohan got St. Paul's first goal, and just before intermission Kahler made it 2–0 on a rebound. Portage Lake drew to within one early in the second half as Coughlin also got a rebound goal. The score held until very late in the game, when Goheen netted his first on a pass from Fitzgerald and then assisted on Conroy's goal to make the final 4–1. Much of the credit for victory went to Bonney, who had played a particularly strong first half.

By the time the puck was dropped for game two the following night, both Whalen and Wellington had arrived and would see action. Less than a thousand fans were on hand for the second game. The visitors took a 1–0 lead at the seven-minute mark of the first half. Briden stick-handled his way out of a center ice scrum and passed to Sicotte, who beat Bonney. After the intermission, Bailey scored from Cullman, Sicotte, and Trathen for what today would be a natural hat trick. Down 4–0, St. Paul rallied on

*Poster announcing the AC's first game in their pursuit of the MacNaughton Cup as a member of the American Amateur Hockey Association.*

goals by Wellington and Mohan, but that was as close as they would get.

The season-opening split was viewed as somewhat less than satisfying, and Gawley was given wider authority than was previously assumed by the public. "Dad" was still not pleased with the club's teamwork and devoted a stiff workout to sending the forwards up and down the ice practicing short passes. He decided to sit out Nick Kahler from the team's exhibition game against Port Arthur on January 17 and use Bert Mohan at rover. Kahler had still not recovered from a foot injury suffered the prior season, and it hampered his skating.

Gawley had coached Port Arthur in earlier times, but if there was a desire to show up the old coach in his new role, it was severely lacking. Despite being leaders of the Thunder Bay League, the visitors were hammered 7–0 before approximately 1,250 fans. St. Paul led 5–0 at the half and wound up with the victory on a hat trick by Mohan, two goals by Conroy, and single tallies by

Adams and Wellington. (The term "hat trick" actually did not come into common usage until the late 1930s.) The crowd was treated to a between-halves skating exhibition by James McGeever and music from the Athletic Club's own drum and bugle corps. The local press was understandably pleased with the win, and the January 18, 1916, *St. Paul Pioneer Press* commented:

> The St. Paul Athletic Club hockey team came to life last night . . . and showed how the game should be played . . . all the other goals [six] were notched as a result of team play in which not less than three forwards took part. This is as it should be and it shows that Coach Gawley is beginning to achieve the results for which he has been striving . . . Individually the A.C. team is composed of stars; when they play together they should be unbeatable in the company in which they are playing.

*The St. Paul Athletic Club Drum Corp*

## On the Road (Mostly)
## in Michigan's Upper Peninsula

The team now readied for its first road trip, leaving St. Paul on Sunday night, January 23, for games in Calumet and Sault Ste. Marie. It would be a long train ride to Michigan's Upper Peninsula, approximately eighteen hours to Calumet and then another nine to American Soo. There was some question as to whether Bill Adams would make the trip—he had come down with bronchitis—but he was cleared to go. He would have the opportunity to play against his brother Jack, later to gain fame with the Detroit Red Wings. Jack Adams played right wing for Calumet, which was led by former Duluth players Joe Linder at point, Jack Mahan at left wing, Russ Barkell at center, and Nicholson in goal. Murray was at cover point and "Scoop" Skinner was the rover.

The rinks at Calumet and Sault Ste. Marie were much smaller than the large Hippodrome surface, and this was thought to handicap St. Paul in the first game of each series. This may have been a factor on January 24 when Calumet triumphed 1–0. Johns wired back to St. Paul:

Last night's game was a heartbreaker. It was anybody's game all the way. The ice was very soft and it was impossible for either team to do any passing. The boys made friends last night by trying to play clean hockey. The same cannot be said for Calumet. Jack Adams laid out Mohan with his stick in the first half, and Skinner tried the same thing in the second half . . . We kept Nicholson busy in the first half. Fitzgerald and [Bill] Adams showed great form . . . Goheen out-played Jack Adams all the way and his body checking was great. Wellington, Mohan and Conroy played hard games but could not get together on the soft ice . . . It is colder today and we should have good ice.

*Frank "Moose" Goheen at 21*

Gawley put Nick Kahler back in the lineup the following night, and Am Whalen rejoined the team. Those moves and better ice seemed to help St. Paul as they left Calumet with a split. The game was scoreless in the first half, but the locals took a 1–0 lead early in the second, as Skinner raced the length of the rink, went around Mohan, and then put the puck behind

Bonney. A first-half Calumet goal had been disallowed by goal umpire R. Kahler (yes, brother of the St. Paul captain) and resulted in the umpire's removal. In today's context it is difficult to imagine someone so close to either team being placed in such a position.

About two-thirds into the second half, Frank Goheen tied the game for St. Paul on a rink-length dash to match Skinner's. Then, with three minutes to go in the game, Kahler picked up Mohan's rebound, following a face-off close to the Calumet goal, and got the game winner. The team left immediately after the 2–1 victory for Sault Ste. Marie in order to practice on January 26 for games on the next two nights. Sault Ste. Marie, better known as American Soo, were the defending MacNaughton Cup co-champions and held the early league lead.

American Soo was captained by Hugh "Muzz" Murray, who would later become only the second American to play for the Stanley Cup, when he was with Seattle of the Pacific Coast Hockey Association. Tallion, described by the *St. Paul Daily News* on January 28, 1916, as "one of the greatest in the United States," was in goal. At point was Cliff Elliot, paired with Murray at counter point, while Maine-born Levi Godin was the rover. Coutu was at center with W. Wilson and Ray Thompsett at right and left wings, respectively. Both games were expected to draw capacity crowds, including fans from Sault Ste. Marie, Ontario (Canadian Soo), for whom special train service had been established.

The teams traded goals in the first half, with Goheen and "Duke" Wellington scoring for St. Paul and Thompsett and Murray for the home side. There were more disputed goals and the resulting replacement of goal judges, but the visitors broke the tie in the second half on goals from Whalen and Mohan. Ray Bonney was injured in this half when struck on the head by a

Soo stick. He was carried from the ice, but the injury was minor and he resumed play as the visitors went on to a 4–2 victory. The local paper, the *Evening News*, on January 28, 1916, was suitably impressed by St. Paul's play:

> It was expected that in the small rink that the local team plays on, the visitors would be at sea, and that a victory was a foregone conclusion.
>
> But, to the surprise of every local player and fan, the A.C. team played like firebrands from the tap of the bell … The Canadian stars on the Soo team could hardly believe that two of the St. Paul players who distinguished themselves last night, Fitzgerald and Goheen, are home products, having learned their hockey in St. Paul. Conroy, who did not play last night, is said to be as good as either of the other two.

Back home, the *St. Paul Daily News* on January 28, 1916, reported that the victory was received with "wild enthusiasm" as the club secretary read a wire from the Soo with the results. The St. Paul Winter Carnival was on and the club was filled with revelers, who would not celebrate the next evening as the team suffered what would be their worst defeat of the regular season. American Soo scored five goals in the first half and two in the second en route to a 7–2 victory. St. Paul managed to play the home team even in the second half on

*The blanket toss at the winter carnival*

goals by Wellington and Mohan, but the Soo lead was too great to overcome.

The teams were scheduled to resume their rivalry in St. Paul on February 3 and 4 in the midst of the winter carnival. The carnival's King Boreas and his court, as well as numerous costumed fans and members of marching clubs, were expected to be on hand. Nonetheless, Johns was quick to point out in the *St. Paul Dispatch* on February 2, 1916, that many good seats remained. American Soo had followed up their victory over St. Paul with a sweep of Calumet before heading for the Minnesota

*The Sherman Hotel on Sibley Street in St. Paul*

capital. These two victories solidified their hold on first place with a 5–2–1 record, followed by the Athletic Club at 3–3–0, Portage Lake at 2–3–1, and Calumet at 3–5–0.

The Sherman Hotel was the hockey hotbed in St. Paul. It was where the Soo would stay, along with teams from Two Harbors, St. Croix Falls, and Duluth, who were playing in a carnival-related tournament. The Soo team arrived there about midnight on Wednesday, February 2, which precluded any workout on the big rink until the morning of the first game. The day before, Gawley had split his squad, with some players involved in a game with the Minneapolis Athletic Club while others practiced at the "Hipp." Both teams knew the series was critical in their quest for the MacNaughton Cup and were confident of a sweep. A. L. Ferguson, Soo manager, told the *Dispatch* on February 3, 1916:

> Our team should not lose another game this season. The boys have struck their stride now, and I doubt if there is an amateur team anywhere in the United States or Canada that can hold them. It is true we will be handicapped on your large rink . . . but even that won't stop us.

"Dad" was just as optimistic and countered:

> The Soo team isn't the only one that is playing regular hockey by any means. Our boys are faster skaters than the Soo bunch and they are playing as well together as the other fellows. Our defense is a hard one for any attack to penetrate and I am expecting the Soo to lose both games here.

While Ray Johns was looking for a sellout, he didn't get it. Some four thousand fans did turn out to see the locals draw within a half game of first place. In the first half, Ed Fitzgerald and "Muzz" Murray collided, with the former coming out of it with a wrenched ankle. He finished the half and expected to be replaced for the second, only to have the visitors object. The matter was settled by both teams playing with six skaters each in the second half, after Fitzgerald suffered another injury. Soon after Fitzgerald's return, St. Paul scored when Wellington picked up Whalen's rebound and beat Tallion.

The Athletic Club's marching band performed on the ice between the halves, and when play resumed, the home team frequently found themselves playing shorthanded as Wellington was penalized three times. The club killed off the penalties, and Bonney kept the puck out of the net to get his first shutout at 1–0. The score

*Ray Bonney was the AC's prime goaltender
in the 1915–16 season.*

got his second goal on a dash from mid-rink. Like the previous evening, most of the second half was also played with six skaters a side. Thompsett's skate was broken, and now it was St. Paul's turn to deny a replacement. Gawley pulled Conroy off the ice, and Bonney went on to collect another shutout at 2–0. "Dad" had made good on his prediction of a sweep—St. Paul was now in first place.

The league leaders were in a commanding position. They were scheduled to play Portage Lake in Houghton on February 7 and 8 and then come home to host Calumet on February 14 and 15 in the final games of the regular season. A sweep of these four games would give St. Paul undisputed possession of the MacNaughton Cup, even if American Soo won its remaining three games. If the regular season ended in a tie for first place, a play-off series would then take place to determine the cup holder.

The team left at 4:30 P.M. on February 6 for Northern Michigan, but Ed Fitzgerald had not recovered sufficiently to make the trip. The Houghton rink was slightly smaller than the one at Calumet but larger than the one at the Soo. Despite having to continually make adjustments from their big playing surface, Gawley expected no difficulties. He predicted another sweep— and St. Paul's first-half play seemed to point in that direction. Wellington picked up a hat trick. With a comfortable edge, the league leaders sat back and let the home team come at them after the intermission. Bailey, the Portage Lake center, scored twice for the green and white within a two-minute time frame early in the second half. But the locals couldn't get the tying goal, and St. Paul notched the 3–2 victory. Johns described the action in a wire back home:

might have been higher, but Kahler failed to finish on more than one occasion.

No doubt that resulted in Gawley sitting the Michigan native down for the next game. With Fitzgerald unable to play, Goheen moved back to cover point and Tony Conroy came off the bench to take his place at left wing. Wellington moved from rover to center and Mohan came in at rover. The first half was scoreless, but a major brawl erupted after the break when Bill Adams and Thompsett collided. Adams went down unconscious, and Mohan, thinking that he had been struck by Coutu, pounced on the latter as Peppin scored what he thought was a Soo goal. The referee disallowed it, ruling he had rung his bell (in lieu of today's whistle) before the puck entered the net. The Soo played the rest of the game under protest, which was subsequently withdrawn.

Before this incident, St. Paul got its first goal when Wellington passed to Whalen, whose shot eluded Tallion. After play resumed, Whalen

> Boys played a wonderful game last
> night in the first half, showing the best
> team work of the season. Portage Lake

came back strong in the second half. The referee permitted body checking into the boards, which our players are not accustomed to, it being against the rules ... The Calumet team is doing a lot of talking about what they are going to do to St. Paul next week.

The next night saw a season-high thirteen goals scored between both teams as the AC's tried to live up to Johns's prediction. The game was spent trading goals, with Sicotte getting the first for Portage Lake within the first three minutes. Am Whalen tied it after a scramble in front of the home team's net, only to have Bailey score on a pass from Jerry Coughlin off the face-off. Briden put the locals up 3–1 after a long dash, but the half would end at 3–3. Portage Lake goalie Monette let in a mid-rink shot from Bert Mohan, and Nick Kahler tied it on a close-in effort in heavy traffic.

It was more of the same after the teams returned from the intermission. The home team went ahead 4–3 when Dailey scored from Sicotte, but Mohan tied it almost immediately. Coughlin, who had been injured the night before, then put the locals back on top 5–4 with a shot from the side of the net. That lead held for only two minutes until Wellington tied it again for the visitors. Briden for Portage Lake and Mohan for St. Paul then swapped goals, before Sicotte settled the issue for the home team on a shot from in front of the net.

The 7–6 defeat was critical to the Athletic Club—a victory would have made their quest for the MacNaughton Cup so much simpler. They now had to come back home and sweep Calumet and hope that the Soo would lose at least one of their three remaining games. A loss to Calumet would be fatal to St. Paul, while sweeps for both teams would create a tie, and a play-off for the championship would be necessary. On the way back from Houghton, the team stopped in Duluth for a mid-season exhibition game with a picked team taken from the local amateur league. St. Paul led at the half 3–0 on two goals by Wellington and one by Goheen and then fought off a strong second-half challenge to win 8–4. Wellington got another for a hat trick, Mohan scored twice, and George Henderson added two more for the visitors in the last half. Henderson had joined the team for this game, as Kahler, Whalen, and Mohan were all hurting with various injuries.

## Personnel Problems

As if those problems were not enough—and it appeared that Kahler could be lost for the season—there was an even greater problem once the team got back home. The Pittsburgh team had made attractive offers to both Ray Bonney and "Duke" Wellington, and they would be gone before the final games with Calumet. The legalities of today's professional sports were not yet in place, and players were free to go where they wanted—though Bonney pleaded unsuccessfully to remain for the last series. "Dad" would now have to go in goal with Cy Weidenborner, who had not seen game action since late the previous December. Jack Ryan of Port Arthur was brought in to take Wellington's place at counter point. Kahler would miss this series, Mohan and Whalen were well enough to play, but Fitzgerald was still out of action.

Surprisingly all of this turmoil hardly mattered, as the AC's won their most decisive game of the season, 10–3. Mohan, who had been described as "battered" by the *St. Paul Dispatch* on February 11, 1916, scored five times. Conroy had a hat trick, while Adams and Whalen added single goals. St. Paul led 7–0 at the intermission and then suffered a second-half let-down, as the teams played evenly. Late in the game, the type of frustration shown by today's hockey commentators reared its ugly head. Calumet's Russ Barkell tangled with Goheen, while the high-scoring Bert Mohan battled with Jack Mahan. The local beat writers were duly impressed with the effort. The *Pioneer Press*'s Al Evans, on February 15, 1916, praised Weidenborner and Ryan, while commenting that "the loss of Bonney and Wellington ... was not seriously felt by the local team ... and the reorganized team showed plenty of confidence and pep from the beginning." The *Dispatch*'s E. R. Hoskings (February 15, 1916) presented his kudos this way: "These results show the reserve material on the team has been as strong at least as the first string talent. Goheen was a dazzling star and Conroy played a wonderful game last night, justifying the faith of Coach Dad Gawley, who, when he first came to St. Paul, pronounced him the most promising young player he had ever seen." Despite his five-goal night, no one seemed overly impressed with Bert Mohan's work!

Perhaps feeling slighted, Mohan went out the next night and collected a hat trick, all of St. Paul's goals, as the team claimed a share of the league's championship with a close 3–2 win. Calumet scored first on Mahan's close-in effort that was countered by Mohan's first goal on a pass from Whalen. Before the intermission, Mohan got his second on a feed from Conroy behind the Calumet net and his third on another assist from the St. Paul native. The visitors dominated play in the second half but could come no closer than 3–2 when Mahan scored on a pass from Jack Adams. Adams had earlier taken a swipe at his brother Bill's legs that brought this reaction from the *Pioneer Press* on February 15, 1916:

> Fortunately Billy's legs received only part of the force of the blow or he might have been laid out. The incident was noticed by Goheen who informed Jack that if he hit his little brother again, he would toss him up among the spectators. Goheen is a pretty muscular athlete, and Jack was a good boy for the rest of the game.

The Soo had swept their final series with Portage Lake to give them a 7–4–1 season record, to St. Paul's 8–4–0. The two-points-for-a-

victory and one-point-for-a-tie system was not then in use but would have given the AC's the MacNaughton Cup, 16 to 15. Since the Soo's tie had been with Portage Lake, the league decided that a further Soo-Portage game was necessary. A Soo victory would create a tie for first place, while a loss would send the Cup to the Minnesota capital. Johns protested this arrangement to Secretary George Cudlip of the AAHA, but it was denied. He then attempted to have the play-off game staged in Duluth as a neutral site, but that too was rejected. The Soo went to Houghton on February 18 and beat Portage Lake 3–1, setting the stage for another play-off to decide the cup winner.

Using a play on today's parlance, how would "Cup Crazy 1916" be contested? Johns very much wanted a two-game total-goals series staged in neutral Duluth, while the Soo were anxious to have two games at home. The compromise worked out at a league meeting in Chicago on February 20 was a best-three-of-five series, with games in St. Paul on February 28 and 29, to be followed by at least one game in the Soo on March 2 and another, if needed, the next night. Should the series be tied at that point, the deciding game would be played in Calumet on March 6. Even with this arrangement in place, Johns did his best to reduce the series to a best of three, but to no avail. The present Stanley Cup finals are a best-of-seven series.

Before the series could get under way, both teams had other games to play. The Soo met Canadian Soo in an intense two-game series for the Soo Falls Trophy. They won both games, 5–3 and 3–1, and then headed for St. Paul. The Athletic Club was scheduled to play a best-of-three series for the unofficial Twin Cities championship against the Minneapolis Victorias. Strengthened by the loan of cover-point Jack Ryan, the Mill City team tied the game in the last minute and then won it in overtime 5–4. Apparently fearing that his team might overly exhaust itself in meaningless exhibitions, Johns delayed the remaining games of the series.

*The American Soo 1915–16 hockey team. Capt. "Muzz" Murray was later enshrined in the United States Hockey Hall of Fame.*

### Battling the Soo for Mr. MacNaughton's Mug

Gawley ran his team through practices that the February 27, 1916, *Dispatch* described as "anything but slow" and was delighted to learn that both Bonney and Wellington would be allowed to return for the series. They both arrived from Pittsburgh on the morning of February 28. About the same time, the visitors checked into the Sherman Hotel and then left to test the Hippodrome ice that the February 27, 1916, *Pioneer Press* had said was "splendid." Members of the Athletic Club planned to attend the game in a body and would be accompanied by the drum corps and torchbearers. Large crowds were expected for both games and additional trolley service would be in place.

Large crowds could logically be expected, and

they were desperately needed, as C. K. Blandin's February 25 letter to the membership reflects:

> Considering the wonderful hockey put up by our team, the attendance . . . has been surprisingly light, and the club is facing an appreciable deficit . . . and it therefore becomes necessary to call upon the full membership to rally to the support of the team . . . To those members who have not attended these games assurance is given of most interesting and exciting evenings where hockey will be seen at its highest development. We must fill the Hippodrome and show proper appreciation of our team in the climax of its effort to secure the championship cup. Two tickets are

enclosed herewith in hope that each member of the Athletic Club will respond to this first and only call.

The price of the tickets are 50 cents each … Tickets presented for admission for which no remittance has been received, will be charged to members whose name appears on the back of the tickets. These tickets entitle the holder to admission either night.

St. Paul had won the season series three games to one, but Soo fans pointed out that their team had lost the two games in Minnesota after a hard stretch of four games in seven days. Now, however, the *Dispatch* said that "the Soo players are confidence personified. They say they are fresh and on edge … and expect to win" (February 28, 1916). Gawley predicted two close wins at home, followed by success on the Soo's small rink once the venue changed. The "Hipp" was filled with the hoped-for large crowd. Even before all were seated, the visitors took a 1–0 lead in the first game, as Peppin won the opening face-off and took a long shot that eluded Bonney. Three minutes later Goheen scored on a similar long shot, but the Soo took the lead at the halfway point when Bonney misjudged Donnelly's shot. The Soo made it 3–1 seven minutes into the second half, when Levi Godin's shot skipped over Bonney's stick and into the net. At this point it hardly looked like "Dad" would make good on his prediction, but now things started to go the Athletic Club's way. Bert Mohan scored on a shot through heavy traffic, and then, with three minutes to go, Wellington fed Whalen from behind the Soo net. His clean effort beat Tallion for the tying tally.

There was no set procedure for overtime, and the Soo would have been content to let the tie stand. But St. Paul would have none of that, and it was agreed that as many five-minute periods as necessary to determine a winner would be played. Bonney, who had not played one of his better games, was brilliant in overtime.

Whalen gave St. Paul a 4–3 victory in the fourth extra period on a pass from Mohan. This was not today's "sudden death," so play continued for another three minutes and the lead held.

Gawley had not used either Kahler or Conroy in the first game, but he put them both in the lineup for game two. Goheen and Mohan, described by the *Pioneer Press* on March 1, 1916, as "pretty well used up in Monday night's mix," were held out for use in the game(s) in Michigan. The move seemed debatable as the two players had accounted for two of the team's four goals in the comeback victory in game one. The Soo went up 3–0 after the first half as Godin scored twice and Thompsett once. That score held until eleven minutes into the second half, when Gawley suddenly looked like a genius. Within a space of but two minutes, Nick Kahler not only scored three goals but was injured as well.

The first came when the St. Paul captain picked up the puck on the back check, went around two defenders, and beat Tallion. Am Whalen fed Kahler for the second and then was struck in the face with a stick. After being quickly bandaged up, he returned to the ice to convert another Whalen pass for his third goal. The teams then battled for another nine minutes with neither scoring. Once again the matter would be settled through extra play.

After a scoreless first overtime, Kahler struck again (*Pioneer Press*, March 1, 1916):

Halfway through the second five-minute period of extra play, the puck was passed from behind the Soo goal in a scrimmage. Whalen attempted to shoot it in, but it struck Tallion amidship and as it fell on the ice the Soo's speedy goaltender attempted to pass it out of dangerous territory. But Kahler was too fast for him, and, catching the rubber as it tumbled off Tallion's shoe, he passed it into the net with a short, quick jab, and the second game of the championship was settled.

The scene shifted to Michigan's Upper Peninsula for game three, and a possible game four, as each coach assessed the situation. The *Pioneer Press*, March 1, 1916, reported their comments:

COACH DAD GAWLEY, St. Paul—We shall win the first game played on Soo ice and the MacNaughton Cup will remain in the St. Paul Athletic club. [It had been on display there since early in the season.]

COACH (PUDGE) HAMILTON, Soo—I am more than ever convinced that our team is better than yours in St. Paul. We shall take two games on our ice, easily, and then win the third, on neutral ice.

Arrangements were made for a special telephone line to be connected to the lounge of the Athletic Club, where accounts of the game could be heard by the membership. Nine players made the trip along with Gawley and Johns: Bonney, Adams, Ryan, Goheen, Whalen, Conroy, Mohan, Wellington, and Kahler. Fitzgerald was still out of action. The *Daily News* on March 1, 1916, cautioned against too much optimism:

The St. Paul boys say they will make it three straight, but that's some task. On their home floor, much smaller than the hippodrome rink, and smaller than the rinks at either Portage Lake or Calumet, the Soo team is a wonder.

Every player is an excellent shot and they bombard their opponents' net from beginning to end. The light is also faulty, and a goaltender not familiar with the conditions finds it difficult to stop the many shots directed continually at him from all angles.

As the game played out, Ray Bonney was to appreciate just how difficult it was to play goal in the Soo rink. He was kept more active than

his counterpart, "Zickey" Tallion, but got the early lead when Nick Kahler took Whalen's pass out from behind the Soo net and fired it home. Before the half was over, the locals tied it when "Muzz" Murray's shot struck Goheen's stick and rebounded past a slipping Bonney. Once play resumed in the second half, St. Paul made it look like they would make good on Gawley's sweep prediction. Within the first twelve minutes, Wellington and Mohan put the Minnesota team up 3–1, but Levi Godin wouldn't let them take the cup that easily. He beat Bonney, who had been brilliant all night, on two long shots to send the game into overtime. The first was a drive from the far right wing. The second went from alongside the Soo net the length of the rink. In today's terms, these would be described as "soft" goals and would produce the third overtime game in the series.

As in St. Paul four nights earlier, the teams battled into the fourth extra session before "Muzz" Murray gave the Soo their first victory. Within the last minute of play, the home team captain dashed along the boards and produced the game winner on a shot from the left wing. The packed crowd of twenty-five hundred went wild as their hopes for the MacNaughton Cup were resurrected. Murray's heroics caused L. B. Chittenden of the Soo newspaper, the *Evening News* (March 3, 1916), to become a poet:

It seemed like the cup was slipping,
When the score stood three to one.
But Godin was only starting
On his big rampage of fun.

Then Captain Murray soon decided
That the game should end at once,
And he scored the winning tally,
With his usual vim and "punch."

We'll hand it to old St. Paul,
They're sure some hockey team,
But of all the teams—we figure,
The Soo has got the cream.

We'll take off our hats to Bonney
For the grand game he put up,
But all the same, we have a "hinch,"
That the Soo will win the cup.

The teams went back at it the next night, and it was apparent that the strain of playing four games in five nights with a travel day in between was taking its toll. And the toll, which also included overtime play, was greater on the Soo than on St. Paul. The *Evening News* on March 4, 1916, described the play in game four as "not near as speedy as the former contests. It dragged laboriously at times, and the Soo did not get into the fray with its usual pep."

The Soo did get into the fray in the early going, but the visitors gained the upper hand about nine minutes into the game when Goheen scored on a long rush. A minute later, Conroy made it 2–0 from a scramble, but the home team closed the gap with a pretty goal from Godin on passes from Coutu and Thompsett. That was as close as the defending cup holders would get, as Kahler scored from another scramble for a 3–1 lead at the intermission. The second half was marred by two ugly incidents. Coutu and Wellington got into an altercation, followed by an exchange between "Muzz" Murray and referee Carlos Haug. Coutu had hit Wellington with his stick, and when "Duke" regained his feet, the Soo center punched him. Haug sent Coutu off for five minutes, but Gawley felt he should have been given a game misconduct. When Haug demurred, Gawley pulled the AC's off the ice.

St. Paul was persuaded to resume the game, and soon after "Muzz" Murray became annoyed at Haug's failure to call tripping penalties on the visitors. Murray became so angry that he threw his stick at Haug but missed. Amazingly, nothing resulted, and the *Evening News* on March 4, 1916, observed that "the referee . . . showed his good will toward the Soo team by not penalizing Murray." So play continued, and Kahler collected his second goal shortly before the end, with the final score 4–1. St. Paul had captured

the MacNaughton Cup in only its first year in the AAHA.

One Soo fan showed his disappointment at the outcome by poking Gawley in the eye as he left the rink. Gawley was more than happy to dismiss the matter, saying, "Shucks, what does a little black eye amount to compared to winning the American hockey championship." The next day on the streets of the Soo, before onlookers more generous than this assailant, the victors paraded with toy musical instruments and pennants in celebration of the victory. Manager Ray Johns saluted his team's efforts in a piece for the *Pioneer Press* on March 4, 1916:

Our boys are the happiest bunch of boys in America today . . . If the St. Paul fans could have seen them play in the last two games they would be just as proud of them as I am . . . Every boy on the team played a whale of a game last night. Bonney never played a better game in his life . . . Adams . . . played the best game of the season last night . . . Frank Goheen played his usual flashing game. His defensive work and his rushes were a feature.

Nick Kahler kept up his good work at center, and always was in front of the net . . . Mohan kept shooting at the Soo goal from all parts of the rink . . . Conroy played a hard game on right wing and kept

*The* St. Paul Dispatch, *March 4, 1916, pokes fun at "Dad" Gawley's championship black eye.*

*The 1915–16 MacNaughton Cup championship Athletic Club team. Standing (l to r): unknown, Wellington, unknown, Fitzgerald, Gawley, Conroy; kneeling (l to r): Kahler, unknown (Goheen missing)*

his man covered all the time. Wellington played when he should have been on the bench with the other cripples, Ryan and Whalen.

The team left the Soo on Saturday night, March 4, and arrived back in St. Paul on Sunday morning at about 9:25. A delegation from the Athletic Club, which featured the drum corps and band, met them at the station and escorted them to the club's room for an informal welcome. The formal acknowledgment of their victory came that night at a banquet. Neither Bonney nor Wellington attended. They returned immediately to Pittsburgh after the victory to resume play with that team. Once the celebrating was done, Ray Johns was looking for other worlds to conquer and found one in eastern Canada.

Before that new challenge could be addressed, however, there was the more immediate matter of the second game of the city series

with Minneapolis. The teams met on March 7 at the "Hipp," with the Athletic Club playing with a revamped lineup. In an early adoption of the two-referee system, Gawley allowed Jack Ryan and Am Whalen to serve as officials, while Cy Weidenborner and Ed Goheen returned to play goal and counter point. Despite the revamped lineup, there would be no upset loss to Minneapolis this time. Frank Goheen got three goals, Mohan two, and Conroy and Adams one each in the 7–4 victory. There was no third game.

### Winning and Losing the Ross Cup

Prior to the Soo series for the MacNaughton Cup, there had been considerable speculation about future games. There was mention that St. Paul might take on the St. Nicholas Club of New York, which featured Hobey Baker. Other possibilities included games in Ottawa, Montreal, and Boston. What evolved was a game for the Art Ross Cup against Lachine, Quebec, to be played in Montreal on March 16. The Ross trophy was emblematic of the amateur championship of eastern Canada. On March 9, Ray Johns told the *Dispatch* about preparations for the game:

> There will be no let-up in the training grind until we have landed this trophy. After we have it in our possession, the boys may relax a little in the other games. [A three-game series in Pittsburgh on March 24, 25, and 26.]. But for the present we are after the Ross cup just as hard as we were after the McNaughten trophy all season . . . Daily practices will be in order until Sunday night when the team starts East.

Jack Ryan and Am Whalen left a day earlier, and plans were made for both Ray Bonney and "Duke" Wellington to rejoin the team from Pittsburgh. After a four-day train trip that included several hundred miles in a blizzard, the St. Paul team arrived in Montreal on March 15 and was met by Riley Hem, a trustee of the Ross Cup and a former goaltender with the Montreal Wanderers. Hem indicated that the game would be played under National Hockey Association (NHA) rules that provided for six players a side and three periods. The Lachine team had reached the cup finals by winning the Montreal league championship and then defeating the Montreal AAA and the New Edinburghs of Ottawa.

Controversy erupted on game day when Perry Norton, Lachine manager, challenged the amateur statuses of Bonney, Mohan, Wellington, and Whalen. The issue was Bonney and Wellington's time with Pittsburgh, Mohan's with the Crescent Club of Halifax, Nova Scotia, and Whalen's with Galt, Ontario. Johns insisted all were legitimate amateurs under the rules of the AAHA. Norton agreed to go ahead and play the game under protest, with the matter awaiting resolution by a meeting of the cup trustees the day following the game.

Ed Fitzgerald had recovered from his injury and was in the lineup on March 16 at the arena

*The American Soo team sends their congratulations to the St. Paul winners.*

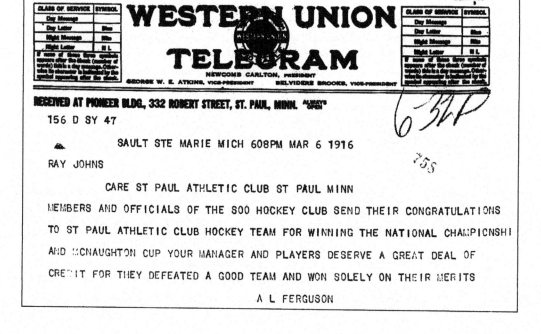

as Frank Goheen gave St. Paul the early lead on an angle shot. The teams then exchanged goals, with Ryan and Whalen scoring for the visitors as the first period ended at 3–3. Lachine took a 5–4 lead after two periods, as Whalen got his second goal for the Minnesotans. The latter broke open the game in the final period as Adams and Wellington (two) scored to provide a 7–5 lead. Norton got the game's last goal for Lachine to make the final 7–6. On March 17, 1916, the game was described by the *Evening News* of Montreal as "fast [and] clean," but there was an exception to that. Goheen was slashed on the head in the second period by Tannahill's stick and knocked cold. The wound required two stitches. Amazingly, Tannahill got only a three-minute penalty.

The cup trustees met the following afternoon and ruled in favor of St. Paul, awarding them the Ross Cup. The Athletic Club had claimed another coveted piece of hockey hardware. But three days later, on March 20, the trustees reversed themselves and stripped the team of the trophy. While accepting the amateur status of Bonney and Wellington, they ruled that Mohan had never been reinstated as an amateur after his professional play. Whalen's status does not appear to have been addressed.

Apparently reeling at the loss of the Ross Cup, St. Paul was defeated by the Sons of Ireland of Quebec 10–2 before leaving Montreal. Carlos Haug, the man who refereed in the MacNaughton Cup finals, took over in goal from Ray Bonney, who returned to Pittsburgh. Though Haug suffered a broken nose in this game, he was well enough to play in the three tilts in Pittsburgh. Bonney was slated to play for St. Paul in these games but came down with appendicitis. Haug was brilliant in the first clash in the Steel City on March 24 but gave up the winning goal in the first overtime period as the locals triumphed 1–0. He was less than brilliant the next night as Pittsburgh routed the visitors 10–4. Goheen (two), Wellington, and Conroy scored for St. Paul. Perhaps reeling from that

*The MacNaughton Cup*

one-sided affair, an ugly incident erupted at the team's hotel the next morning. *Pioneer Press* sports reporter Perry Dotson recounted the happening almost thirty years later in his column "Dotson Dashes," on February 6, 1946:

In case you don't remember, the team that season was about evenly divided between Americans and Canadians . . . The storm between the two groups had been brewing for weeks and it was only a question of selecting a battleground and setting the date. The club had just won the Art Ross [revoked] and McNaughton [*sic*] trophies . . . and had moved into Pittsburgh for a big game(s) . . . It was a bright Sunday morning when the team gathered in the lobby, hungry and completely lacking in good will. The Canadians asked for breakfast money and Nick Kahler . . . told the boys merely to sign their cafe checks and turn them in to the cashier. That was as good an excuse as any for the battle and what a one it was.

The lobby palm trees fell as in a typhoon. There were at least a half dozen separate punching duels and in a matter of minutes the free-for-all was attracting many from among the church-going throngs passing the hostelry. The teammates finally were quelled and urged to retire to their rooms where the struggle flared again a half hour later when one of the Canadians was caught wearing one of the Americans' favorite ties.

Dotson described the AC's as "torn by dissension throughout all its . . . games" but commended them as a team that "could win in spite of its internal and external disputes."

The series ended on March 27 with another Pittsburgh victory, 4–2. Trailing 2–0 at the intermission, the AC's tied the game on goals by Henderson and Wellington before succumbing.

While the loss of the Ross Cup and subsequent defeats in Montreal and Pittsburgh took some of the luster off the season, the *Dispatch*'s Canadian correspondent paid them tribute on March 17, 1916: "The showing of the St. Paul experts was a revelation to local followers of the game, who had supposed that a team accustomed to playing seven-man hockey would be at sea playing under the six-man rule prevailing in Quebec."

# 3

# 1916-1919

## *No League and a War to Fight*

"We wanted to show members of the Club, the citizens of St. Paul, the people of the United States, that in hockey St. Paul was second to none."

*Tom Charlton, team manager, letter to St. Paul Athletic Club members, January 26, 1917*

A month after returning from Pittsburgh with the team, Ray Johns was gone. The man who had created a champion team in a mere two years left St. Paul on April 26, 1916, to pursue a better business opportunity with the Schmelzer Arms Company of Kansas City, Missouri. While building the AC's and amateur baseball in the city, Johns's "real" job had been with the William R. Burkhard Company, sporting outfitters. Although he left on a tentative basis, Johns did not return. In a letter to Athletic Club president Oscar Taylor in early July, he suggested that a manager or committee be appointed at once to plan for the coming season. He would be available to lend whatever assistance he could from his new location.

Johns's words were heeded. M. E. Harbin was named chairman of the hockey committee and Tom Charlton was named coach/manager. Johns would not be back, and neither would "Dad" Gawley. Charlton's role is difficult to determine—he actually appears as a player in a team photograph, though he never played a game. As the season proceeded, it is apparent that the on-ice leadership came from Ed Fitzgerald, who was selected captain by his teammates after an organizational meeting on December 8. Fitzgerald took over from Nick Kahler, the star of the

MacNaughton Cup team—the ex-captain moved across the river to develop the sport in Minneapolis. The team had held a light workout at Lake Como on November 19 amid rumors as to who the returning Canadian players might be. While Ray Bonney's and "Duke" Wellington's names were mentioned, neither would return that season. But Herb Drury would make his St. Paul debut.

Drury was a native of Midland, Ontario, who had "burned up the ice," according to the *St. Paul Pioneer Press*, with the Port Colborne, Ontario, Seniors the prior season. Along with the returning Bert Mohan, Drury would help provide the offense for the team. At 5 feet 7 inches and 165 pounds, he was described by the St. Paul paper as a "midget." He would later play for the United States as a naturalized citizen on the 1920 and 1924 Olympic teams. Between Olympics he would perform for the Pittsburgh Yellowjackets in the United States Amateur Hockey Association (USAHA), followed by a journeyman's career in the NHL with the Pittsburgh Pirates and the Philadelphia Quakers.

The team's first regular workout of the 1916–17 season got under way at the Hippodrome on December 14. Besides Fitzgerald, others answering the call were Tony Conroy, Herb Drury,

Frank Goheen, Bert Mohan, Cliff Neilson, Vern Peterson, Ransome Tregelone, and Cy Weidenborner. Coach Charlton was assisted by Homer Sweeney, who had played one game the previous year, and Lucius Ordway. The December 15, 1916, *St. Paul Pioneer Press* noted:

> COACH CHARLTON PLEASED. The club has an unusual number of speedy skaters ... The combination play of Drury and Mohan, especially, was noteworthy ... Conroy and Goheen seemed as fast as ever on the steel blades. [Cliff] Neilson of Winnipeg impressed, as did Tregelone, a defense man, formerly of Calumet.

## Playing Independently

As workouts continued, the question now arose as to who the AC's would be playing. Portage Lake had dropped out of the AAHA, and if Calumet did the same, it would leave only St. Paul and American Soo, hardly enough teams for league competition. While that question was being resolved, the team warmed up for whatever season might be in the offing by routing (no score was kept) the local senior Olympias the day after Christmas. The new year opened for the team on January 2 with a 14–0 thrashing of Thief River Falls at the Hippodrome. Five minutes into the game, Ed Fitzgerald went the length of the rink to score and Bert Mohan quickly followed. Before the half was over (this game was played in two twenty-minute halves), another seven goals had been scored. Mohan would finish with five goals, Drury with four, Fitzgerald with three, and Conroy with two. The *St. Paul Pioneer Press* writer covering the game gave high marks to Drury, Fitzgerald, and Mohan, as well as the Thief River Falls goalie, Ralph Bennet. He calculated that on average St. Paul had fired three shots a minute at Bennet, which give him 106 saves on 120 shots! Perhaps the most interesting development to come out of the game was the innovation of numbering

*The newly built St. Paul Athletic Club, 1917*

the players. The game program shows Weidenborner with the number 1, Hodgeman (the second goalie who did not play) with 2, Fitzgerald 3, Goheen 4, Drury 5, Mohan 6, Tregelone 7, Conroy 8, and Peterson 9. The professional Pacific Coast Hockey Association began having players wear numbers in 1911, and the NHL followed suit upon its founding in 1917.

The schedule was finally set when it was announced on January 13 that the AAHA would not function, as Calumet had dropped out of the competition. This left St. Paul with no other course than to pursue an independent schedule, as it had done in its first year, although the team would be allowed to retain possession of the MacNaughton Cup. Lucius Ordway laid out a tentative slate of games with the idea that visiting teams could play American Soo on the same trip. First among the visitors was Fort William, which featured Percy Nicklin, also a Midland native, on defense and goalie Bernie McTeigue. Both would eventually play for Eveleth in the USAHA. Frank Goheen had been slightly injured in practice, but he was ready for the first of the two-game series on January 18.

Fort William, however, was not really ready for the game. The team had been on a train for thirty-six hours in a regular coach, having missed connections for their special car. Arriving at 3 P.M. for an 8:15 P.M. start time at the Hippodrome, the team members showed the fatigue of their long travel when, after Mohan had given the AC's an early lead, the visitor's Fraser accidentally kicked the puck into his own net. Unlike today, at that time such a goal was not awarded to the closest opposing player. The two-goal lead grew to six at the half, as Goheen, Mohan, Conroy, and Tregelone scored. Fort William regrouped at the break to play a creditable second half, actually outscoring St. Paul 2–1 as Mohan added his third tally to end it at 7–2.

The *Pioneer Press* (January 19, 1917) was delighted with the play of Herb Drury, who, it was later determined, had injured his hip in the game:

> Herb Drury played like a festive streak
> of lightning, winding in and out among
> the visiting players with such bewildering
> speed that they were completely at sea.
> Times without number he wormed his
> way throughout the opposing lineup, and
> invariably he passed the puck to one of
> his own players in front of the nets. That
> Drury's rushes did not result in twenty
> or more goals was due to the remarkable
> defensive playing of McGeah and Nicklin.

Fred McGeah had taken Bernie McTeigue's place in the Fort William nets for the first game, but McTeigue was back in place for game two after the visitors had a presumably restful night at the Sherman Hotel. The rest helped, as the game was scoreless until the eighteen-minute mark of the first half, when Mohan took a pass from Drury to give St. Paul the lead. A minute later Tony Conroy made it 2–0 at the half. Following the intermission the visitors drew to within one on Foreman's goal, but that would be all as Mohan scored two and Conroy and Goheen each scored one to close out the 6–1 win.

Fort William had taken seven minutes in penalties to only one for the locals, which was attributed to their "not being acquainted with the rules in force and [being] fouled [penalized] for back checking near the boards," according to the *Pioneer Press* (January 20, 1917). The meaning here is not clear, but perhaps the penalties were for boarding. The game was witnessed by six hundred fans, many of whom were dressed in colorful costumes. The St. Paul Winter Carnival would soon be under way.

Two days after the Fort Williams sweep, St. Paul fans awoke to find that Ray Bonney was apparently on his way back to join the AC's for their two-game set in Sault Ste. Marie, Michigan, on January 25 and 26. Bonney had been in Pittsburgh since the previous March, and his failure to play since that time was supposedly due to poor health, which seemed to rule out playing in the current season. Whatever the reason, when the puck was dropped in the American Soo, Cy Weidenborner was still in the nets, where he would stay for the rest of the season. Bonney's future would be in Pittsburgh.

"Muzz" Murray was still very much Mr. Hockey in the Soo, as the locals took both games by 3–2 counts. On the team was a young Vic DesJardins, another Soo native who would, along with Murray, find his way to the United States Hockey Hall of Fame. After a 1–1 first-half standoff in game one, the Soo outscored the AC's in the second half 2–1. Tony Conroy and Herb Drury got St. Paul's goals, as the latter scored on a sensational dash. Murray got one of the Soo's goals and picked up two more the following night when he scored both the tying and winning goals. His mid-ice shot glanced off Ed

Fitzgerald's stick and past Cy Weidenborner to give the "Lock City," as the local *Evening News* described the town, the victory.

St. Paul had been swept and Vern Peterson and Bert Mohan had been injured, but the team had been quite competitive. Peterson had received an ugly gash to his right temple in game one, and Mohan had strained his ankle, keeping him out of the second game. He was replaced by White Bear Lake native Dick Conway on left wing as Tony Conroy went to rover and Herb Drury moved over to center. Peterson shook off his injury to score both of St. Paul's goals in game two. The *Evening News* gave the visitors their due:

> Drury was the "big noise" on the St. Paul team. He is one of the speediest players ever seen here and also a clever stick handler. Once he got the puck he was generally sure of taking it down for a shot. Goheen, again, played a wonderful game, as did Conroy and Peterson on the wings. Weidenborner is a good goaltender. He displays excellent form and shots that tally on him are usually earned.

## Sweeping the Soo

The scene would now shift back to St. Paul as the Soo came south to play the AC's on January 30 and 31. Looking ahead to those games, Tom Charlton, who seemed to have settled into the position of manager, issued a letter to the membership on January 26 that featured the directive "PLEASE READ THIS" at the top: "Do you know that OUR Club has been active in the one branch of athletics since its inception? Do you know that we have been wonderfully successful in that sport? If you don't, you should, so we will acquaint you with the facts. Now absorb the following . . ." After recounting the team's 1915–16 performance, the letter continued:

> Expecting to defend the McNaughton [*sic*] trophy [which by the way is on

exhibition at the Club] in league competition this year, our team was reorganized. We wanted to show the members of the Club, the citizens of St. Paul, the people of the United States, that in hockey St. Paul was second to none. WE BELIEVE ABSOLUTELY THAT THIS IS TRUE. The team we have this year is even faster than the one we had last year. We have already played three games at the Hippodrome and won all three.

> Carnival week we will play two games . . . with the American Soo, from whom we wrested the McNaughton Trophy [*sic*] last year after very exciting competition. We are arranging to have different Marching Clubs attend in body and are reserving sections for them.

> Four admission tickets are enclosed— they can be used at either game. If these tickets are used, we will charge them to your house account.

> Now is the time for you to boost and support a very deserving team and sport. You will be well entertained at an exceedingly low cost. Should you have a coupon book it is of course good, yet you might need these tickets also.

> Get into the procession—right up with the band wagon—because it is an actual fact that our team has been receiving better support from outsiders than from our own members.

> We expect you to be present. Wear your uniform, please.

The desperate tone of the letter, close to both begging and directing support, was echoed in E. R. Hosking's piece, which appeared in the *Pioneer Press* at about the same time:

> Though possessing the fastest hockey team in the United States . . . fans of the Twin Cities have been unaccountably slow in appreciating the game, which without

*Early pond hockey and public skating at the St. Paul Winter Carnival, 1917*

question is the fastest and most exciting indoor pastime yet invented.

The team is handicapped by the situation of the Hippodrome rink which while midway between the two cities, is several miles from the downtown sections of both. But in spite of these drawbacks the St. Paul Athletic club team has a right to expect much greater patronage than it has received to date.

The Athletic club team is proving a costly luxury for the club that has assembled it, for although it is an amateur aggregation, the cost of bringing other teams to play it here has proved a heavy drain on the club's treasury. There is a considerable deficit already, and unless the patronage picks up largely in the remaining games it is certain that the club will not again attempt to provide the fans of this city with a championship team.

The Athletic Club's situation was not unlike that of today's New Jersey Devils, who, despite three Stanley Cups, have difficulty in selling out the Continental Airlines Arena at the Meadowlands. The Arena usually sells out only for games with the New York Rangers, and the team is looking for a new facility in Newark. The AC's would find a new place to play in two years, but it would prove to be only a temporary move.

With such dire predictions for the future of the game in the air, a smaller-than-hoped-for crowd showed up for the first game of the series. They would witness, as best described by the *Pioneer Press* on January 31, 1917, "tripping, slashing, fisticuffs, cross checking, penalties galore and one hockey stick thrown into a box . . . narrowly missing a woman . . . [a] style of hockey that prevailed in the good old days before the rules were made as strict as they are today."

Frank Goheen started the scoring three minutes into the game by taking a pass from behind the Soo's net and putting it in from thirty feet out. Two minutes later, Vern Peterson retrieved the puck from heavy traffic and got it to Tony Conroy, who made it 2–0. By the time the half was over, Herb Drury and Peterson had scored, the latter after stealing the puck from Soo point Jack Murray. As the half ended, Bert Mohan and Soo rover Levi Godin exchanged blows at mid-ice and were joined in the unpleasantness by Herb Drury and Soo captain "Muzz" Murray.

Referee Ray Fenton got things under control, but the Athletic Club's domination continued after the break. Mohan got two more, Ed Fitzgerald victimized Jack Murray again

when his shot went off Murray's skate into the net, and Tony Conroy made it 8–0 on a goal similar to his first. With his team being blown out, "Muzz" Murray decided to liven things up. After Goheen lost his stick attempting to check him and it wound up between Murray's legs, the Soo cover point picked it up, skated twenty feet, and threw it into the seats. The stick hit close to a box occupied by several women. This prompted Fenton to give Murray a one-minute penalty, which, the *Pioneer Press* (January 31, 1917) reported,

Murray refused to accept, and he took his team off the ice. A heated colloquy, with Murray, Fenton and Manager Charlton . . . ensued in the dressing room, in the course of which Murray and Fenton nearly came to blows. Finally the Soo captain brought his team back on the ice and the game was finished.

Halsey Hall, longtime Twin Cities sportswriter and broadcaster, would recall Murray in the early 1950s as "a rampaging offensive defense man from the Soo country. The only man I ever saw who could really bother the great original Hippodrome outfit." The bother would come the next night, but Goheen and Mohan scored again to close things out at 10–0.

It had been a convincing thrashing of a major opponent, but not without cost. Herb Drury had taken a beating, with injuries in both calves. Play was halted for fifteen minutes for treatment of the first injury, and he left the game after the second incident. The teams played six each for what little time was left. Drury was back the next night, when nineteen hundred fans turned out to see a complete reversal of game one, though Drury once again had physical problems. The AC rover collided with teammate Vern Peterson and was knocked unconscious. Carried toward the locker room, he soon awoke and demanded to return to action. "Struggling to his feet he skated slowly back to his position and in five

*A St. Paul Dispatch cartoon illustrates an early AC game at the "Hipp."*

minutes was going at lightning speed, again thrilling fans by his shifty, elusive spectacular tactics," as the *Pioneer Press* put it (February 1, 1917). Hey, "he was a hockey player," as the ESPN crowd likes to remind us today.

On the ice it would be Tony Conroy's night. He would score three goals in the last six minutes to break a 1–1 tie and give St. Paul the victory. Soo rookie Vic DesJardins gave the visitors an early lead, but Bert Mohan tied it just before the break. The teams battled on until, with six minutes to play, the durable Drury skated be-

hind his own net, dodged a forechecker, leaped over another's stick, and eventually got the puck to Conroy who put it away. The Soo disputed the goal, but referee Homer Sweeney let it stand. Conroy got two more to propel a close game into a decisive victory. Besides Drury, Mohan and Fitzgerald had also been injured, but nothing that impaired their play.

The Soo would move across the river to play Minneapolis the next night and salvage their Minnesota trip with a close 8–6 win. The new team in the Flour City had been assembled by former AC captain Nick Kahler and played its home games at the Casino Rink, which had an ice surface only a quarter the size of the Hippodrome's. It was there that the second of a two-game set would be played against the AC's. The team was billed as the Minneapolis All-Stars, but All-Stars they were not. Composed largely of Canadian imports, one of whom was George Henderson, who had been with St. Paul the season before, they fell 9–2 on February 6 at the Hippodrome and 9–0 two nights later in Minneapolis.

St. Paul quickly went up 3–0 in the first five minutes of game one and led 6–0 at the half. In an attempt at damage control, Kahler had his players form a half-circle in front of his net, but the AC's still added three more goals. The All-Stars recovered well enough in the second half, perhaps inspired by Kahler's tussle with Herb Drury, to hold St. Paul to three more goals while getting two of their own. It was small consolation, and the *Pioneer Press* described the opposition as "kids . . . outclassed. They were lost on the big rink" (February 7, 1917). Conroy, Goheen, and Mohan each had two goals, and Drury, Fitzgerald, and Peterson added singletons.

The All-Stars barely found themselves in game two, despite the hampering of Drury's speed on the smaller ice surface. St. Paul romped, with Conroy, Drury, Goheen, and Mohan each scoring twice and Peterson getting one. Despite the easy win, manager Tom Charlton complained that playing on such a surface left the players open to injury because of crowded conditions with seven players on each side. Charlton would now have greater concerns, as Duluth was due at the Hippodrome on February 13. Memories were still fresh from the last very physical game against them two years before.

Duluth manager Al Swanstrom had put together a team made up principally of players from the city league's best team and supplemented by the stars of the two other clubs. The AC's would once again face Russ Barkell and Arni Olsen, who had seen action against them

in their first year of play. Six hundred fans had turned out for the Minneapolis home game, and the crowd would double for this one. They would see Bert Mohan put St. Paul ahead 1–0 after five minutes, but Barkell would tie it at the half, "eluding six St. Paul puck chasers, dodging and boring to the net, [scoring] though knocked to his knees," as the February 14, 1917, *Pioneer Press* described the action.

Despite numerous rushes by Conroy, Goheen, Fitzgerald, and Mohan, Duluth goalie Richards kept the game tied until the final seconds when Vern Peterson got the game winner on a pass from Drury. If Richards was great for Duluth, Weidenborner was superb for St. Paul. The *Pioneer Press* wrote:

> If there was one man of the fourteen who shone brighter than the others, that man was Weidenborner. The chubby goal keeper had been waiting for a chance to show fans what he could do.
>
> How many times and in how many ways he saved St. Paul from defeat no one stopped to reckon. Shots at him came too thick and fast. Fans saw him block one after another, deflect them with his club, catch them in his hands, scooping like a shortstop or poking the most convenient piece of his anatomy in the way.

The victory brought the team's record to 8–2 on the year, but the earlier financial concerns reared their head again the day following the Duluth victory. The Athletic Club's Executive Committee, of which Tom Charlton was a member, met on February 14 and directed the Hockey Committee to negotiate for a game in Duluth. However, no other games were to be scheduled beyond that contest until the executive committee examined the overall situation. The deficit in the Hockey Committee accounts was running about $1,500.

Charlton attempted to arrange the Duluth game, but the guarantee proved to be prohibitive. On February 25, the *Pioneer Press* reported that the season was over. It had been an artistic, but not a financial, success. The lack of league play, the failure to attract large crowds during carnival week, and the distant location of the Hippodrome were the reasons cited for terminating the season. As to the future, Charlton indicated that it was too early to make a final decision, but the need for a good surface, closer to residential areas, was critical. Housing development of the area in the vicinity of the fairgrounds where the Hippodrome was located was still in the offing.

The executive committee met on February 27 to close things out, and the minutes showed the financial side of the players' involvement. Though hockey was amateur, payments were made as follows:

> The Secretary was authorized to make settlement with the hockey players according to the following schedule:
> Mr. Goheen is to receive $200 minus his house account or any other charges in the house against him and an additional $50.00 which we are to pay Mr. O. L. Taylor for an advance made to Mr. Goheen.
> Mr. Drury [is] issue[d] a check for $35.00 for his transportation back to Port Colborne, Ont.
> Mr. Mohan is to receive no money.
> Mr. Fitzgerald $75.00 less his house account.
> Mr. Conroy $75.00 less his house account and an advance of $25.00.

It should be remembered that these young men were in their twenties. Conroy and Drury were both twenty-two, Goheen was twenty-three, and Fitzgerald was twenty-four. The expense money was important to them as a supplement to their regular incomes. No mention was made of payments to any of the other team members. The season was now over and the future somewhat clouded. Well, not exactly.

## Belated Action

On March 4, the *Pioneer Press* reported that the team might be reconstituted as an independent organization in order to oppose one of two possible Toronto teams passing through to Winnipeg for the Allan Cup finals. The Allan Cup was played off to determine the best senior amateur team in Canada. All players except Bert Mohan, who had departed for a railroad job in Montana, were available for such a game. Five days later, the game seemed a sure thing, with the opponent now determined to be the Toronto Dentals, yet the contest never took place. What did take place was a two-game series against the Pittsburgh Athletic Club at Duquesne Garden in that Pennsylvania city on March 23 and 24. St. Paul would be returning to the site of their three-game series of the previous year.

The AC's would oppose a squad that the *Pittsburgh Sun* described as a team that "has demonstrated beyond the shadow of a doubt that it is one of the speediest septets ever put together here or in any other city." Pittsburgh's big stars were the McCormick brothers, Joe and Larry, who were natives of Buckingham, Quebec. Both would play for the United States at the 1920 Olympics as naturalized citizens, and Joe would eventually join St. Paul in the early 1920s. St. Paul replaced Bert Mohan with Dick Conway and Chubby McBride.

While St. Paul was competitive in both games, the results were no better than in 1916, as Pittsburgh swept again 2–1 and 4–0. McBride had the only Athletic Club goal of either game when he scored on a pass from Ed Fitzgerald as time ran out in game one. The visitors held Pittsburgh to one goal in the first half of game two, but Cy Weidenborner gave up three more in the second half.

Concerns about St. Paul's hockey future soon seemed of little concern when, two weeks after the return from Pittsburgh, the United States entered World War I on April 6, 1917. While the war would preclude any high-level hockey in the year ahead, one of Tom Charlton's concerns, the need for a new rink closer to residential and commercial areas, would become a reality late in 1917. The Lexington Rink, also known as the Coliseum, was constructed adjoining the St. Paul Saints' baseball park at the corner of Lexington and University avenues. The center field wall of the park was used as the west wall of the new rink, which was designed to seat eighteen hundred spectators, who would view games on a 250-by-90-foot ice surface. This was smaller than the Hippodrome, but still quite large, even by today's Olympic standard of 200 by 100 feet. Skaters would have access to a clubhouse, skate storage lockers, and food concessions. In what must have been state-of-the-art construction for the times, a boiler would circulate warm steam through pipes that would form foot rests for each row of seats. Construction superintendent MacMicking told the *Pioneer Press* (November 6, 1917):

> Our new rink will be the finest west of Cleveland. We will spare no expense in completely equipping the entire building, and, as for the ice, we will have the best sheet of aqua in the country. St. Paul skaters are due for a pleasant surprise when we have our grand opening. And the best part of it all is that we are only twelve minutes away from the loop district by street car.

The war in Europe, which had been raging since 1914, ultimately found its way to the United States when the nation entered the conflict on the side of the Allies. While prewar sentiment in St. Paul tended to be divided along business and labor lines, with the former favoring U.S. entry and the latter opposing it, once the decision was made, the city's population supported the effort. Registration for the draft took place on June 5, and more than twenty-two thousand men reported without incident. Of particular note, the traditional anti-British

stance of Irish-Americans was virtually non-existent in the city.

Conroy, Goheen, and Fitzgerald would all see service in the war, with the latter two serving overseas in France. Fitzgerald's service was particularly noteworthy. He was commissioned an artillery second lieutenant in June 1917 following graduation from officer's candidate school at Fort Snelling. Sent to France in September, he received additional training at the French Artillery School before serving in the Champagne, Chateau Thierry, St. Mihiel, and Argonne campaigns. By the time the 1918–19 hockey season rolled around, he was with the army of occupation in Germany.

With both Fitzgerald and Goheen unavailable, it was left to Tony Conroy to revive the game after the one-year war layoff. Conroy's war service was in the United States, allowing him to take a leadership role. (The team is called both "St. Paul" and "Company G" in the two local newspapers. The latter designation is explained in a *St. Paul Daily News* article that appeared when Conroy retired from playing in early 1928. The newspaper commented that Conroy had been with the AC's (and the subsequent minor pro team) "every year excepting in 1917 and 1918, when the club failed to operate because of the war, and 1918–19, when some of the star players still in France made it necessary to form a National Guard team." For the sake of consistency, the name St. Paul will be used in recounting the 1918–19 season.) Public skating resumed at the Hippodrome on Christmas Day 1918, and the Lexington rink opened a day earlier. Hippodrome manager Gale Brooks expressed optimism that high-level hockey would soon be under way, and on January 8 Tony Conroy held his first practice. He would be able to hold only one more training session before the team's first game, but this proved to be quite enough. Conroy had attempted to schedule Calumet. When those efforts failed, he settled for the Great Lakes, Illinois, Naval Training Station. Great Lakes may have had a great football team

*Drafted men leaving St. Paul for World War I duty*

*Canteen workers serving soldiers at Union Station in St. Paul, 1917*

*American troops disembarking from ships at a French port during World War I*

during World War II, but their World War I– era hockey effort left much to be desired. St. Paul won both games easily when the season finally began on February 4 at the Hippodrome.

Conroy, who served as captain and also played rover, was able to put the St. Paul regular Vern Peterson at point, paired with occasional fill-in Dick Conway at cover point. Future AC regulars Emmy Garrett and Everett McGowan were at center and right wing, respectively. Al Wilzbacher played left wing, and Forest Henkel was in goal. Conroy set the pace by scoring first at the three-minute mark and was followed by counters from Garrett (two), Wilzbacher, and

McGowan. Great Lakes tightened things up in the second half, holding St. Paul to goals by Wilzbacher and McGowan, while getting one by Henkel to end things at 7–1. It was 10–1 the next night, as once again twenty-five-minute halves were played, and the sailors blanked St. Paul until the ten-minute mark of the first half, when McGowan opened the scoring. It was only 3–0 at the half, but then "in the second half the [St. Paul] team scored their first goal in six minutes, Garrett registering after worming his way through almost the entire opposing team. Then he scored three more in the next eleven minutes," as reported by the *Pioneer Press* on February 6, 1919. The newspaper was impressed with Everett McGowan's speed, as well it might be, as he would ultimately have both a hockey and speed skating career. Others enjoying the evening were Wilzbacher with three goals, Conroy with two, and McGowan with one.

While sinking the Navy was no doubt great fun, it was hardly a true test of the team's abilities. That would come in a two-game set in Sault Ste. Marie on February 19 and 20. Conroy would drop Dick Conway for the trip and add his brother George and former AC star Nick Kahler. The Soo team carried the name "Fields'

Nationals" and featured players from two years earlier, such as Ray Thompsett, Roy Hill, and Vic DesJardins. Newcomer "Taffy" Abel, who would later play in the NHL and join Murray and DesJardins in the United States Hockey Hall of Fame, was at point. "Muzz" Murray had departed for a professional career with Seattle in the Pacific Coast Hockey Association.

DesJardins would be the star of the first game with three of the Soo's four goals, as the home team shut out St. Paul on their far-smaller ice surface. The second game developed into a total shootout, with the Soo coming out on top 7–5. McGowan and Garrett had a majority of the visitors' goals, "playing in better form than they did the first night," according to the *Pioneer Press* special correspondent on February 21, 1919. A scheduled contest with Sault Ste. Marie, Ontario, was cancelled, and it would be two weeks before the team saw action again.

Conroy, who was a lieutenant in the National Guard, took the team north for two games with Duluth on March 3 and 4, 1919, with two more planned for the Hippodrome on March 5 and 6. Vern Peterson was dispatched to the Great Lakes to see if he could schedule further games with the sailors or anyone else. Nick Kahler and Everett McGowan stayed at home, making the playing mix somewhat different, with Al Corboy being added at point, while Frank Rogers played both right wing and rover. The results were offensively better than the two games on the Upper Peninsula, but no better on the scoreboard.

Joe Linder was back with Duluth, as were Russ Barkell and Jack Mahan, so, as with the Soo, the home team had the edge in experience. The teams fought to a 2-all draw at the half, before the "second half [when] Duluth featured some great team work, and fairly swept the St. Paul crew off the ice for about five minutes," as the *Pioneer Press* reported. That effort was enough to make the final 7–4, as Garrett, Wilzbacher, and both Conroys had the St. Paul goals. The following night, Duluth piled up a 5–1 lead at the half to ensure an 8–5 victory, as the visitors won the second half 4–3. Tony Conroy was St. Paul's star with numerous rushes, two of which resulted in goals, while his brother, Garrett, and Wilzbacher each had one.

Vern Peterson failed to come up with any additional games, and the last two Duluth games were dropped. The short season ended at 2–4, but it was not without value. Tony Conroy was able to keep playing with only a year lost to the war, while his younger brother, George, Emmy Garrett, and Everett McGowan made their debuts. George Conroy and, particularly, Emmy Garrett would go on to play significant roles on postwar AC teams.

Those postwar teams would see St. Paul solidify its status as a hockey power and go on to challenge for national honors in a new league. Before that happened, there was still the matter of proving who was best in the Upper Midwest by once again challenging for the MacNaughton Cup.

# 4

# 1919-1920

## *Sharing the Cup and an Olympic Role*

"Hockey occupies the center of the sport stage at present in St. Paul. For dazzling
speed, for sensation and thrill after thrill, the great ice game cannot be beaten."

St. Paul Dispatch, *February 24, 1920*

Ray Johns had been the driving force behind early St. Paul major league hockey. That role in the post–World War I era would now fall to Frank Weidenborner, brother of goaltender Cyril, the backup on the MacNaughton Cup team and a regular in 1916–17. Frank was both a baseball and a hockey player, seeing service in the latter capacity in the days of the Twin Cities League. But, like Johns, his forte was organizing, not playing. The "war to end all wars" was over, and the nation was on the cusp of the Roaring Twenties and "the golden age of sport." It would be the age of Prohibition (championed by Minnesota congressman Andrew Volstad), speakeasies, flappers, jazz, and a raging bull market. By the end of the decade, it would all come tumbling down, but that's another story. There was hockey to be played in St. Paul in these postwar years, and Frank Weidenborner would see to it that it was played.

By December 1919, Minnesotans were back from the war and ready to compete. But how would the team now be organized and where would it play? The *St. Paul Pioneer Press*, December 14, 1919, wrote that

through the civic patriotism of a group of young business men, St. Paul is to get back

on the hockey map this winter with a team that will revive the memories of 1917, when the fastest amateur team in the United States played under the colors of the St. Paul Athletic club . . . The team, which is now in the process of organization, will be known as the St. Paul Athletic club team, but that organization is not to assume the responsibility of meeting a possible deficit at the end of the season. The guarantors have agreed to take full charge of financing the undertaking . . . The team will be managed by F. F. Weidenborner.

The new postwar team would play most of its games at the new Lexington Rink. Side boards had been installed, as well as sufficient seating to handle all but the largest crowds. A small number of games in which sizeable numbers could be expected would be played at the Hippodrome. Thus, Tom Charlton's hope for a more urban facility, with easier access by streetcar, was now a reality. With the organizational framework now in place, the work of forming the team and determining what kind of competition it would be facing had to be addressed. In the previous four years of high-level competition, there had been league play only in 1915–16. Now such play would become the norm. Frank

Weidenborner was off to Marquette, Michigan, on December 20 to attend a meeting that re-established the AAHA for 1919–20. It was hoped that Duluth and Calumet would be able to join, but the final membership along with St. Paul was American Soo, Canadian Soo, and Portage Lake. The schedule called for four games against each opponent—two home and two away—which allowed sufficient opportunities for independent play against non-league opponents.

Workouts had begun on December 7 at the Lexington Rink under de facto coach Ed Fitzgerald. He would once again assume the captain's mantle amid speculation over the return of Herb Drury. He would not be back, but Nick Kahler, who had played such a key role the first two years and had resurfaced briefly the previous season, would be. The *St. Paul Daily News*, December 28, 1919, wrote: "At center will be old reliable Nick Kahler. He may not be near as fast as many of the others, but knows the game thoroughly, is a steady, dependable player and should more than hold his own." Among the "others" skating with the AC's this year would be Canadians Frank McCarthy and A. C. Gehrke along with Minnesotans George Conroy, Emmy Garrett, Everett McGowan, and Vern Peterson. McCarthy and Garrett would see the most playing time, while local goalie Ernie Byers would serve as backup to Weidenborner. These players would complement the established core of Tony Conroy, Ed Fitzgerald, and Frank Goheen,

*The 1919–20 AC's. Standing (l to r): George Conroy, Vern Peterson, Nick Kahler, Emmy Garrett, Frank Weidenborner; bottom (l to r): Cy Weidenborner, Capt. Ed Fitzgerald, Frank Goheen, Tony Conroy*

who had been with the team since its inception in 1914. They would play together until Ed Fitzgerald went behind the bench for the 1922–23 season.

### The Postwar Era Begins

League play would not get under way until January 6, but Weidenborner had scheduled Duluth for the season opener on December 30. Joe Linder was gone, but Russ Barkell was still a force to be reckoned with for the Zenith City skaters. He was joined by locals Ivor Anderson in goal, Gus Olson at rover, and Jimmy Owens on defense, as the terms "point" and "cover point" started to fade from use. Anderson and Olson would see considerable service when Duluth returned to league competition in the years ahead. The promising Owens would die prematurely.

It would be Olson who opened the scoring as his shot caromed off Weidenborner's skate. The 1–0 lead held at the half, but Nick Kahler would score twice after the intermission to put the AC's ahead, only to have Duluth's Owens tie the game as his shot deflected off a defender's stick and into the St. Paul net. Kahler got the winner after taking a pass from Tony Conroy, who had maneuvered through heavy traffic to make the play. It had been a good start to the season, not only on the ice but also at the box office. E. R. Hosking, on December 31, 1919, wrote for the *Pioneer Press*:

> It has frequently been remarked . . . that fast hockey could be made more than self-supporting in St. Paul if the fans were able to see games played within a reasonable distance of the residential and business sections of the city . . . Fifteen minutes before [play] began there was a line of fans standing from the door of the rink down University avenue. The capacity . . . of the Lexington avenue plant . . . is 1,600, and the rink was jammed to the doors.

> If St. Paul had been provided with a good downtown rink, easily accessible . . . hockey would, years ago, have become the leading winter sport of this city.

As to the game itself, Hosking described it as a "creditable beginning" with "many rough spots" in the play. He was critical of the first-half positioning of the center and rover and viewed right wing as a problem. Rookie Everett McGowan played that position, and he would be gone after two games to pursue his speed-skating career. Kudos went to just about everyone else, including Duluth goalie Ivor Anderson. He was described as "an entertainment in himself" when he used a baseball mitt as an early version of today's catching glove.

Weidenborner attempted to strengthen the team by signing Leo Archibald from the Winnipeg Victorias, but he was dropped after a few practices. There was still speculation concerning the return of Herb Drury, and Bert Mohan was also mentioned as a possible returnee. None of this came to anything, and when the team opened against American Soo, the only change in the lineup of the AC's saw Goheen moving to rover while McCarthy took his place on defense. The rink was described by Ed Shave in the January 7, 1920, edition of the *Daily News* as "packed" and included a contingent of Soo fans, who saw their team, after dominating a scoreless first half, go down 4–0 before Roy Hill got the last two goals to make the final score 4–2. Three of St. Paul's goals came in rapid succession after the break, with Kahler, Conroy, and McCarthy getting the tallies. Ed Shave recounted the last goal:

> Frank Goheen, the most spectacular player on the ice, carried the puck down alone, evaded, leaped . . . around some four of the Soo players. Just as he shot he was sent sprawling on the ice, but while he was sliding the puck shot past the astonished goal keeper.

Attendance dropped off to about a thousand fans for the second game on January 7, but the result was the same, as the AC's skated to a 7–4 win. Nick Kahler got four of the seven goals. Conroy and Goheen added two and one, respectively. The outcome was never much in doubt, although Vic DesJardins, now Soo captain, had two goals. Most of the game's excitement came when Soo goalie Buzzo threatened Goheen with his stick after the White Bear Lake native charged the visitors' forward, Matt Kokko.

## North to Duluth and the Range

As the team headed out on their first road trip, it was announced that Port Arthur, Ontario, was scheduled to play either one or two games with the AC's on January 19 and 20. As it happened, Port Arthur never came to St. Paul, but by the time the team returned home, they had extended their winning streak to five. The three-game trip opened in Duluth on January 12 at the Curling Club rink. The home team had played well after their opening loss to St. Paul, twice defeating Eveleth and Hibbing.

After Nick Kahler gave the visitors a quick one-goal lead after only ninety seconds of play, Duluth took a 2–1 lead when Gus Olson and

Jimmy Olson scored. That would be the high point for Duluth, as Kahler got two more and Goheen one. By the six-minute mark of the second half, St. Paul had upped the score to 7–2 on goals from Conroy, Goheen, and Garrett. A late goal by the home team made the final 7–3. Louis Gollop, writing in the *Duluth News Tribune* on January 13, 1920, summarized things quite well when he reported: "St. Paul has a defense that is almost impossible to break through and as an offensive team, boy, oh boy!" It was more of the same the next night—early competitiveness followed by an AC onslaught. The AC's led at the half 2–1 on Conroy and Goheen goals, but Russ Barkell tied the game early in the second. It was as close as Duluth would get as Goheen, Kahler, and Fitzgerald scored before Barkell got another. Nick Kahler managed to pick up a five-minute penalty when he hit Oreck Gow while the latter was flat on his back.

It was off to Eveleth the next day for the team's third game in three nights. The Hill Top City had not yet established its unique status in American hockey. The seeds were being sown though they were not evident this night. The locals kept St. Paul off the scoreboard until the twenty-minute mark of the first half, when Kahler made it 1–0. Goheen added another in

*The Duluth Curling Club*

the first half, and Garrett and Conroy got two more after the break. "Squel" (Cy) Weidenborner picked up the 4–0 win, the first of four he would record for the season.

The AC's were done traveling to the Range, but not with Range teams. Back in the Lexington Rink on January 20 they took on Hibbing in a game that was purportedly for the "state title." The basis for that description is unclear, but in any event the team made the *Pioneer Press* headline writer look good. The scribe had proclaimed that the "AC Hockey Team Wins State Title" on January 21 as he reported St. Paul's 8–1 pasting of Hibbing. The home team was coached by St. Paul native Bob McMenemy, who also played on occasion, but not on this night. Goheen and Kahler each scored twice in the first half, while Hibbing got its only goal early in the second period, before Conroy, McCarthy, Goheen, and Kahler closed things out.

### Confronting Portage Lake and the Soos

St. Paul was now 7–0 on the season, but only two of the wins had come over league competition. After the one-game home stand, it was off on another road trip, this time to Michigan's Upper Peninsula to play Portage Lake twice before returning for two games with Canadian Soo. Then it would be back on the road to Canadian Soo and American Soo for two game sets. All of this was AAHA competition and would play a large role in determining the next holder of the MacNaughton Cup. The *Duluth News Tribune,* January 2, 1920, had reported:

> Portage Lake proposes to put on the ice one of the strongest amateur hockey teams in the United States . . . [All players are] American developed . . . with the exception of Travers and Dietz . . . [T]he hockey season for Portage Lake is most promising.

The season would prove to be less promising once the AC's finished their stay. On January

22 the visitors won handily 7–1, as Kahler celebrated his return to his home area (Dollar Bay is across the lake from Portage Lake) with a four-goal game. Goheen and Garrett added solo goals while another went unassigned, finding its way home from heavy traffic in front of the net. Kahler continued his happy homecoming the next night with two more goals, Garrett added two, and Conroy had one as St. Paul completed the sweep 5–1. The local *Daily Mining Gazette,* January 23, 1920, was duly impressed:

> The playing of the St. Paul men who are a good set of upstanding men, rather tall and rangy, is worth seeing. With the exception of Garret[t], the men have been playing on the team for about four years either as regulars or spares. Goheen, one of the men who [has] been on the team for the longest time, is the star player and he ranks high. Khaler [Kahler], the former Dollar Bay boy . . . Fitzgerald, McCarthy, and Conroy are all able men, who follow the puck and don't lose it readily.

The team returned to St. Paul to prepare to host Canadian Soo on January 27 and 28 at the Lexington Rink. Ed Fitzgerald had told the *Daily News* on January 25, 1920, that a great effort had not been required to beat Portage Lake and that Conroy and several others were not at the top of their game. Conroy had played with a slight cold. All would be ready for the next series, which he expected to be the most difficult of the season. The two Soos had just completed a very physical two-game set in which players from both teams had been carried from the ice.

Before Frank Weidenborner came back from Michigan he had to take care of a not-so-small matter. For some unknown reason, the MacNaughton Cup, which had been in the physical possession of the St. Paul Athletic Club in 1917, had found itself in Calumet, Michigan, a few miles north of Portage Lake. Weidenborner retrieved the trophy, and it went on display at Rockstruck's jewelry store and at Spaulding's, a sporting goods outlet, before returning to the club headquarters, "where, if the men from across the border [Canadian Soo] are vanquished, it will, beyond all doubt, remain for another year," as the *Pioneer Press*, January 27, 1920, so aptly stated.

St. Paul now led the AAHA with a 4–0 record. Canadian Soo was also undefeated in league action, but it had played two fewer games. The team was regarded as the most formidable opponent for the AC's in their quest to retain the MacNaughton Cup and were led by their goaltender, James Patrick Walsh. No one ever called him Jim—he would be known forever as "Flat" and would ultimately play in the NHL, mostly with the Montreal Maroons. Former teammate Herb Drury was in the Soo lineup, but Soo captain Gerry Munro, another future Maroon, was injured and didn't make the trip.

"Squel" Weidenborner would have two superb games in goal as he came up with consecutive wins, 2–0 and 3–0. In game one he turned back close to twenty-four shots, while Fitzgerald and McCarthy played superb defense. Emmy Garrett, another product of St. Paul, would be the offensive star the first night with two goals. The *Pioneer Press*, January 28, 1920, said of him:

> Garrett . . . was the surprise of the evening. This fleet skater was in practically every play, defensive and offensive, and his passing, dodging and play-making propensities brought deep discouragement to the Dominionites . . . [I]t is quite unlikely that he will be removed from right wing.

Garrett got his goals in each half, the first off a bad clearing effort by Walsh and the second from a scramble in front of the Soo netminder. The *Daily News,* January 28, 1920, observed that the visitors' attacks were "stemmed [and] greeted with cheers mingled with piercing feminine screams."

The next night Garrett got his third consecutive goal very early in the first half when he picked up the puck behind the Soo net, drew out Walsh, and put it by him. After the break, Garrett set up Kahler for the second AC goal, while Goheen did the same for the Dollar Bay native's second tally of the game.

St. Paul was in great shape as the team headed back to Michigan and Western Ontario for games with both Soos. The home and home series with Canadian Soo resumed on February 2 with the AC's realizing that a split with both home teams would keep the MacNaughton Cup in the Minnesota capital. That certainly looked like a real possibility when the visitors came away with a 3–2 win the first night. St. Paul dominated the first half on goals by Vern Peterson, Goheen, and Garrett. Peterson was making his season debut, taking Kahler's place—the team's scoring leader was unable to make the trip. The AC's would sorely miss his presence in the second half and in the two games back across the border. Canadian Soo matched St. Paul's first-half dominance in the second half, but fell short of getting the equalizer.

They would get more than the equalizer twenty-four hours later, when "Gloomy" Lessard broke a 1–1 tie late in the second half on a high overhead drive that eluded Weidenborner. All of the game's scoring had occurred in the second half as Quesnelle and Garrett had traded earlier goals. The loss ended the AC winning streak at a dozen games, but a sweep back in Michigan would still clinch the Cup. That was not to be, as the team now experienced its first real slump of the season in a pair of nasty games with a team they had dominated a month earlier.

St. Paul would suffer a loss on February 5 in a game rife with discord and penalties. American Soo took a 1–0 lead in the first half, but the visitors protested that the goal was scored while a penalized Soo player was still on the ice. The goal was allowed to stand—the referee ruled that the player in question was on the penalty bench. Earlier in the period, "Taffy" Abel and Goheen came to blows that precipitated a bench-clearing brawl that brought fans on the ice. Abel and Roy Hill got second-half goals for the home team to give them a 3–0 win. When it was all over, Frank Weidenborner vented to the special correspondent for the *Pioneer Press*, February 6, 1920:

> At the beginning of the game the referee ruled a player off the ice and the man did not leave. The Soo scored during this time and the referee permitted the score, not giving any additional penalty. We never had a chance until the last five minutes of the game when it was too late. Every time our men started they would be tripped or checked in some illegal manner. We would have left the ice during the first five minutes, but we needed the money to return. We are disgusted with the treatment received here.

If Weidenborner was angry after the first game, he would be livid after the second. Play resumed two nights later with the AC's forced to play one man short. Peterson had injured his leg in the first game, and the Soo would not play with one fewer skater, claiming that St. Paul should have brought an extra player. There would be more of the violence of game one, as the home team built up a 3–0 first-half lead. The *Pioneer Press*, February 8, 1920, described things this way:

> Deliberate slashing and tripping prevailed throughout the contest which was one of the roughest ever witnessed. Goheen struck Matt Kokko in [the] head with [his] stick and the latter was carried from the ice, but returned after three minutes.
>
> Abel, 225 pound Soo defense man, deliberately struck Garrett across [the] back with [his] stick but the blow glanced off and the Saint[s'] player was not badly injured. Fans thronged the ice during the progress of both fights which resulted from unclean tactics and many blows were exchanged with telling effect.

When play resumed in the second half, Goheen got two quick goals to bring the AC's close, but it would not be enough. The Soo got a late goal to seal their 4–2 victory. Weidenborner again sounded off to the correspondent from the *Pioneer Press* on February 8, 1920:

> Almost every minute of the contest was marked by tripping, kneeing, and offside checking with body and stick, also slugging over the back and body. We got a raw deal in both contests, but the team played good hockey considering the difficulties. Will arrive home Sunday and our protest [to AAHA president A. L. Ferguson] will be taken up before leaving.

Nothing came of the protest, and the team returned home having gone 1–3 on the road trip, their worst stretch of the season. St. Paul still led the AAHA with a 7–3 record (12–3 overall), while American Soo trailed by two games in second place. The MacNaughton Cup might be safely resting in the Athletic Club's rooms, but its 1919–20 status was still up for grabs.

## Securing the Cup and Returning to Pittsburgh

"Smarting under three defeats inflicted upon them on the tour into the copper country, the St. Paul A. C. hockey players are determined to 'take it out' on the Portage Lake septet," commented the *Pioneer Press* on February 8, 1920. And take it out they most certainly did. Portage Lake came to St. Paul at the bottom of the league with a 0–7–1 record and would leave still looking for a first victory. Things started well enough for the visitors on February 10 when Bill Trathen got the game's first goal. The visitors would earn four more, but the AC's got twelve for their most lopsided win of the season. Emmy Garrett had a six-goal game, while Conroy had three, Kahler two, and Goheen one. In the entire history of the NHL, there have been only eight six-goal games, and Garrett's effort is particularly impressive in an era in which passing was allowed only within each zone and then only laterally and backwards. He was good enough to be described by the *Pioneer Press* as "the big noise" for the home team, while Conroy's work at wing was "better than at any time in his career."

K. T. Robertson, Portage Lake manager, laid the defeat at the hands of a tired team that had made the train trip the previous night without benefit of sleeping berths. It would be different in game two—but not by much. St. Paul got two first-half goals from Kahler, while adding four more in the second game from Goheen (two), Conroy, and Garrett. Cyril Weidenborner got his final win of the season. That night's "first star" would be Goheen. The *Pioneer Press,* February 12, 1920, would describe him as a "wizard [who] treated the spectators to a lot of clever skating." Most importantly, the victory clinched a tie for the MacNaughton Cup for the AC's. However, if either of the Soos won all of their remaining games, a tie would result and a play-off series would be necessary to determine the Cup holder for 1919–20.

While the two Soos played out the remainder of their schedules attempting to force a play-off, St. Paul players busied themselves with three non-league contests. All of these would be shifted to the Hippodrome, and, in order to reacquaint his players with the larger surface, Ed Fitzgerald began practice there on February 16. Duluth would be the first visitor on February 19, followed by the Winnipeg Monarchs on February 23 and 24. Admission prices would be dropped from 85 cents to 55 cents. Box seats were $1.10. The higher admission rates were required for league games. (Movies, which were often accompanied by vaudeville acts of singers, dancers, and jugglers, typically charged 15 to 25 cents for tickets, while live theater prices ran from one to three dollars a performance.)

Duluth came to the Hippodrome having improved considerably since their last game with the AC's. The night before they had staged a late four-goal rally to beat Hibbing 6–5. Much of the improvement was attributed to the addi-

tion of Bill Bogan and Jack Mahan to the lineup. Both were veterans who had played for Duluth in the past. Ernie Byers took over from "Squel" Weidenborner in the nets due to a death in the latter's family. Mahan did not make the trip, and his absence was felt as the home team quickly put the game away early in the first half. Kahler and Garrett got the first two of six goals. Duluth countered with two, though they played St. Paul to a 4–4 draw in the second half. Kahler caged three more, Goheen had three, and Garrett added another for the home team. So much for an improved Duluth team—bring on the Manitobans.

The Monarchs had won the Allan Cup in previous years, but were not having one of their better seasons. Nonetheless, they featured future NHL'ers Ivan "Ching" Johnson and Walter "Perk" Galbraith, both of whom would see action against the AC's in the years ahead. Johnson's career was good enough to get him elected to the Hockey Hall of Fame in Toronto in 1958. Fitzgerald drilled the locals on Sunday morning, and when game time arrived on Monday night, "Squel" Weidenborner was back in the nets. The crowds had not been large at recent games, so Frank Weidenborner must have taken some satisfaction when two thousand fans were on hand for game one.

No doubt adding to that good feeling was the 2–0 game his brother—about a year older—pitched at Winnipeg. In a game that the *Daily News* of February 24, 1920, described as "one of the speediest of the year with both teams skating furiously from start to finish," Kahler scored ten minutes into the first half on a pass from Fitzgerald. Soon after, Conroy assisted on Garrett's fifteenth goal of the season. There would be no further scoring, as Weidenborner, aided by Fitzgerald and McCarthy, protected the lead despite a Monarch burst in the last ten minutes. The term "shutout" made its first appearance in contemporary press accounts when W. F. Keefe, the *Pioneer Press* writer covering the game, reported on February 24, 1920, that "Nick [Kahler] took the puck every time and otherwise made the shutout a possibility." Keefe also lauded McCarthy for having "played his best game since donning the colors of the A. C.," as well as for showing some offense when "on one occasion [he] came within an ace of scoring."

Things would not go as well for St. Paul the following night, perhaps due to the rink conditions that the *Dispatch,* February 24, 1920, described after game one:

> The change in the rinks has something to do with the change in the passing game. The Hip rink, being so much larger gave more opportunity. The ice . . . was sticky and the puck would not carry well nor true. The lights also grew hazy, due to smoking, and the deep breathing of the players.

In a game in which they would take five penalties to Winnipeg's one, the AC's went down in their first and only home defeat of the season. After a scoreless first half, "Ching" Johnson gave the visitors an early lead while Goheen was off tending to an injured arm. Garrett, who had returned to play after an errant Monarch stick gashed his throat, soon tied it up on a long shot from the side. With under two minutes to go, Winnipeg's Finkelstein stole the puck at mid-ice and beat Weidenborner for the game winner.

In the race to force a play-off with St. Paul, Canadian Soo had defeated their American counterparts in a hard-fought two-game series. This left the Canadians and the AC's with identical 9–3 records and forced a two-game total-goals play-off series with one game in St. Paul and the other at Canadian Soo. St. Paul had hoped to avoid this scenario through a successful protest of the two-game series at American Soo in early February. League president A. L. Ferguson and secretary K. D. Robertson had previously disallowed the protest. When Frank Weidenborner pointed out that St. Paul had not been represented at the meeting in which the protest was denied, he requested another meet-

ing. The *Pioneer Press,* March 4, 1920 reported that the meeting

> was attended by Frank F. Weidenborner of the local club. When the protests came up they were promptly disallowed and when Mr. Weidenborner attempted to appeal to the league rules, President Ferguson said: "What do we care about the rules?" [Ferguson was from American Soo and Robertson from Portage Lake.] Captain Fitzgerald at first was for refusing to play the Soo team again though this would mean forfeiting the cup, but later was prevailed upon to comply with the league mandate . . . The A. C. players have decided . . . these will be the last games the team will play against either Soo team. This means that St. Paul will not be in the league next year if either of the Soo teams are in it.
>
> As things are now in the circuit, the league is being run to suit the convenience of President A. L. Ferguson, in the opinion of St. Paul players, who say that his policies may suit such small communities as the Soo and Houghton [Portage Lake], but they savor too much of minor league tactics to suit St. Paul.

The first St. Paul–Canadian Soo game was scheduled for March 5 in Minnesota, with the return engagement slated for March 8 in Ontario. Neither game was ever played—the Twin Cities was hit by a severe snowstorm that first led to a one-day delay and then to cancellation. The AC's and Canadian Soo were declared co-champions, but St. Paul was allowed to retain possession of the MacNaughton Cup.

There was, however, still hockey to be played, though none of it in St. Paul. This was an Olympic year, and the games had been awarded to Antwerp, Belgium, in order to assist that nation in recovering from the ravages of World War I. There were two reasons for the inclusion of hockey. First, the

*Le Palais de Glace, Antwerp*

International Olympic Committee was able to secure the commitments of five European countries to participate: Belgium, Czechoslovakia, France, Sweden, and Switzerland. Second, the administrators of Antwerp's Le Palais de Glace would not stage the figure-skating competition unless there was hockey. International Ice Hockey Federation (IHHF) vice president Paul Laroiq, a Belgian, had convinced Olympic founder Baron Pierre de Coubertin to include both hockey and figure skating in the games. Both were regarded as demonstration sports included within the Games of the VII Olympiad. There was as yet no official Winter Olympics. Competition would be staged April 20–30 with the regular summer sports getting under way later in the year.

St. Paul, along with Boston and Pittsburgh, played hockey at the highest level in the United States at this time. However, while St. Paul came the closest, there was no one team composed entirely of American players that could be selected to represent the nation at Antwerp. The national governing body for the sport was the International Skating and Hockey Union (ISHU), headed by President Cornelius Fellowes of New

York. It became apparent to the ISHU that their original idea of staging an elimination tournament among the Boston, Pittsburgh, and St. Paul teams and sending the winner to Antwerp was unworkable. It was simply not possible to come up with a fourteen-man team of American citizens since clubs in this era usually carried no more than nine or ten players.

There still remained a scheduled three-game series between the AC's and Pittsburgh to be played in the Pennsylvania city. These games would now be a means for Olympic and Pittsburgh team manager Roy Schooley to evaluate St. Paul's talent—he had previously seen Boston when they played his squad earlier in March. The AC's left for Pittsburgh on March 9, changed trains in Chicago the next morning, and arrived in the Steel City on March 11. The team had worked out at the Hippodrome on March 8 and would do the same on the Duquesne Garden ice soon after their arrival. Part of the rationale for playing the last three games at the Hippodrome was that the ice surface was similar to, though somewhat larger than, that of the Pittsburgh rink.

There would be a significant difference in these games in that they would be played with six men to a side and in three fifteen-minute periods. The forerunner to the NHL had gone to the six-man game for the 1911–12 season and to three periods a year before. The rover position would be gone, so Goheen, who had periodically played defense, would be teamed with Fitzgerald on the back line. Kahler would center Conroy and Garrett, while McCarthy and Gus Olson would be the spares. The latter was a late addition off the Duluth team. "Squel" Weidenborner would be in goal as usual.

Despite giving up the first goal at 1:09 on the first period, St. Paul had no problem in adjusting to the six-man game. Ray Bonney, who had been so instrumental in helping the AC's to the MacNaughton Cup in 1915–16, was in the Pittsburgh nets and gave up two goals to Goheen within two minutes to give the visitors a 2–1 first-period lead. Conroy made it 3–1 in the second period, and Russ McCrimmon got his second for the home team in the third period. It was too late to affect the outcome, and a hopeful Frank Weidenborner wired the *Daily News,* March 13, 1920:

> Every man played a good game. Goheen played center [a change in plans], Olson right defense and Kahler (spare) and Garrett right wing. The ice was slow, but our boys outplayed Pittsburgh every minute. Weidenborner . . . starred. Goheen, as usual, electrified the fans. All our men outguessed and outskated their opponents. We will try to duplicate tonight.

Howard Cassidy, a reporter for an unidentified Pittsburgh newspaper, was more ecstatic about the team's play than the manager:

> These young Lochinvars out of the West, flushed with victories, brought all the wizardry of the ice sport for the delight of the fans at Duquesne Garden last night. They

won because they were more consistently good. They were quick as a flash to turn any advantage, they frequently outskated Pittsburgh and their speed at times was bewildering. And they had Goheen, the marvel. And more than that, they threw a barrier across the ice, with Capt Fitzgerald as its backbone and Weidenborner like a curtain at goal, that the locals could not batter down.

But batter it down they did the next night, when St. Paul appeared to run out of gas— "Squel" Weidenborner had his worst night of the season, allowing six goals, as Pittsburgh romped to a 6–1 triumph. McCrimmon again scored first, this time fifty-five seconds into the game. Former AC'er Herb Drury quickly followed at 2:06. The home team got another before the end of the period, and then, after a scoreless second period, closed things out with three more goals in the final canto. Kahler got St. Paul's only goal on a pass from Goheen after Pittsburgh had made it 5–0. Both Goheen and Drury had more than their share of physical play. In the second period, they collided near St. Paul's goal while going for the puck. Pittsburgh sportswriter Raymond Coll, in an unidentified Pittsburgh newspaper story on March 14, 1920, observed:

> Herb went down and out while Frankie was forced to hang his head over the side boards for a few minutes before play could be resumed. Herb retired for the remainder of the period, but came back in the final stanza . . . Herb . . . played a bang-up game last night . . . a marked improvement . . . on the previous night.

The first two games had been played on Friday, March 12, and Saturday, March 13. The teams would now rest on Sunday and play the deciding game on Monday night. At stake, in addition to Olympic evaluations, would be the Cornelius Fellowes Cup, symbolizing the amateur championship of the United States. The trophy was named for the ISHU president, who would later succeed Roy Schooley as manager of the United States Olympic Team.

First-period action was at a furious pace as the teams battled to get the all-important first goal. When it happened it went to the AC's Gus Olson and would prove to be the visitors' high-water mark, as Frank Manners would get two for the locals by the end of the first period. Like the previous game, there was no scoring in the second period, but Goheen was injured when an errant stick caught him in the face as he fought for the puck. But he continued to play. The White Bear skater was not so lucky in the final period, when a flying puck struck him again in the face and he was forced to leave the game. St. Paul had gotten the better of the play in the second period, but once Goheen was gone, fortunes sagged. McCrimmon scored twice for Pittsburgh after the ten-minute mark, and the home team claimed the Fellowes Cup.

*Daily News'* sportswriter Ed Shave had predicted the outcome on March 11, 1920:

> I hope that the Saints [this nickname starts to come into common usage at this time] beat Pittsburgh, but I fear very much that we will suffer two defeats there. The Pitt six is strong in every department. Although St. Paul has done very well this season I do not think they have been meeting teams which have the class that Pittsburgh possesses . . . St. Paul has a number of players who with more coaching, more experience will develop into high class hockeyists, but right at the present are still developing. If the Saints win one game at Pittsburgh they will do all that can be expected of them.

Nonetheless, while the team's fate was similar to that of the 1915–16 squad, Frank Weidenborner felt that St. Paul had made its mark. The *Pioneer Press,* on March 25, 1920, reported that

Manager Weidenborner . . . said the St. Paul boys by their manly conduct and their furious work in combat have given western hockey the biggest boost it ever had received in the East, and that [if] the St. Paul team had more reserves, especially when Frank Goheen was hurt, they would have been able to go the same pace in the second and third battles as they displayed . . . in the first encounter.

## On to Antwerp

Hockey was over only for Garrett, Kahler, and McCarthy—on March 16 Roy Schooley named the 1920 United States Olympic Team. Schooley was a naturalized American from Welland, Ontario, who had come to Pittsburgh in 1901. He had begun his career as a referee and subsequently had become manager of both Duquesne Garden and the Pittsburgh team. As manager of the Olympic squad he had full power to select the players. Schooley knew his own team well enough and now had evaluated the talent on the Boston and St. Paul clubs. Off the AC's he selected Goheen and Conroy as forwards, Fitzgerald on defense, and subsequently, Cyril Weidenborner as the back-up goaltender.

The four would join Joe and Larry McCormick plus Herb Drury from Pittsburgh. Also on the team were George "Gerry" Geran and Frank Synott of Boston, as forwards. Irving Small and Leon Tuck, both of Boston, were the other defensemen, and Pittsburgh provided Ray Bonney in goal. Joe McCormick was named captain a day later.

At the same time Schooley was making this announcement, William S. Haddock, the number two man at the ISHU, unveiled plans to fund the team's trip to Europe. Approximately $15,000 was needed, and revenue from exhibition games would be the source of funds. The intent was to play two series of two games each at Duquesne Garden. The first series on March 22 and 23 would be against the Winnipegs (not to

*The newly chosen 1920 U.S. Olympic team*

be confused with the Monarchs or the Falcons). An opponent remained to be scheduled for the March 29 and 30 games. All money beyond the guarantee paid to the visitors and overhead expenses would go to the Olympic team. Haddock urged local fans to think of the admission prices as a means of supporting the team.

Schooley also indicated that the team would assemble in Pittsburgh on March 20 to prepare for the games against the Winnipegs. Conroy and Goheen were inserted into the Pittsburgh lineup on March 20 in a season-ending game against the Toronto Dentals. Pittsburgh won 3–2, and the *Pittsburgh Post,* March 21, 1920, reported that "the St. Paul players played flashy hockey and were applauded by the large crowd."

In the time between the announcement of the team's selection and its assembly in Pittsburgh, questions concerning the citizenship status of certain players were raised in the *Ottawa Journal,* on March 18, 1920. The Canadian newspaper commented that "the majority of the players on this team are practically all Canadian" and then recounted the playing careers of the McCormick brothers, "Dinny" Manners, Ray Bonney, Ed Nagle, and Russ McCrimmon.

The McCormicks were from Buckingham, Quebec, and had served in the U.S. Army in France during World War I. They had just become citizens on March 17. Herb Drury, from Midland, Ontario, had had similar service, but no question was raised about his eligibility, or that of Frank Synott of Chatham, New Brunswick. Ray Bonney was American-born but Canadian-developed, but that was not an issue. Manners, Nagle, and McCrimmon were Canadian citizens and clearly not eligible. A day later, the *Journal* further raised the issue of the professional status of "Gerry" Geran, a Holyoke, Massachusetts, native who had played four games for the Montreal Wanderers in the 1917–18 NHL season.

Reviewing this issue some eighty-three years later, there appears to be no reason to doubt Roy Schooley's comment, in the *Post* on March 17, 1920, that "all of the men selected can make the trip and are eligible from the standpoint of American citizenship." The McCormicks had just become citizens, Drury was naturalized, and Synott was presumably already a citizen. Bonney's U.S. birth gave him citizenship, while all the AC players were Minnesota natives. Tuck, like Geran, was a Massachusetts native, but from Melrose. Thus the team would be seven native-born and four naturalized players. Small was unable to make the trip, and Geran's previous brief professional career was not raised further as an issue.

Geran, along with Tuck and Synott, arrived on the morning of March 22 in time to work out with the team for the first exhibition game against the Winnipegs that evening. The Winnipegs' most notable player was defenseman Mervyn "Red" Dutton, who would have a Hall of Fame career as a player, coach, and NHL president. Despite the late integration of the Boston players into the Olympic team lineup, the Americans triumphed 4–3 as Geran and Joe McCormick each scored twice. The Winnipegs came back the next night to edge the U.S. team 3–2. Geran and Drury got the American goals. Although they lost, the *Pioneer Press*, March 24, 1920, described Geran and Goheen as "bright stars" and added: "Goheen thrilled the large crowd by his sensational dashes down the ice, but was unfortunate in his shooting."

Since each team had won a game, it was decided to hold the Winnipegs over for a third game on March 25. Drury had had an unruly first game in which he was ordered off the ice after a physical altercation with the referee following a roughing call in the second period. He had returned for the third period, but there were now calls for his removal from the team. It was rumored that Frank Downing of Boston, whom the AC's would face in 1922, would take his place. When the puck was dropped for the final game, Drury was back on the ice.

The Winnipegs took the lead at 11:01, but soon thereafter St. Paul made its presence felt. "Conroy came down the ice like a streak of lightning after shooting three times unsuccessfully [and] finally managed to pull Tupper away from the net and sent the disc in for the tieing score," reported the *New York Times* on March 26, 1920. There was no further scoring in regulation or in the first five minutes of overtime, but Joe McCormick gave the United States the 3–1 victory with two goals in the second. (Sudden death was not necessarily played outside the NHL at this time.)

The *Pittsburgh Post* on March 26 reported that any shortfall in funds raised by the Winnipeg series and the two that Pittsburgh would play on March 26 and 27 would be covered by Duquesne Garden. The Hamilton Tigers would furnish the opposition for the locals as the *Post*, on March 25, 1920, observed that these were not Olympic team games. (The March 29 and 30 dates had been dropped.) Despite that fact the Boston players were in the lineup on the first night as Goheen and Fitzgerald officiated. The other Olympians rested. Hamilton, with future NHL players Carson Cooper and Leo Reise, won 4–3. Geran had one of the Pittsburgh goals.

The following night it was Boston's turn to rest as the Pittsburgh and St. Paul players gave the Steel City team a 5–0 victory. The *Pioneer Press*, March 28, 1920, reported:

> For the greater period of the game the forwards who will play on the American Olympic team . . . were used, this being done to perfect team play, and the work of Captain Joe McCormick, Goheen, Drury and Conroy was a revelation . . . Goheen, skating through the opposing team, shot a pretty goal. [Olympians Drury and Joe McCormick also scored.]

The team was now slated to assemble in New York on April 6 for departure on the steamer *Finland* the next day. Prior to leaving for New

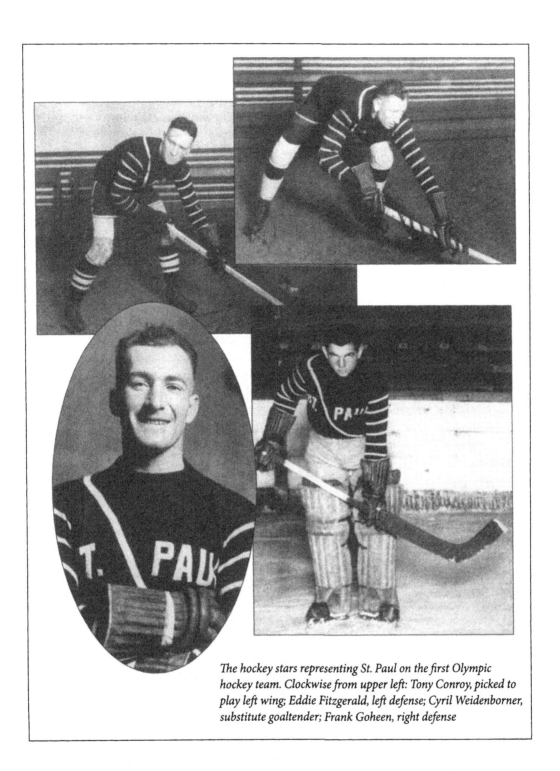

*The hockey stars representing St. Paul on the first Olympic hockey team. Clockwise from upper left: Tony Conroy, picked to play left wing; Eddie Fitzgerald, left defense; Cyril Weidenborner, substitute goaltender; Frank Goheen, right defense*

York, Pittsburgh played two games against Kitchener, Ontario, winning both by 5–4 and 3–1 scores. It was another opportunity for Pittsburgh's Olympians to prepare for Antwerp. All played, and Drury scored twice in the first game.

As the Olympians traveled to New York, the *Post* on April 6, 1920, reported that Schooley had resigned as manager amid rumors of unspecified friction, which he denied. He cited a family illness as the reason and was succeeded by ISHU president Cornelius Fellowes. Schooley's departure would be sorely felt in the weeks ahead as the newspaper prophetically observed: "The absence of the man who organized and coached the Olympiad team since its formation will be a distinct loss to the American team."

Once in New York, the team practiced at the 181st Street Ice Palace for two and a half hours on April 6 before sailing a day later from the West 17th Street pier. Speakers included Schooley, Fellowes, and Gustavus Kirby, president of the United States Olympic Committee. Kirby made a brief speech warning that the team would face its most formidable opposition ahead and expressing confidence that the United States was sending its best team.

After stressing the need for clean play, he gave way to Fellowes, who replied on behalf of the players. He indicated that they "are anticipating the hardest fight from the Canadians" and expressed confidence in ultimate victory (*New York Times*, April 8, 1920).

The voyage to Antwerp featured rough weather, but periodic workouts on the liner's decks helped keep the players focused. The *Finland* docked in Antwerp on April 20 and was met by the Belgian Olympic Committee. Fellowes tersely wired back to the U.S. Olympic Committee: "All well. Practice tonight. Seven entries in hockey. Elimination draw Thursday. First match Friday. Canada only serious opponent" (*New York Times*, April 21, 1920). The team worked out at Le Palais de Glace (180 by 62 feet) as Canada's Winnipeg Falcons, the Allan Cup winners, looked on. Then it was off to their accommodations, which the *Daily News* on May 18, 1920, would describe as "sleeping quarters in third class hotel and food and water not of a quality suited for a training table." Fellowes, on the other hand, moved into the first-rate Grand Hotel.

The tournament was played under the "Bergvall" system of elimination, which employed a

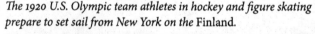

*The 1920 U.S. Olympic team athletes in hockey and figure skating prepare to set sail from New York on the* Finland.

*The U.S. team on ice at Antwerp. From left: Cornelius Fellowes, Cy Weidenborner, Ed Fitzgerald, Joe McCormick, Gerry Geran, Herb Drury, Frank Goheen, Tony Conroy, Frank Synott, Larry McCormick, Ray Bonney, and Leon Tuck*

unique knockout format between nations in the first round. Those who won went on to compete for the gold medal. Those who lost to the gold-medal winner played another knockout series for the silver, and those who lost to the silver medalist played for the bronze. The games would be played in two twenty-minute halves with a ten-minute intermission. If there was a tie at the end of regulation play, additional ten-minute periods would be played until the winning goal was scored.

The United States began play on April 24 with a 29–0 crushing of Switzerland. The *New York Times* on April 25, 1920, reported:

Scoring almost at will, the Americans baffled their opponents not by the clever-est hockey . . . but by their adroit skating. From the very outset the Americans took the offensive, scoring their first goal within two minutes.

They finished the first half with the score 15–0, and even though Drury was put out of the game by the referee after the third minute of play in the second half for kicking the puck, the Americans continued

to score with six men against their opponents' seven.

Only once was the American goal threatened. That was after Conroy had also been ruled off, and the Americans, playing with five men, were forced to put up a brisk defense for a few minutes.

When it was all over, the St. Paul players had accounted for slightly more than half of the U.S. goals. Tony Conroy finished with eight, Goheen had six, and Fitzgerald one. Joe McCormick's seven, Drury's six, and Tuck's one rounded out the scoring. As Canada had disposed of Czechoslovakia 15–0, the Americans were now in for what essentially was the gold-medal game. The winner would have to play Sweden, who had beaten both Belgium and France, for the big prize. However, that outcome was never in doubt.

The North American nations met on April 25 for the battle. Canada's Winnipeg Falcons were largely of Icelandic heritage and led by future Hall of Famer Frank Fredrickson. The other players were Bobby Benson, Chris Fridfinnson, Mike Goodman, Haldor Halderson, Connie

Johannesson, and goaltender Wally Byron. Goodman and Johannesson would later play for Duluth and St. Paul in the USAHA.

Before play got under way, a controversy erupted over the referee, a Canadian named Garoon, who was serving with the American Red Cross. Since he had worked an afternoon game, Canada agreed to accept him on condition that he could be removed if fatigue affected his work. Garoon refused to serve under that condition and was replaced by De Rauch, a Frenchman. The delay was considerable, but once the puck was dropped Canada attacked aggressively. The *Pioneer Press* on April 26, 1920, described the game this way:

> Bonney . . . stopped the puck twice in the first two minutes of play. Goheen . . . shot hard for a goal a moment later, and from then on during the first half it was a nip and tuck exhibition, the fast work and cleverness of the men of each team bringing spectators to their feet every minute. McCormick . . . tried hard several times for a long drive from near the center of the rink, but each time his try was blocked.
>
> Canada's forwards, Halderson, Fredrickson and Goodwin [Goodman] frequently took the puck from the Americans by lightning like tricks, only to lose it a second later to Conroy, Drury, or Goheen . . . [Finally] Fredrickson penetrated the American defense after a long skate in the tenth minute of the second half and scored. In the fifteenth [eighteenth] minute Johanneson [sic] also scored. Both Canadians' goals were shot from scrimmages after hard fighting.

The 2–0 victory pitted Canada against Sweden the next day, and the result was a predictable 12–1 rout and the gold medal. The United States now had to play the Swedes and Czechs for the silver.

Sweden fell 7–0 on April 26 as Geran scored on three successive long shots within a one-minute time frame of the first half to give the United States a 3–0 lead. Conroy added two more in that half and two in the second to account for all the American scoring. The next day "Squel" Weidenborner got a chance to play in goal against Czechoslovakia as the United States went on another scoring spree in a 16–0 rout that clinched the silver medal. The *Pioneer Press,* April [?], 1920, trumpeted the role of the AC's:

> In winning second place, the American hockeyists—with the St. Paul boys all scintillating—ran up a larger score on the Czechs than did the Canadians. To Tony Conroy of St. Paul goes the honor of scoring more goals in a single game than any other man competing in the Olympic games of 1920. Tony scored eight times . . . and he was "ousted" before it was over. Frank Goheen, always brilliant, scored six times in the same game, and Eddie Fitzgerald did well enough that his feats were worth cable-chronicling when he went in merely as a substitute. Cyril Weidenborner, the fourth St. Paul [player], helped his mates beat the Czechs worse than the Canadians did, playing throughout that contest.

Medals were awarded on April 29, and the Canadian team, which had been honored by Canadian Pacific seagoing personnel in Antwerp two nights previous, returned home to civic fetes in Toronto and Winnipeg. While such honors were certainly not appropriate for finishing second, the treatment afforded the United States team was deplorable. After the game with Canada, Fellowes gave the players their return tickets and departed for Paris. It was not the last that some would hear from their replacement manager. Once they arrived in New York, Drury, the McCormicks, Synott, and Weidenborner all received cablegrams indicating that they each owed Fellowes $1.80! This indignity occurred after the players had used their own money for legitimate expenses.

Weidenborner made it back home before the three other St. Paul players, who delayed their returns to sightsee in Paris. Voicing displeasure with Fellowes's management of the tour, he shared some other observations with the *St. Paul Dispatch* on May 17, 1920:

*Frank Goheen's original Olympic jersey, program, and Olympic pass*

> The Swedes had never played a real game of hockey until they reached Antwerp. They had a game of their own somewhat resembling shinny, but after a couple of practices under the instruction of an American coach they picked up the rudiments of the game rapidly and in time became good players because they are good skaters and seem to have hockey instinct.
>
> None of the other teams in the tournament except the Canadians and ourselves had a team that the average high school team of this country could not defeat.
>
> The referee, a European, knew so little of hockey that he ruled players off for legitimate body checks . . . The European players in their games between themselves used the equipment of the two teams from this country [continent]—as they had little of their own and when the series was over they bought all the sticks, gloves and pads of the Americans and Canadians.

In the light of hockey's subsequent development in Europe, it is interesting to note the St. Paul goaltender's view on the potential of Swedish players. It is almost as if he could foresee the arrival of today's NHL Swedish stars Peter Forsberg and Mats Sundin. And comments on the quality of European officials

were still being frequently heard late into the twentieth century.

Besides Weidenborner, Goheen also later reminisced in a 1972 story written by Lionel Spartz (most likely for the *White Bear Press Weekly*):

> The Swedes, French, and Czechs didn't know how to shoot hard. All they did was backhand stuff, not winding up and shooting like we did . . . In the game against the Czechs, I remember all their goalie wore was a pair of shorts, a jersey and a pair of gloves. He had never seen any real, hard shooting. I felt so sorry for him that I didn't even shoot at him.

The St. Paul Athletic Club could look with pride at their role in the American silver-medal achievement. The *Daily News* on May 24, 1920, echoed the *Pioneer Press* in expressing that pride, perhaps a bit boastfully, by declaring that "the St. Paul boys, particularly Goheen and Conroy, were the stars of the series."

# 5

# 1920-1921

## A New League

"Frank Goheen, who captained the team this year, deserves a world of credit for his splendid playing and also for his good spirit which he kept in the team, at all times. Earlier in the season he was painfully injured and never was in the pink of condition at any time thereafter."

The ACE, *March 1921*

While the four AC players were off with the Olympic Team, Frank Weidenborner was in Pittsburgh attending a three-month training course in life insurance offered by Carnegie Tech. Weidenborner's "day job" was with the Provident Mutual Life Insurance Company—insurance would be his life work. Conroy, Fitzgerald, and Goheen would visit him there before returning to St. Paul after the Olympics. Just before Weidenborner's departure for the course, the *St. Paul Dispatch,* on April 3, 1920, would comment:

> Mr. Weidenborner is largely responsible
> for the success of the A. C. hockey team
> this year. He steadfastly refused, from
> the start of the season, to resort to the
> common practice of building up a hockey
> team by importing [players] from Canada.
> He maintained that there was enough
> talent here in St. Paul to win the league
> championship.

Well, not quite. The trademark of the AC's was their homegrown players, exemplified by the core four of Conroy, Goheen, Fitzgerald,

and Cy Weidenborner, and later supplemented by George Conroy, Emmy Garrett, and George Nichols. Michigan's "Taffy" Abel and U.S.-born, Canadian-developed Dennis Breen would also play key roles. However, such Canadians as George Clark, Jeff Quesnelle, "Babe" Elliott, Joe McCormick, and Wilfred Peltier were essential to St. Paul's success, both under Frank Weidenborner's reign and that of his successor, Ed Fitzgerald. Under Ray Johns and Nick Kahler, imports Bill Adams, Herb Drury, Bert Mohan, and "Duke" Wellington helped put St. Paul on the hockey map.

Quesnelle would prove to be Weidenborner's blue-chip acquisition for 1920–21. But before play could get under way, the matter of how the sport would be structured in the new season remained to be determined. The AAHA was done after the 1919–20 campaign, and those that ran hockey in the United States decided it was time for a new organization devoted solely to their sport. They met at Philadelphia's Ice Palace on October 25, 1920, and formed the United States Amateur Hockey Association (USAHA). Representatives from Boston, Philadelphia, Pittsburgh, and St. Paul (Frank Weidenborner) were

*The 1920–21 AC's. From left, standing: George Conroy, Wallie Elmer, Blaine Meyers, Frank Weidenborner, Ed Fitzgerald, Emmy Garrett. Sitting: Ernie Byers, Tony Conroy, Frank Goheen, Jeff Quesnelle, Cy Weidenborner*

on hand, and they elected William S. Haddock, Pittsburgh, as president and George V. Brown, Boston, as secretary-treasurer, serving as temporary officers. The action had the blessings of the ISHU, the previous governing body, as well as of the Amateur Athletic Union (AAU). The ISHU would drop the "H" and concern itself with only figure and speed skating.

In recognition of his prior services to hockey—one wonders what these services might have been considering his management of the Olympic Team—Cornelius Fellowes, ISHU president, was named an honorary president of the new USAHA. An executive committee consisting of Weidenborner, Roy D. Schooley, Pittsburgh; Percey Winsor, Boston; and Joseph Drexler, Pittsburgh, was appointed. The executive committee assembled in Pittsburgh on December 12 and reelected Haddock as president. Weidenborner became vice president and Schooley became secretary-treasurer. George V. Brown had resigned the latter position—the new organization had adopted a ruling that no one involved in rink ownership could be involved directly or indirectly with a team. Brown was involved in the Boston Arena and Schooley presumably had divested himself of any connection with Duquesne Garden.

Each club was to be self-governing and in full control of its own funds. If called upon, clubs would be required to explain their financial operations. Since the October meeting, a number of cities had expressed interest in joining the USAHA, which resulted in the formation of three groups of four teams. The AC's would play in Group Two along with Cleveland, Duluth, and Pittsburgh, and the schedule would get under way on January 3 and 4, 1921. Group One was made up of the Boston Hockey Club, Boston Athletic Association, New York, and Philadelphia. Group Three members were American Soo, Calumet, Eveleth, and Portage Lake. Pittsburgh would subsequently drop out of Group Two, and Canadian Soo would join Group Three.

The schedule was so arranged that the group winners would be determined by February 22. There would be no intergroup play until the postseason play-offs got under way. At that time the winners of Group One and Two would play off and then meet the winner of Group Three for the national championship. All games were to be conducted using officials who were non-residents of the cities of competing teams.

### A New Era Begins

St. Paul was scheduled to begin league play in the new circuit against Duluth on the first weekend of 1921, but as usual there would be earlier non-league play. Off-ice training had begun in late November. The *St. Paul Pioneer Press* on December 5, 1921, reported:

> Proceeding on the reasoning that eventually winter must strike . . . members of the St. Paul Athletic club hockey squad are in hard training for the season they hope will open December 20 or 21, with the Fort William, Ont., team, at the Hippodrome.
>
> The squad which now numbers twelve huskies worked out three times last week in the club gymnasium, two hours of work superintended by Physical Director E. O. Hoppe, being topped up with [a] two mile run around the track.
>
> So the boys have not had an opportunity to put on their skates, but they are hop-

*The St. Paul Athletic Club gymnasium*

ing the weather will turn cold enough this week to permit them to do some outdoor practice at [Lake] Como.

Some practice at the lake occurred under Ed Fitzgerald's direction, but the squad did not hit the Hippodrome ice until December 20, when cold weather finally arrived. Two days earlier, Frank Goheen, who was now starting to be referred to more frequently as "Moose," was elected captain. Tony Conroy would reminisce about Goheen to Phil Bronson of the *Pioneer Press* on January [1?], 1948:

> He had only one thought in mind—to score. The shortest distance between two points is a straight line, and that's the way he went—down the center. He had terrific speed and fight . . . I coined the term, "Moose." He had a chest like a house and huge strong legs, with thighs as big as Emmy [Garrett]'s waist. No man ever trained more.

Training was what was needed—the AC's had only a week to get ready for their non-league opening series with the Winnipeg Wanderers on December 27 and 28. Russ McCrimmon, who had played a major role with Pittsburgh a year earlier, was reported ready to join the club. McCrimmon never came to St. Paul, but Jeff Quesnelle and S. McPherson did. Quesnelle had been a key cog at center ice in Canadian Soo's late season charge a year earlier, while McPherson had played for Port Arthur, Ontario. Quesnelle would be the team's center. The *Pioneer Press,* December [?], 1920, reported:

> The acquisition of Harry [Jeff] Quesnelle . . . will go far to make the St. Paul hockey team one of the very best in the United States . . . Quesnelle has a natural gift for playing this position. He is fast, clever and seemingly tireless. In the games in which his team was seen here last winter, Quesnelle seemed to furnish about 50% of the Soo's punch.
>
> Quesnelle is a native of [Sault] Ste. Marie, Ont., and learned the game in that city.

Kingston, Ontario, native Wallie Elmer would be the other significant addition to the team, seeing service as a forward. All of the Minnesotans would return, as well as Toronto native Frank McCarthy. Over the course of the season, a sprinkling of others, both Canadians and locals, would see spot duty.

One thousand fans attended the Hippodrome opener. Box seats were priced at $2, reserved seats were $1, and general admission was 75 cents. Subzero temperatures had now hit the Twin Cities, and the huge unheated arena offered limited protection from the cold. However, those attending by car were able to park their vehicles in a nearby building at no charge. Not quite what we experience today.

The Wanderers were an all-star aggregation formed from various senior teams, but they did have the advantage of an additional week of on-ice practice. Goaltender "Babe" Elliott would later join the Minneapolis independent team and then become the regular netminder

for the AC's the next season. He would play a strong game against the home team in a 2–2 tie, as six-man hockey, played in three periods of fifteen minutes each, made its debut in St. Paul. Six-man hockey with the rover position being dropped had been played in Canada since 1911, though the Pacific Coast Hockey Association held out until 1922. While the elimination of the position would offer more open ice and increase the possibility of scoring, such impact would not be as great for St. Paul because of the large Hippodrome ice surface. The playing portions of the game would drop from sixty to forty-five minutes, but the extra time generated would provide for two intermissions rather than one and would hopefully keep the players refreshed. The four Olympians had experienced the new game during the Olympic tryout period the prior March, but it was new to the others, who would have to adjust to one less player. The December 27 game was played in twenty-minute periods, but hereafter fifteen minutes would be the norm for both league and non-league contests.

Winnipeg appeared to take an early 1–0 lead at the end of the first period, but it was ruled that time had expired. The visitors got the first goal a minute into the second period and followed that with another, before Jeff Quesnelle made his St. Paul debut a happy one with his first goal on a pass from Fitzgerald. Goheen tied it early in the third period, and Tony Conroy appeared to have the game winner with less than a minute to play, but the puck was ruled to have gone through a hole in the side of the net. Frank Weidenborner wanted to play overtime, but the Manitobans would have none of it since it was not regular league competition.

Quesnelle continued to make the St. Paul manager look good the next night when he scored on a difficult angle after taking a pass from Goheen. The second-period tally stood as the margin of victory for the AC's, as the Wanderers mustered little in the way of offense. E. R. Hosking, writing in the *Pioneer Press* on

December 29, 1921, thought the transition to the six-man game could have been smoother:

> Captain Goheen and . . . the St. Paul Athletic club's hockey team have discovered . . . that they still have a lot to learn of the intricacies of the six man game . . . [T]he new style of play puzzled them a lot especially when near their opponents goal . . . [I]f the A. C. forward line had played as it should, it probably could have scored nearly ten goals, but on almost every rush down the ice Quesnelle was boxed and the wing men were obliged to shoot from impossible angles.
>
> In the seven-man game there are two forwards in center ice, the center and the rover, and it is more difficult for the opposing defense men to box them.
>
> The remedy for the defects shown in the two games is, of course, better team work and passing.

While the AC's pondered their adjustment to the new game, significant off-ice developments were taking place that would affect the nature of St. Paul's play in the USAHA's first season. A dispute concerning the eligibility of former St. Paul and Pittsburgh player and U.S. Olympian Herb Drury would result in Pittsburgh dropping out of the competition. While there was considerable speculation that Nick Kahler's independent Minneapolis team would take their place, that would not happen. Minneapolis would eventually join the league, but not until the 1923–24 season. For this year, Group Two would consist of just Cleveland, Duluth, and St. Paul. As in other years, the AC's would fill in the rest of their schedule with a variety of non-league teams.

Duluth would be St. Paul's first opponent on January 3, as the USAHA made its debut in Minnesota that night. The game would also be the first for Oscar Aubrey, a Moose Jaw, Saskatchewan, native, whom Frank Weidenborner has just signed. Aubrey's career in St. Paul would prove to be brief, but his arrival at the time was viewed as significant. Some eleven hundred fans were on hand to see the newcomer assist on Jeff Quesnelle's third-period goal, which put the locals ahead 2–0. Tony Conroy had made the first goal in the second period. The AC's dominated play, which was slowed by soft ice, and the visitors didn't score until the game's last minute, when Gus Olson's thirty-foot shot eluded "Squel" Weidenborner.

The ice was better the next night when St. Paul took an early 2–0 lead as Aubrey continued to shine by scoring his first goal. Quesnelle added a second. Duluth tied it up late in the first period on two long shots, and that would be their high-water mark. The AC's scored four times in the second period, but only two by Goheen and Quesnelle counted. Two others by Quesnelle were disallowed. Leading 4–2 going into the third period, Goheen gave Ernie Byers some work in the nets and he gave up a late goal, while Emmy Garrett got the home team's fifth counter. Between the first and second periods, former AC player Everett McGowan, who was now pursuing a professional speed-skating career, gave a demonstration of his work by circling the rink several times. McGowan would soon compete against Norval Baptie on Hippodrome ice. He would ultimately resume his hockey career with Vancouver of the professional Western Canada Hockey League. The *Pioneer Press* on January 5, 1921, was pleased with the victory:

> Playing on better ice last night, the St. Paul Athletic club hockey sextet displayed flashes of the class that has been expected of it. The team work, without which it is impossible to win in fast company, showed a distinct improvement . . . The second match . . . produced some great playing by the forward line, Conroy, Quesnelle, and Aubrey. There has never been any doubt as to the class of the defense with Eddie Fitzgerald and Frank Goheen in front of

"Squel" Weidenborner. What the team needs now is one or two high class reserve players, because in the six-man game the regulars cannot go through an entire game without some rest.

With a start of two victories the A. C. team seems certain to fight it out for first place . . . with the Cleveland club, and it will have the advantage of . . . practice games before it tackles the fast sextet from Ohio.

The "practice" games would be with the Winnipeg Columbus team, a club that had won the city intermediate championship for the past two years. Columbus arrived on the morning of January 10 via the Great Northern Railway and went straight to the Hippodrome to get acclimated to the big ice surface. This familiarization process seemed to work very well that night. For two periods Columbus dominated play and took a 1–0 lead into the final session. When play opened in the third period, Goheen went to center from defense to rest Quesnelle, and McCarthy took the "Moose's" spot. The change jump-started the AC's offense, and eventually they tied the game when Fitzgerald copied Goheen's rink-length dashes with one of his own before feeding Conroy, who put it in from a far left angle. As in the Wanderers' series, overtime was not planned, but Columbus agreed to play six five-minute periods to determine a winner. E. R. Hosking's game story, in the *Pioneer Press*, January 11, 1921, tells it best:

> But with three minutes of the second gone, Quesnelle took the puck as it glanced from the skate of a visiting player, darted through three opposing athletes, and shot. Gillis caught the puck in his left hand, but it hopped over his fingers and fell just inside the net.

As there was no "sudden death," play continued, but there was no further scoring and St. Paul had a 2–1 victory. They would do it again

on January 11, but it would be a costly win. Quesnelle put the AC's ahead 1–0 in the first period as the locals out shot Columbus 14 to 5. After eight minutes of play in the second period, the visitors tied the score before misfortune struck St. Paul. Late in the period, as he tried to recover a loose puck near the sideboards, Frank Goheen lost his balance and skated straight into an iron pillar. He was knocked unconscious and carried from the ice.

Frank McCarthy would take his place, and the team would recover to win 3–2 on third-period goals by Aubrey and Fitzgerald. While it was first thought that Goheen had dislocated his shoulder, the injury proved to be a bad bruise, and he spent the night at his White Bear Lake home. It appeared that he would be able to make the road trip to Cleveland for the key league series on January 14 and 15. However when the squad boarded their Chicago, Burlington, and Quincy train at 7 P.M. on January 12, Moose was not among them.

St. Paul had won five of six games and tied one other, but Cleveland was expected to be a championship contender. It had a tradition of strong independent teams before the USAHA was launched and was led by Nelson Stewart, a Montreal native. After his Cleveland days, he would win a Stanley Cup and league scoring championship with the 1925–26 Montreal Maroons and would later see service with the Boston Bruins and the New York Americans. Stewart was an early NHL superstar who would also win two most valuable player awards, be the first to score three hundred goals, and be inducted into the Hockey Hall of Fame in 1962.

In the second game of the series, on January 15, Stewart would virtually single-handedly destroy the AC's, scoring five of Cleveland's seven goals in the 7–1 rout. After the three-minute mark of the first period, Jeff Quesnelle gave St. Paul an early lead, which held for only four minutes until Stewart scored his first. He followed it with three more and added number five in the second period. This game had followed a 9–2

*Nels Stewart in a Cleveland uniform. "Old Poison" would go on to a Hall of Fame career in the NHL, principally with the Montreal Maroons.*

national series between the USAHA champion and a representative of the Canadian Amateur Hockey Association. The series winner would receive the Wills International Trophy, donated by Hamilton B. Wills, an American from Boston now living in Toronto. Circumstances precluded the series from being played until 1939, when the USAHA was long out of business. The meetings also gave the president the authority to decide positional standings of tied teams at the season's end and brought the Collegiate Hockey League under the organization's banner.

The team returned to Minnesota to face a two-game series with Minneapolis. The games had been "on and off" before the Cleveland trip for various reasons and were now on again. The *Pioneer Press* on January 17, 1921, reported:

> The Mill City team is [certain] to give the Saints . . . a battle. [It] is composed largely of Winnipeg stars, Chambers, Dunlop, and Elliot . . . in addition to Nick Kahler . . . and Fosdale and Thompson, Mill City local talent.
>
> Under ordinary circumstances the Saints would be top-heavy favorites, but in view of the two hard games at Cleveland, and the long rail trip which will not end until today . . . the locals are likely to find the . . . opposition rather stiff. In fact a battle royal is expected.
>
> "Moose" Goheen, who was so badly injured . . . that he was kept out of the Cleveland series, is expected to play. And his presence, local followers hope, will inspire the boys to a decisive triumph.

A battle royal it would be, but Goheen would not be there to participate. The AC's had just arrived after a fifteen-hundred-mile train trip and would be playing their fifth game in eight days. Under the circumstances their 2–1 overtime win on January 17 was impressive. Cy Weidenborner had given up sixteen goals in Cleveland, but he came back with a solid effort. After being out-

thrashing administered by the home team the night before. In that game St. Paul had trailed only 2–1 after one period as Quesnelle registered the visitors' tally, but Cleveland broke the game open with four goals in the second and three in the third. Stewart scored "only" twice in this game. Garrett got the other AC goal. In a comment that could apply to both games, the *Pioneer Press* on January 15, 1921, said, "Minus Captain Goheen, speedy defense star, the St. Paul team was unable to cope with the whirlwind attack of Cleveland."

League meetings were held concurrent with this series and resulted in establishing an interplayed in the first period and going down 1–0, the "Goheenless Goheens carried the brunt of the battle," said the *Pioneer Press* on January 18, 1921. Tony Conroy tied the game with five minutes left in the second period, and the game remained that way until the end of regulation play. Frank Weidenborner was always eager to play overtime, and this time was no exception. Nick Kahler took some convincing, but Weidenborner and Hippodrome manager Gale Brooks were adamant, and Emmy Garrett responded with the game winner.

The series contract called for a second game. It would be played two nights later, but at the Lexington Rink. With Goheen still out and Fitzgerald and his brother hurting, Frank Weidenborner attempted to get the game cancelled, but to no avail. Under the circumstances the manager held out Fitzgerald and "Squel" and went largely with the reserves. Conroy, Emmy Garrett, and Quesnelle were inserted for the final five minutes of each period. Byers took over in the nets while Bill Garrett, Emmy's brother, and Wallie Elmer were on defense. Newcomer Blaine Meyers, a Winnipeg native, started at center, while George Conroy, Tony's brother, and Walter Gosweich were the wings.

The result was a 4–1 Minneapolis victory played on soft ice before a crowd of only five hundred, far below the usual one thousand fans that were turning out at the Hippodrome. Meyers scored his first goal to tie the game early in the second period, but that was all St. Paul could do. In an interesting development before the game, Oscar Aubrey defected from the AC's to Minneapolis and played against his former team in this game. While player movements were presumably regulated by the USAHA, they had no control over players leaving to nonleague teams. The *Pioneer Press* on January 20, 1921, expressed disappointment with the game:

It is unfortunate that it was necessary for Manager Frank Weidenborner to use his second team last evening. If he knew

beforehand that he was going to do so, the fact should have been announced as some of the people who went out and paid their money to see the game expected to see the regular A. C. club.

The regular members of the A. C. were somewhat battered up . . . They were completely fed up on hockey. The game did not draw and it was foolish to have placed the regulars on the ice in the condition they were and take chances of any more injuries or staleness with the games coming on Tuesday and Wednesday [January 24 and 25] with Ft. William.

"Moose" Goheen, now recovered from his shoulder injury, would return to the lineup for the series with the strong Fort William squad, which had battled the Winnipeg Falcons a year earlier in the quest for the Allan Cup. Despite the strong opponent and the captain's return, attendance continued to be sub par. Crowds of only six hundred and five hundred, respectively, turned out to watch St. Paul return to form with two one-goal victories. The first night Goheen celebrated his comeback by scoring the AC's first goal on passes from Quesnelle and Conroy. The latter made it 2–0 early in the second period when he stripped the puck from Fort William defenseman P. Flanagan at mid-ice and went in to score. The visitors, who had been badly outplayed for two periods, made it close in the last period but could come up with only one goal.

Twenty-four hours later the teams would be knotted after regulation play at 3–3, as the home team got goals in each period from Quesnelle, Conroy, and Garrett. There was no question about overtime in this game, and it would be conducted in a manner unheard of today. There would be two five-minute periods, and the teams would change goals at the end of each overtime session. Thus, when Fort William went ahead 4–3 in the first five minutes, play simply continued into the second five minutes. Jeff Quesnelle then put the game away with two goals, the last set up in classic Goheen fashion. The *Pioneer Press* from January 26, 1921, noted:

> When the Maple Leafs took the disc up the ice and it was shot wildly, Frank Goheen, skating like a demon, sped all the way across the ice, "nursing" the puck through the first five Fort William players, then at the proper second, flipped it to the waiting Quesnelle, who again sent it into the cage, winning the game.

## Confronting Cleveland and Honoring the Moose

The two wins gave St. Paul a 9–3 record at mid-season and good reason to believe that they could still catch Cleveland in the Group Two race. Frank Weidenborner believed that Fort William was every bit the equal of the Ohio team and that a sweep of the coming series was possible. Two wins were essential in order to stay in the running since Cleveland was 4–0 in league competition to the AC's 2–2. Duluth was not expected to be a factor.

Except for his wartime service, Frank Goheen had now been in a St. Paul uniform since 1914, a total of four playing seasons. He had become the team's franchise player, in today's jargon, and his service in the Olympics and captaincy enhanced that image. The folks in his hometown of White Bear Lake felt it was time to show their appreciation to the local star, who, though born in St. Paul, had grown up and learned his hockey in the community near the lake. They decided that the first game of the Cleveland series, January 31, was the time to honor him. In a piece titled "Are You Going?," the *White Bear Press*, on January 21, 1921, recounted Goheen's career and asked: "Now isn't this sufficient proof to yourself that you owe Frank a little support?"

When game time arrived, hundreds of White Bear residents were on hand to honor Goheen. They had chartered a number of street cars and sat in a special reserve section. The thirty-five-

*Streetcars in the Snelling Shops car house, 1920*

piece village band provided music. Between periods animal trainer Heine Brock entertained on the ice with a white bear. Ultimately, "Moose" was presented with a special gold watch from the organizing committee.

Goheen provided some excitement for both the hometown contingent as well as the overall crowd, but it was a case of too little, too late. Cleveland had arrived the evening before and apparently had spent a restful night at the very elite St. Paul Hotel. They dominated the first two periods and took a 3–0 lead into the final fifteen minutes. Goheen had been on the receiving end of some chippy play in the second period, but perhaps pumped up by the gold watch ceremony, which occurred after the middle session, he went out and scored two goals. However, the visitors added another to make the final 4–2.

*Collecting streetcar tolls*

The game had drawn the season's best crowd at twenty-seven hundred, some no doubt there because of the Goheen honors, but the numbers dropped to seventeen hundred the next night while the AC's level of play rose. Quesnelle put the locals up 1–0 in the first two minutes, only to have Nels Stewart tie it five minutes later. Cleveland got another before the end of the period, and Stewart made it 3–1 early in the third. Then, according to the *Pioneer Press* on February 2, 1921:

> Undaunted, the Saints came on with a furious rush and scored twice in the few remaining minutes. Elmer, who was playing his first game at wing in place of "Emmy" Garrett [injured the night before] ... carried the disk to the cage, pushed it to Quesnelle, who fell, but poked it in for his team's second score. Debernardi and

Goheen went out again as the result of a mixup and when they got back in Tony Conroy whizzed the disc past Turner for the tying score.

USAHA overtime rules were the same as those used in the Fort William game, and St. Paul carried their momentum into the first overtime. Fitzgerald, Conroy, and Goheen all had excellent chances on Cleveland goalie Vern Turner, but his "eagle eye and coordinating hands, feet and body always intervened" (*Pioneer Press*, February 2, 1921). Stewart wouldn't score in the second overtime, but three of his teammates did, and the visitors had the sweep.

The second period of both games had been penalty-filled, and one of those picking up some time in the box for Cleveland was veteran defenseman Frank "Coddy" Winters. The night before game one he had been feted at a party given by his Minnesota friends. Winters was Cleveland's only American, a Duluth native who had moved to Ohio after visiting with his hometown team. He became a fixture on the local hockey scene and played a key role on Cleveland's strong 1912 and 1914 teams. Winters played through the 1925 season and then spent the rest of his life in his adopted hometown working in the sporting goods business. "Coddy" became a charter enshrinee of the United States Hockey Hall of Fame in 1973.

The two victories clinched the Group Two title for Cleveland, but they would not leave St. Paul without a critique from E. R. Hosking of the *Pioneer Press* on February 1, 1921:

> There is no doubt that the Cleveland team plays the best hockey seen in St. Paul for several seasons, but it is a pity that such clever exponents of the game find it necessary to indulge in unnecessary roughness.
>
> The visitors ... seemed to have decided to "get" Captain Frank Goheen and they made numerous attempts to do so.

Then when Referee Sexsmith ... properly penalized the offenders, they became indignant, contending he was favoring the home team.

There was not the slightest excuse for the rough house tactics of the Cleveland players, because they were in the lead throughout the game.

With the Group Two champions properly chastised, Hosking went on to renew the plea for a rink closer to downtown St. Paul despite the existence of the Lexington Avenue facility, which was, of course, not quite downtown:

The attendance at the Hippodrome rink this winter is demonstrating that a profitable return awaits any one who has sufficient courage to build a rink adapted for hockey in the downtown section.

The principal defect of the Hippodrome from a hockey standpoint is the immense size of the ice sheet, which is nearly 300 [270] feet in length and about 125 [119] feet wide. A sheet of 200 × 90 feet would be infinitely better for fast hockey.

The fifty or more feet of ice behind the goals at the Hipp permits defense players to stall, with the result that when the puck is brought down the ice the attacking team invariably finds itself facing the whole six men on the opposing team.

That is the principal reason why the scores at the Hipp are lower than on any other hockey rink in the country.

St. Paul would eventually get a downtown rink when the Auditorium on 5th Street added artificial ice and seating for six thousand in 1932. Its ice surface would be 195 by 87, close to what is now the standard for professional hockey. Interestingly enough, USAHA regulations provided only for a minimum of 160 by 60. For now, the AC's would have to get by with the Hippodrome, and it would serve the team well,

except for the finals in 1922 and 1923, when the visitors found it more to their liking.

The team would now be idle until February 14 and 15, when play would be resumed against Minneapolis. This time there would be no resting of players in game two, though Goheen would allow Ernie Byers to relieve "Squel" Weidenborner for the third period of that game. Minneapolis was coming off a split with Duluth, but the sharpness presumed by active competition proved illusory as St. Paul easily won both games 2–0 and 5–0 before crowds of 750 and 900, respectively.

Moose put the AC's ahead early in the first game when he executed a version of what is now called the "wraparound," which was then viewed as being unusual. According to the *Pioneer Press* on February 15, 1921:

Goheen swept across the full length of the rink, passed to Tony Conroy in front of the net, and Tony barely missed. Goheen then outwitted the opposition by doing something unhockeylike. He took the disc when it flashed on the net, swung around the cage in a circle, skated right through the grouped Millers ... and shot from ... about two feet.

The captain added another soon after the beginning of the second period, after which the visitors resorted to tactics designed to slow him down. In the third period, the Minneapolis left wing, Chambers, put his stick around Goheen's neck and then grabbed the other end and started to whirl him. "Moose" retaliated in the same manner, and both went down and then off to the penalty box. Before the end of the period, Fitzgerald and Dunlop tangled and were similarly banished.

If all this might lead one to think that the next game would be a bit physical, that conclusion would be wrong. Weather intervened to cool tempers. Game one had been played on soft ice, and with colder weather not expected to arrive in the next twenty-four hours, the second contest was delayed until February 18. Only one penalty was called in this game, and five different St. Paul players scored: Elmer and Conroy in the first, Garrett in the second, and Goheen and Quesnelle in the third. Only Babe Elliott's superb goaltending prevented the AC's from doubling the final score.

The Group Two race had been decided, but there were still two league games left on the schedule against Duluth in the Zenith City on February 21 and 22. With nothing more at stake than pride, the teams split two epic overtime games, each by a 3–2 count. Fifteen hundred fans were on hand at the Curling Club for the first game, which was not settled until the home team's Jimmy Owens beat Weidenborner from a difficult angle with a minute left in the fourth overtime session. It was the Duluth native's second goal of the game—he had tied the score in the second period after St. Paul had taken a 1–0 lead on Conroy's first-period effort. Goheen and Gus Olson had traded goals in the first overtime before Owens's game winner. Louis Gollop, writing in the *Duluth News Tribune* on February 22, 1921, reported this reaction to the game:

> A Canadian called up while we were writing this story and insisted on telling what a wonderful game it was. "I didn't think that two such teams could be found in the United States. I have seen and played hockey all my life but never have I even dared to dream about seeing such a contest."

They would do it all again the next evening as the crowd doubled to three thousand. This time the AC's would come out on top. Down 2–0 after two periods, St. Paul rallied to tie things at the end of regulation on Goheen and Quesnelle goals. It would be Goheen who came up with the game winner at the eight-minute mark of the first overtime period. It was a fitting conclusion to a difficult series for the captain of the AC's. He had been temporarily put out of action in the opening period of game one with a vicious chin gash, only to return in the third period to be injured again in a collision with a Duluth player. He quickly rebounded to play the remainder of the period and all of the overtime periods and then starred in the second-game victory.

Frank Weidenborner had booked the Winnipeg Falcons into the Hippodrome on March 3 and 4, but warm weather would delay by one day the series against the team that had represented Canada at the 1920 Olympics. The Falcons had not repeated their Allan Cup success, and only goalie Wally Byron, defenseman Bobby Benson, and left wing Mike Goodman were left from the gold-medal winners. Nonetheless, the Falcons were viewed as a formidable opponent, but that was not enough to get any more than nine hundred fans out for the first game.

Those that came were delighted to see St. Paul, which, of course, had four players off the 1920 U.S. silver-medal team, break open a previously tight game and send four pucks past Byron. Goheen and Elmer had provided the AC's with a 2–0 lead heading into the third period, but the Falcons made it 2–1 on an early goal. It was no contest after that, with Quesnelle, Goheen (two), and Elmer closing it out at 6–1. The rout no doubt kept the gate down the next night, as only four hundred attended a far more competitive game. After the Falcons had taken a 1–0 first-period lead, Conroy and Elmer provided the 2–1 victory with two second-period goals.

The Falcons' manager was so impressed with St. Paul's performance that he indicated he would return home and attempt to arrange games there for the AC's against the Manitoba senior champions from Brandon. This apparently noble action would be in lieu of accompanying his own team to Duluth for games with the USAHA entry. One suspects that perhaps Mr. Axford was motivated by the financial potential for such a series. In any event, St. Paul stayed in Minnesota and ended the season with three games in the northeast, sometimes referred to as the "Arrowhead." The *Pioneer*

*The 1920–21 Eveleth team. "Ching" Johnson is sitting second from right.*

*Press* on March 7, 1921, predicted that there would be more hockey:

> Frank F. Weidenborner, hustling manager of the St. Paul A. C. hockey team, mopped the perspiration off his brow last night, remarked about the sultry weather and then hinted that he is dickering with Eveleth for a game at the northern town. Frank simply won't let hockey die. Soon we may expect to hear that he is taking the battling Goheens to the North Pole for a Fourth of July match.

Weidenborner might better have let Axford schedule the Brandon games—the two with Eveleth would prove to be disastrous. Eveleth had won the Group Three crown with a 14–1–1 record to Canadian Soo's 13–3–0. They were led by 5-feet 11-inch, 210-pound, aggressive defenseman Ivan "Ching" Johnson, a Winnipeg native who gained the title "Babe Ruth of Hockey." The balding, smiling Johnson made his way to the NHL through Minneapolis and then to the New York Rangers. With the "Broadway Blueshirts," he would sip from the Stanley Cup in 1928 and 1933. Johnson was elected to the Hockey Hall of Fame in 1958.

The March 9 opener didn't get under way until 8:35 P.M. The AC's had taken the late afternoon train to the Hilltop City where they had won decisively the year before. This time things would be quite different. Eveleth was waiting for the outcome of the series between Cleveland and the Boston Athletic Association. The winner of that play-off would face Eveleth for the Fellowes Cup. In order to prepare for the league championship, the Group Three winners played various teams and St. Paul was first in line.

Eveleth quickly showed why they had been the class of Group Three by scoring four first-period goals and four more in the second before the visitors could get on the board. The *Eveleth News* on March 9, 1921, described things in this way:

> The game at this point was perhaps the fastest of the evening, and the crowd went

wild when Goheen scored the first goal for St. Paul. He made a long clean shot and was cheered for fully three minutes. Goheen played a great game all the way through, scoring again in the third period for the final goal of the game.

The Eveleth crowd reaction to the twenty-seven-year-old Goheen reflected the stature that he had achieved in the sport at this point in his career. But the cheers of the opponents' fans could hardly temper the disappointment in being hammered 11–2. If that was bad, it got slightly worse the next evening when the final was 12–2, although the score stood at only 4–2 early in the second period. Trailing 4–0 after one period, the AC's got back in the game on goals by Conroy and Garrett before disaster struck. According to the *Eveleth News* on March 17, 1921:

> Goheen, who played a wonderful game, was injured and had to be carried off the ice . . . Weidenborner was a busy man at goal and after Goheen was out of the game, the St. Paul defense was weak and it was impossible for one man to [stop] all the shots directed at him. Conroy and Fitzgerald did fine work for St. Paul, but on the whole the team was outclassed.

Reported as "outclassed" may reflect the real possibility that the AC's made the trip to the Iron Range without any spares. Newspaper accounts of the two Eveleth games do not mention any subs, and there is no box score reported for the team's last game in Duluth on March 12, when they beat the hometown team 5–3. Playing without any substitutes and therefore finishing the second game with only five players against one of the league's top teams may account for the one-sided scores in Eveleth. Cy Weidenborner saw more rubber go past him in these two games than in any other two during the season.

In any event, the season ended on a positive note with Goheen presumably back in the lineup. Much was made at the time of the team's dominant home record and the fact that they had defeated all Canadian-based squads. A closer look at the results indicates an inability to defeat Group Two and Three opponents, Cleveland and Eveleth, who were nearly as Canadian as any of St. Paul's other opponents. It was apparent that the level of play was higher in the USAHA than the AAHA, but the AC's would meet the challenge. The ability to be competitive would start with the 1921–22 season, the beginning of a "golden era" that would see St. Paul vie for a national title over the next two years.

*The ice rink in Eveleth, circa 1920*

# 6

# 1921-1922

## *Winning the West I*

Come on Tony, Emmy, Wallie
Rush right down that ice,
Shove the puck right in the goal there,
One will not suffice.
Rah! Rah! Rah!

Onward Goheen, Jon, and Shifty
Little Garrett, too.
Break down our foe's defense.
And go right through.

Our goal tender, watchful, nimble,
Elliott, you're right there
Then our subs—Cass, Squeal and Rothschild,
You have done your share.
Rah! Rah! Rah!

Weidenborner and Fitzgerald,
To you much credit's due.
Three cheers for St. Paul's lineup
We're for you.

(To the tune of "On Wisconsin")

The ACE, *February 1922*

*These women's fashions typified the "Jazz Age," as Twin Citians found excitement in sports, movies, cars, radios, and dancing. Some activities were rather mundane, such as the annual Easter egg hunt and an archery contest.*

If the AC's were to compete for the Group Two title in 1921–22, they would have to deal not only with defending champion Cleveland and in-state rival Duluth, but with Pittsburgh as well. The Steel City skaters were back, allowing for a more balanced and competitive four-team structure within the group.

The 1920–21 season had been a good one for the Cleveland Athletic Club. After securing the Group Two title they went on to defeat the Group One champions, the Boston Athletic Association, in a four-game total-goals series.

The teams split the first two games at Boston before returning to Cleveland for another split, but the home team had a 10–6 edge in goals. It had been a tough series, and Eveleth, the Group Three champion, would be just as tough in another four-game total-goals set. This time Cleveland took the first two games at home and Eveleth won the next two, which were played at Pittsburgh because of the lack of ice on the Iron Range. Once again the Ohio skaters won, as they outscored Eveleth 14–12 to take the national title.

Frank Weidenborner was faced with some significant challenges in the new season as last year's scoring leader Jeff Quesnelle did not return and his brother "Squel" became the backup. "Babe" Elliott, who had been with Minneapolis the season before, took over in the nets. The local four, together since 1914, would be no more because Ed Fitzgerald moved behind the bench as non-playing coach. Frank Goheen and Tony Conroy would carry on, with the latter serving as captain.

There would be other changes as well. Most notable among the Canadian imports would be right wing Charles Cassin and defenseman Connie Johannesson, both Winnipeg natives. Cassin was a college player. Johannesson was best remembered for his play with the Winnipeg Falcons, Canada's 1920 Olympic champions. Wallie Elmer would be back on defense, and St. Paul native Emmy Garrett would take over from

*Local outlets like the* St. Paul Daily News *worked hard to report on the growing baseball, football, and hockey news of the time.*

E. GARRETT

A.J. CONROY
-Captain-

J.E. FITZGERALD
-Coach-

F.X. GOHEEN

FRANK T. WEIDENBORNER
-Manager-

**St. Paul Athletic Club Hockey Team**
- 1921-1922 -

Member of United States Amateur Hockey Ass'n.—
Playing in Regular scheduled League games won championship of Group 2 (Western) and defeated EVELETH, winners Group 3 (Northern), in five games. Lost to BOSTON winners Group 1 (Eastern)- in final series.

H. WILDERMUTH
-Trainer-

W.D. ELMER

B. ELLIOTT

K. JONASSON

E. WEIDENBORNER

GEO. CONROY

C.M. CASSIN

W.J. GARRETT

The 1921–22 AC's

Quesnelle as the team's top goal scorer. This core group would see most of the action, but six others, the usual import/local mix, would play as needed.

Fitzgerald had held some training on whatever ice could be found between thaws, but the continued vagaries of the weather kept the team off home ice until December 19. The late start caused the cancellation of a proposed two-game series with the Canadian National Railroad Team from Winnipeg that had been scheduled for mid-December. When play finally got under way after Christmas there would be a significant change in the ice surface. The *St. Paul Pioneer Press* on December 4, 1921, reported:

> The hockey club has shortened the playing surface of the huge rink by forty feet, taking twenty feet off each end, behind the nets, and this will make the rink about the right length for hockey and will do away with the tiresome loafing behind the nets which has marred games there for several years.

Since fifty feet had already been taken off each end, this would result in an ice surface of 200 feet by 119 feet, today's standard NHL and international length, but far wider than both the NHL's 85 feet and the international 100 feet of the time.

The late start was of particular concern since rivals Pittsburgh and Cleveland, both with artificial ice, had already played games. (Artificial ice was produced by spraying water over brine-filled pipes that had been cooled by a compressor using freon as a refrigerant.) In-state Group Three member Eveleth had been on the ice three weeks, including game action. While falling behind opponents was worrisome, Weidenborner and Fitzgerald soon had even greater concerns. According to the *Pioneer Press* of December 19, 1922:

> St. Paul's hockey prospects were clouded Sunday when it became known that

Frank Goheen and Tony Conroy, two of the stars of the A. C. team, had received very flattering offers ($2200 per season) from the Edmonton professional club in Western Canada [Western Canada Hockey League].

> Goheen and Conroy have not finally decided to accept, but plan to talk the matter over with the Canadian management. They may leave for Edmonton Tuesday night to look the situation over and make a decision on jumping the amateur ranks for the pro game.

The article went on to suggest that Goheen was more likely to take the professional offer than Conroy and that even if both players left, "manager Weidenborner is well fortified with reserve material and his outfit will not be wrecked by the departure[s]." Canadians Jack Chambers and Russ McCrimmon, with Minneapolis and Pittsburgh the previous season, were cited as potential replacements for Conroy and Goheen.

A day later, as practice was now under way, the situation clarified to some extent when it was determined that both players would lose their amateur status even by simply accepting transportation to Western Canada to assess the offer. Conroy and Goheen, regarded by most fans as the backbone of the AC team, were under considerable pressure from friends and teammates to remain in St. Paul. Feelings were high that this could be the year for the AC's. Nonetheless, it must have been tempting to accept the offer, especially considering the economic downturn of the early 1920s. The two delayed their decision another day. The *Pioneer Press* on December 21, 1921, wrote that

> Conroy went to the Hippodrome ready to say goodbye to his mates and tell them he was leaving Wednesday. When he left the rink at 10 P.M. his farewell lacked finality and encouraged his fellow players to hope

that he will not desert the club which he has helped so mightily.

Goheen was equally doubtful about the advantages of the Canadian offer, but all he would say was that he would decide today. The fact that he reconsidered his decision to leave Tuesday evening, and then was out for practice, is taken as an indication that he is finding it hard to leave the team with whose prestige in amateur hockey he has been so prominently identified.

Weidenborner and Fitzgerald, apparently sensing that the duo were close to backing out of any departure plans, simply added to the pressure by commenting that the team looked better than previous editions and could surely capture a championship if the two stars stayed in place. Frank Weidenborner was quoted in the December 21 *Pioneer Press*: "The boys were fighting with mid-season spirit. They are in great form this year and there is every indication that we will develop a winner."

By noon the following day, after conferring with Weidenborner and hockey patron Lucius Ordway (from the same philanthropic family that gave its name to St. Paul's Center for the Performing Arts), Conroy and Goheen announced they would be staying with St. Paul. While it is pure speculation, one suspects that the two were given some incentive to remain. Of course, in today's pro sports jargon, "terms of the agreement were not made public."

## Fitzgerald Picks His Men

With the Conroy/Goheen matter taken care of, Ed Fitzgerald set his attention to structuring the squad for the coming season. The 1920–21 AC's had suffered from a lack of sufficient spares. At this time, when teams were small and the concept of lines (a center with a right and left wing) was still in the offing, it was important to have two to three players who could give the regulars some needed rest during a game. Late in the

prior season it had not been uncommon for the team to have only one or two extra players. This was particularly evident during the March games in Eveleth and Duluth.

Fitzgerald had been impressed with the way "Coddy" Winters, the Cleveland captain, had judiciously substituted his spares and was determined to emulate his style. When St. Paul took to the ice for the season opener on December 27 against the Winnipeg Columbus club, Fitzgerald included himself, Emmy Garrett, and Connie Johannesson as spares. Besides the latter, three other new faces—Babe Elliott in goal, Russ McCrimmon at center, and Charles Cassin at right wing—made their AC debuts. Goheen was at left defense, with Wallie Elmer on the right side and Conroy at left wing. Fitzgerald would not put himself into any games until later in the season, when injuries forced his hand.

McCrimmon made a spectacular first impression when he scored the locals' first two goals, one in each period, as the game moved into the last session tied at two. After Columbus went up 3–2, Fitzgerald sent in his spares and Garrett responded by getting the last St. Paul goal after Goheen and Cassin had given the home team the lead. The 5–3 victory had been achieved with three goals in three minutes, which came close to being repeated the next night. With the AC's up 5–3 early in the third period, Cassin, McCrimmon, and Conroy all scored in rapid succession, though not necessarily within three minutes, to crush the visitors 8–3. For Conroy, it was his fourth goal of the night. Goheen and Cassin each had one. It was an impressive display. The *Pioneer Press*, December 29, 1921, reported:

The local victory was earned by vastly improved team work and much better shooting on the part of Captain [succeeding Goheen] Tony Conroy and his aids. The A. C. leader had a batting eye like Ty Cobb and gave a fancy exhibition of hockey . . . His mates fed him the puck with beautiful accuracy and when Tony wasn't jamming it past the Winnipeg goal tender he was bombarding the anatomy of that much abused individual with hard shots.

The games had been played with the reduced ice surface previously noted, but there was also another change that may have accounted for the nineteen goals scored in the two games. According to the *Pioneer Press*, December 23, 1921:

> The games on the local ice will be faster this season because of the fact that board walls have been erected back of the nets to prevent the puck from getting lost when shot beyond the goal. Heretofore there has been considerable stalling while the players were jockeying around bringing out the puck. Now it will bound back after passing the net and immediately will be in play.

Valuable time would no longer be lost in retrieving lost pucks, resulting in less-fatigued players and an increased pace to games.

Weidenborner had lowered ticket prices for the new season by dropping general admission to 50 cents and box seats to one dollar. While the results would not be seen in the attendance for the early games, the crowds would pick up significantly once the league schedule got under way on January 9. In the meantime there was another two-game set with a second Winnipeg team, the Nationals, as well as a recurring threat from Edmonton.

Bill Tobin, goaltender with the Eskimos, as the Edmonton team was known, was on a scouting mission for his club and watched both Columbus games. It was reported that he had raised the ante to $2,500 per season, but both Conroy and Goheen said there was "nothing to it" (*Pioneer Press*, December 29, 1921). Tobin left to continue his scouting mission in the East and indicated he would return to continue negotia-

tions after finishing his business there. While Conroy and Goheen would stay put, Tobin apparently succeeded in luring away Russ McCrimmon. The *Pioneer Press*, January 5, 1922, indicated that "Silver," as he was known to some, had been called home to Canada because of a sickness in his family. *The ACE*, from January 1922, seems to be closer to the mark:

> McCrimmon, the new man who played several years with Pittsburg[h], made a fine start, but loyalty to the team was evidently not considered when he turned professional and jumped to Edmonton to play there.

Tobin would eventually coach the Chicago Blackhawks in 1931 and 1932 and later serve as their general manager from 1942 through 1954. Perhaps because of this early foray into Minnesota, he knew where to come for players when his Chicago boss, Major Frederic McLaughlin, wanted American skaters. The 1937–38 Stanley Cup–winning Chicago Blackhawks had four Minnesota players—goaltender Mike Karakas, Eveleth; defenseman Virgil Johnson and forward "Cully" Dahlstrom of Minneapolis; and forward "Doc" Romnes of White Bear Lake.

The Nationals would fare no better than the Columbus club, falling to St. Paul 6–1 on January 3 and 4–1 the following evening. In the first game, Charley Cassin scored a goal in each period, and Conroy, Elmer, and Jack Chambers netted one each. The latter essentially took McCrimmon's roster spot and was used as a spare, along with Emmy and Bill Garrett, as "Coach Fitzgerald kept a steady stream of spares skating to and from the sidelines, [with] Emmy Garrett doing the best work of the relief corps" (*Pioneer Press*, January 4, 1922). Emmy Garrett took a two-minute penalty when he and the Nationals' O'Connell wrestled each other to the ice. In game two, he continued his aggressive play with two second-period goals following a scoreless first period. Cassin and Goheen added third period goals, while Elliott beat O'Connell twice before surrendering the shutout late in the game.

About one thousand fans had attended game one, but attendance fell off badly the next night. That situation would change with the first league series against Duluth on January 9 and 10. "5,000 Persons Expected at First League Hockey Game in St. Paul," trumpeted the *Pioneer Press* on January 6, 1922. The article reported an early version of today's professional sports group sales:

> It is the intention of the team management to dispose of as many seats as possible in blocks to various clubs and organizations throughout the city. Realizing the importance of the game, the Kiwanis Club has purchased a block of 100 tickets and will have a large representation at the game . . . Manager Weidenborner has also arranged for special street car service on both . . . nights. Cars will be ready immediately at the conclusion of the game to haul fans downtown.

Duluth arrived in St. Paul on Sunday, January 8, accompanied by enthusiastic fans whose numbers would swell the following day. Like the AC's, Duluth had swept two earlier series, one with Eveleth and the other with the Nationals. Joining the Zenith City skaters for the new season would be Mike Goodman, like Connie Johannesson, a veteran of the Winnipeg Falcons. Goodman was not only a good hockey player but, like Everett McGowan, also an outstanding competitive speed skater.

The visitors worked out at the Hippodrome on Monday morning, and the USAHA season got under way that night before a crowd estimated at four thousand. Roughly that same number returned on Tuesday night, as both crowds would see the games go into overtime with St. Paul victorious both nights. On Monday, Garrett got the game's first goal in the second period, only to have Duluth's Gus Olson tie it up in the closing stanza on a spectacular defense-splitting move.

The AC's got the 2–1 victory when Conroy scored early in the first ten-minute overtime period on a pass from Goheen after "Moose" made one of his long dashes down the ice. Both goaltenders came in for praise from the *Pioneer Press* on January 10, 1922:

> Elliott was a sure and cool buffer for all except one of the shots that came his way. He had little chance to stop Captain Olson's counter, which was crowded into the cage from a scrimmage. Anderson, the Duluth guard who wears a baseball mitt and frequently stops the puck by reaching out and grabbing it like a first baseman, was just about as efficient as Elliott. He had a lot more shots to stop and was in the way of dozens of perfect liners.

Garrett also got his team's first goal the following evening when his shot in front of the Duluth net caromed off of Gus Olson's skate and past Anderson to tie the game in the second period. The visitors regained the lead, only to have Goheen send the game into overtime with "a terrific line drive from far down the sidelines" (*Pioneer Press*, January 11, 1922). It was "Moose" again in the second ten-minute overtime when, with a minute to go, he put Garrett's rebound into the cage for the 3–2 win.

The two overtime victories put the AC's at 6–0 on the year and 2–0 in league play, and the second game also featured the then unheard-of instance of a goaltender leaving his net to play the puck. The *Pioneer Press* on January 11, 1922, described this maneuver:

> Babe [Elliott] looked bad on one occasion when he was forced into leaving the net to play around with the puck. Goodman was quick to notice Babe's aberration and proceeded to steal the puck away from him, dash around the net with it and barely miss crowding it in before Elliott could get back.

*Frank Weidenborner helped put St. Paul on the U.S. hockey map.*

The Duluth victories had been an auspicious conclusion to the first part of the season. It was one thing to beat up on non-league opponents, but these wins counted in the league competition. The AC's hoped they would provide momentum for even better things ahead and sustain the team during a nearly two-week layoff.

### A Break in the Action

St. Paul would not resume play until another Winnipeg entry, the Monarchs, arrived for a two-game set on January 23 and 24. If it was a welcome break for the players, who would continue practice at the Hippodrome under Fitzgerald's direction, it must have been a real relief for Frank Weidenborner. The *Pioneer Press,* January 12, 1922, described his typical game night duties:

> Frank Weidenborner, manager of the St. Paul hockey team, is going into training along with his players because when the A.C. sextet performs Weidenborner is the hardest worker in the outfit. As the crowd assembles he stands with his trusty megaphone and directs the customers to the ticket lines and entrances, while herding wandering automobiles to their parking places.
>
> With folks seeking to enroll on the free list duly discouraged, Frank goes inside to tell the assembled multitude the game is about to begin. After play starts, all he

has to do is to take part in any arguments that may develop on the ice, announce the added attractions between periods [often skating exhibitions], escort a troupe of ushers bearing coffee and hot dogs to the press bench line, run back to the dressing room to find out who made that doubtful assist, settle arguments as to whether Mike Goodman's nationality is indicated by his first or last name, give an expert opinion on whether a player is knocked cuckoo or just resting when he picks out a soft spot on the ice and flops, and last, but by no means least, to gumshoe [do detective work] about the rink scrutinizing mysterious spectators in an effort to discover if they are pro scouts from Canada.

As can be seen, Weidenborner's responsibilities extended to both on- and off-ice activities, though the former was largely the area where Fitzgerald operated. The "free list" refers to what today would be known as the "comp list," those spectators admitted for whatever reason free of charge. It is a list that sports and entertainment organizations like to limit as much as possible.

The Winnipeg Monarchs had split a two-game set with the AC's two seasons before and came to St. Paul fresh from game competition, while the locals had not seen any action for two weeks. The Monarchs were viewed as exactly the kind of opponent needed to prepare the AC's for the coming road trip to Cleveland and Pittsburgh for league play.

Sometime prior to the start of the first game, defenseman Wallie Elmer became ill, and Fitzgerald thought it best to hold him out of this game as a precaution. Bill Garrett took over for him, and George Conroy and Ryland Rothschild made their first appearances as spares. It would be a brief career for Rothschild. Within two minutes of hitting the ice he suffered a broken collarbone and would see no further action.

Goheen gave the home team a 1–0 lead fif-

teen minutes into the opening period when he shoved in Cassin's rebound. Tony Conroy added a second-period goal and then set up his brother for the third marker in the last period. A late Monarch goal kept Elliott from his first shutout of the season. He would do just as well in the second game, giving up only a solitary second-period goal, as St. Paul swept the series with a 5–1 win. Emmy Garrett scored three times, Tony Conroy and Cassin once each, and Elmer returned to see limited action.

The series sweep had been covered by Halsey Hall for the *Pioneer Press*, the second such assignment for the young sports reporter who would become a fixture on the Twin Cities sports scene for the next fifty years. Of this last game before the squad's departure to the East, he would write, on January 25, 1922:

> The game was nothing more than a good farewell workout for the Saints . . . The Monarchs . . . did not offer the opposition they afforded in the first clash . . . The Saints spent most of the time developing their team work and near the end of the game were traveling at the fastest pace they have shown this series . . . [T]he Canadians played as if they were bored with the proceedings.

The AC's boarded the train at Union Station at 8 P.M. the following evening and two nights later, on January 27, faced a Cleveland team that was certainly not bored. After the locals took a 1–0 first-period lead, the two teams went on a second-period scoring binge, which the home team won, getting five goals to the visitors' three. Leading the way for Cleveland was the superb Nels Stewart with three goals. St. Paul got two from Tony Conroy and one from Cassin. The 6–3 loss was the first defeat of the season for the AC's, but Frank Weidenborner was not discouraged. He wired home to the *Pioneer Press*, January 29, 1922:

Superior team play in second period defeated us. Game very rough and full of penalties. St. Paul had edge in first and third [scoreless] periods. The second was wild and our sensational defense weakened just enough to let them beat us.

All the boys played well but there was no particular star. We look for a victory tonight.

Weidenborner proved to be quite prophetic as he got his victory, and a star to boot, in the second game. Actually he got two stars. "Babe" Elliott's goaltending in the third period kept the game tied at two before Goheen got the game winner a minute into the period off a pass from Garrett. The teams had traded a goal apiece in each of the first two periods, with Elmer and Moose getting the St. Paul tallies. The hard-fought win was not without cost as Connie Johannesson went out with a broken collarbone when he collided with Cleveland's Jamieson. The split left the locals in first place in Group Two since they had played two more games than the AC's had.

With Johannesson on the shelf, Eddie Fitzgerald had no choice but to insert himself into the lineup for the games in Pittsburgh on January 30 and 31. St. Paul would be facing two former teammates—Ray Bonney would be in goal and Herb Drury at left defense for the home team. The first game proved as intense as the last contest in Cleveland, and the teams fought to a scoreless draw after two periods. Then, seven minutes into the final session, McGovern's shot grazed off Elliott's arm into the net for a 1–0 Pittsburgh lead, which proved short-lived. Thirty seconds later, Cassin scored off the face-off to tie the game and eventually send it into overtime. Sullivan then won it for Pittsburgh at the three-minute mark when he got the puck behind the St. Paul net and skated out to beat Elliott.

Things went better for the AC's the next night as Elliott got his first shutout in a decisive 3–0 victory. He also drew a penalty late in the second period for dropping to his knees to stop a shot, a practice then prohibited by the rules. Wallie Elmer took his place in front of the net and managed to preserve the shutout as the penalty carried over into the third period. At the time, St. Paul led 1–0 on Garrett's first-period goal, and he would get another on a pass from Fitzgerald in the last period. Goheen then closed out the scoring to make the final 3–0. *The ACE*, February 1922, expressed satisfaction with the trip:

> The boys left here on the 25th of January and invaded the East, so to speak. Getting an even break at Cleveland and Pittsburg was considered a very good week's work, and Cleveland for the first time in many moons was defeated on [its] own rink.
>
> Coming home . . . our boys . . . were a full game out of first place.

The AC's would now face on Hippodrome ice the same two teams they had split with on the road. Pittsburgh was due in on February 6 and 7 and Cleveland on February 13 and 14. The team would have to do

*Ed Fitzgerald's skates, which he may have also worn as a member of the 1920 United States Olympic Team*

better than a split at home if they were to take the lead in Group Two. Despite the major challenge ahead, the club chose to hold only one practice before the first Pittsburgh game. The *Pioneer Press* on February 3, 1922, wrote:

> The men feel that tonight's workout will be all they need to put them in top shape for the Pittsburgh series . . . With the exception of Johannesson's collarbone and minor bruises suffered by Goheen and Elmer, the squad is in good condition. Manager Weidenborner says the morale of the team has never been better . . . and the men are working with but one view in mind, that being the championship

of the United States Amateur Hockey Association.

Pittsburgh arrived a day before the first game and made their headquarters at the St. Francis Hotel. Weidenborner had high hopes of big gates for both games but had to settle for crowds of about twenty-five hundred at each. The contests followed the closely fought pattern of the second Cleveland game and the two at Pittsburgh. Goheen gave St. Paul a 1–0 first-period lead, off a rush that gave assists to both Conroy and Garrett. The visitors quickly countered a minute later when "Dinny" Manners tied it on a shot from the center of the rink. Both goalies then dominated play until game's end,

*The St. Francis Hotel on West Seventh Street in St. Paul, circa 1920–22*

although Pittsburgh carried the momentum. That edge continued into the overtime when former Olympian Joe McCormick got the winner at the first minute of the second extra period. Halsey Hall from the *Pioneer Press* reported that the players conceded they were outplayed and blamed the defeat on overconfidence (February 7, 1922).

There would be no overconfidence in game two as Ed Fitzgerald showed that he could still play the game. According to the *Pioneer Press,* February 8, 1922:

> The veteran coach of the Saints took possession of the puck in his own territory after checking Joe McCormick and started up the rink. Near the Pirate [both Pittsburgh and Cleveland were occasionally referred to by their respective baseball team names] nets, he passed across the ice to Emmy Garrett and Emmy then passed to Moose Goheen who was the right man in the right place. Bonney had no chance to stop Goheen's close-range, lightning-light shot.

The first-period goal was all that the home team needed for the victory, although they may have been aided by a ninety-minute power outage that occurred soon after Goheen's score. The long stoppage may have been enough to take the edge off of both team's play, as the goaltenders again held sway the rest of the way and once again Pittsburgh dominated third-period action.

The split kept the AC's a game behind Cleveland, which had just divided a series in Duluth. The team would be in good physical shape for Cleveland as Connie Johannesson returned after his injury and Emmy Garrett seemed no worse for wear after his collision with Herb Drury in game two. The *Pioneer Press,* February 9, 1922, looked ahead to the Cleveland clashes:

> The Cleveland games promise to be grudge battles. This is the crucial

series of the season, for two victories for either team will virtually cinch the championship.

Nelson Stewart, the crack center ice man, is the man whom the Saints fear most on the Indian aggregation. Stewart is to Cleveland what Goodman is to Duluth and Drury is to Pittsburgh, with the added advantage of fitting better into the team work. The Saints held him in check in the second game at Cleveland only by putting two men on him and will likely repeat this plan next week.

With the Group Two lead more immediately at stake in the series, St. Paul turned out in the kind of numbers Frank Weidenborner always dreamed about. *The ACE,* February 1922, wrote:

> Every hockey fan was awaiting for Cleveland, for at the two games on February 13th and 14th, attendance records at the Hippodrome rink were smashed. 4,032 persons were out Monday night, and 5,500 on Tuesday night. Never before was such a crowd seen at the big rink.

Cleveland arrived in town from Winnipeg, where they had played in a tournament in conjunction with that city's Winter Carnival. On Saturday, February 11, the USAHA team had played to a 6–6 tie with the Manitoba All-Stars for the tournament title but declined to play overtime because of their arduous pre- and post-Canadian schedule. That decision caused the event to be forfeited to the All-Stars, but presumably left the players better rested for the critical St. Paul series.

Nels Stewart had played his usual game in the tournament, scoring six goals and three assists in two games, but the AC's held him in check in game one and even made him look bad. After Emmy Garrett slapped in Connie Johannesson's rebound in the second period to give St. Paul a 1–0 lead, Tony Conroy got the clincher. Halsey Hall was there for the *Pioneer Press*, reporting on February 14, 1922:

> The first came so quickly after the opening face-off of the [third] period that many spectators were still filing from the warming room. Goheen snatched the puck from Stewart as the opening bell sounded, passed to Tony Conroy and the gallant captain lifted one from the side which escaped Turner for the second score.

Conroy had sharpened his game in the Winnipeg tournament as a replacement for Duluth's Mike Goodman, who was out with an eye injury. He scored three times in an 11–7 loss to the Manitoba All-Stars. His goal in this game was the clincher, but midway through the period Elmer got an insurance marker from a scramble in front of the visitors' net, though things were not quite over. Stewart set up Joe Debernardi, and Elliott lost his shutout on a bullet from the Cleveland right wing. Elliott then had to come up with a number of sensational saves to preserve the 3–1 victory. As the losing team left the ice, Hall quoted Debernardi: "Well, we're tied now, that makes it all the more interesting."

Interesting it was—the largest crowd up to that point in St. Paul's hockey history saw the second game go into two overtimes before Goheen's goal won it 3–2. After Garrett had converted Moose's pass for a 1–0 first-period lead, Cleveland came storming back to take a 2–1 lead into the last canto. Then the Goheen/Garrett duo did a repeat of their first-period action to tie the game with three minutes to go. Goheen's winner came four minutes into the second overtime when he took the puck at mid-ice, skated a few feet, and sent a wrister past Vern Turner. Halsey Hall from the *Pioneer Press* described the success on February 15, 1922:

> Before fifty-five hundred shouting fans at the Hippodrome rink Tuesday night, St. Paul's fighting A. C. hockey team achieved its greatest triumph since hockey became a major sport in this city. Coming back with a strength which brooked no resistance and knew no defeat, the A. C. sextet swept the Cleveland champions aside and wrested the mantle of leadership from the Forest City team . . . The victory was all the more noteworthy because Goheen played with an injured knee and Elmer and Elliott were in none too good condition.

St. Paul now led Group Two, and that would be reason enough for considerable civic pride—already expressed two days before in the Cleveland series. In a dinner at the local Elk's Lodge, the team was honored, along with Dr. Carl Haedge, national handball champion, and Everett McGowan, a former AC player who was now a national speed-skating titlist. Frank Weidenborner spoke to the attendees about the problems of contending for a championship. Ed Fitzgerald made brief remarks, and each team member was introduced to a rousing reception. The event brought out the city and state leadership, most notably Speaker of the Minnesota House W. L. Nolan.

The team would now have a two-week layoff before traveling to the head of the lakes for a two-game series with Duluth on February 27 and 28. Fitzgerald held his last practice at the Hippodrome on February 24 and along with Weidenborner declared the squad to be in its best physical condition of the season and not in the least overconfident. The latter may not have been totally true, since the AC's would be facing a Duluth team without its star player Mike Goodman. The Winnipeg native had injured himself in a speed-skating race and despite rumors to the contrary would see no action in this series.

Goodman's absence hardly seemed to matter to Duluth and even appears to have served as a catalyst to inspired play. Lodged in last place in Group Two, the home team played the spoiler role to the hilt. Ten minutes into the

*Everett McGowan, champion speed skater, played briefly with the AC's and later in the professional Western Canada League with Vancouver.*

game, Jimmy Wahl gave the locals a lead, which Garrett soon countered by putting a rebound past goalie Ivor Anderson. Duluth came back with a second-period tally and Conroy sent the game into overtime in the last period. That period featured fisticuffs between Goheen and Wahl, which resulted in both being ejected from the game. The teams then battled into the third overtime, with four skaters each, before Gus Olson, who had been injured earlier in the contest, scored the game winner for Duluth with two minutes to go.

A victory would have clinched the Group Two title because Pittsburgh defeated Cleveland 3–1 the same night. But the clinching would have to wait one more day—and when it came, it came in a flurry. In a game marked by extensive brawling, St. Paul routed the home team 7–1. Goheen scored three times and Conroy and Garrett added two apiece. Wahl was ejected again and didn't take Goheen with him this time, but the AC star had other concerns. The *Pioneer Press,* March 1, 1922, described things this way:

> Olson and Goheen indulged in a fist fight in this period which nearly had disastrous consequences. Several hundred fans swarmed on the ice before the men were separated, and Goheen was badly bumped while police were frantically trying to quell the disturbance. When play was resumed Goheen donned a football headgear as a measure of protection against further outbursts by excitable fans.

## On to the Range

The win gave St. Paul an 8–4 record, and although Cleveland would come back to beat Pittsburgh 5–3 as the AC's routed Duluth, their 7–5 record made St. Paul the Group Two champions. Canadian Soo had won the Group Three title, but they were ineligible for the U.S. national championship, which was now down to three teams: Eveleth, St. Paul, and the Boston Westminsters. The latter had won Group One with a 14–0 thrashing of New York's St. Nicholas Club and would now await the winner of the Eveleth–St. Paul series, which would open in the Hilltop City on March 3. The teams would play two games there before moving to St. Paul for games starting on March 6. Total goals would decide the series.

Meanwhile in Boston, hockey writer A. Linde Fowler, reporting for the *Boston Evening Transcript* on March 1, 1922, would have some interesting observations:

> As between playing Eveleth . . . or St. Paul . . . some of the Westminsters will root for St. Paul in its series with Eveleth, not because they think St. Paul is the weaker of the two but because of traveling and rink conditions. They understand that the Eveleth rink is small and that its lighting arrangement will bother a visiting team, whereas the St. Paul rink is a larger one. Moreover, Eveleth means a longer and more precarious train ride, for to miss a train there from Duluth is said to entail the loss of a full day.
>
> Competitive games . . . would seem to give St. Paul the edge over Eveleth . . . for Duluth went to Eveleth and broke even in two exhibition games, while Eveleth also lost three out of four games to Canadian Soo.

The AC's remained in Duluth and worked out at the Curling Club before boarding a train to Eveleth on Friday morning, March 3. Those fans who had followed the team to Duluth stayed with them while a smaller group traveled from the capital to lend their support. Athletic Club executive F. Charlton wired encouragement to team captain Tony Conroy on the eve of the first game: "Sorry am not with you personally[,] am in spirit[,] bring home the bacon."

Frank Goheen would remember the games in Eveleth ten years later when Joe Hennessay reported in the *St. Paul Daily News*, March [?], 1933:

> Of all of the rough and tumble games in which he has competed the Moose believes the toughest was the playoff series with Eveleth in the winter of 1922 when the penalty boxes were jammed constantly.

St. Paul would be playing for the first time in Eveleth's new rink, also called the Hippodrome, which had opened with the new year. Crowds of more than three thousand would pack the rink both nights and prove more than casual onlookers. Goheen continued wearing his football headgear and put the AC's ahead 1–0 as he finished off a rush by putting Garrett's pass behind the Eveleth goalie. The teams traded second-period goals with Johannesson getting the St. Paul marker before Garrett made the final score 3–1 when he knocked in Conroy's rebound in the last period.

Three minutes before the end, Eveleth's Jim Seaborn was ordered off the ice, much to the crowd's displeasure. When Johannesson became involved in a postgame scuffle, both players and fans rushed the ice for a full-scale donnybrook, which soon brought Eveleth's finest to the scene. What the police couldn't totally control, three Eveleth players did by waving their sticks and charging the crowd. The AC's were then able to proceed to their dressing room, where it was determined that Goheen had a cut over his right eye and Conroy a severe bump on his head.

There was more such postgame bedlam the next night despite Eveleth's 4–3 win, but the police were able to quell things that potentially could have exceeded the previous evening's activities. St. Paul blew a 2–1 lead on second-period tallies by Garrett and Goheen heading into the third session when the home team erupted for three straight goals. It was a penalty-filled game, as Goheen recalled, but Frank Weidenborner would remember it from a different perspective (*Pioneer Press*, April 10, 1922):

*"Ching" Johnson's Eveleth jersey. Johnson was another USAHA graduate to achieve stardom in the NHL. As a New York Ranger he won two Stanley Cups and was elected to the Hockey Hall of Fame in Toronto.*

Ask Weidenborner what the highlight of the past hockey season was and he will probably tell you the caress he got from Ade Johnson at Eveleth. It happened in the timer's box when Seaborn and Nicklin were enjoying one of their frequent penalties.

Weidenborner raised his hand during a face-off to ask the Referee something and Ade Johnson evidently thought this was not fair. Wham, bang, down came his stick with full force on Weidie's felt hat.

Someone asked Frank why he didn't fall down, pretending he was hurt and scare the Eveleth gentleman.

"And let those two eggs run out of the penalty box, I should say not."

The AC's left for home at 7 A.M. Sunday morning, and Eveleth departed at noon with Mayor Victor Essling aboard. The mayor was the driving force behind his city's team and would join them at the St. Francis Hotel as the series resumed in the capital. St. Paul had come out of the first two games badly battered. Goheen was covered with bruises, and the others, particu-

larly Garrett, who was slightly built, were exhausted. The AC's had taken only one spare on the trip, Cassin, and had played four games in six days. One of those games had involved overtime play. Nonetheless the series was tied in both games and goals.

Gale Brooks, the Hippodrome manager, predicted good ice for the resumption of the series on March 6 despite an upturn in temperature. Weidenborner would get his second five-thousand-plus crowd for the game, as George Conroy was now available as a second spare to help spell the regulars. Hockey fever had now gripped St. Paul to the extent that it was front-page news for the *Pioneer Press* on March 7, 1922: "St. Paul–Eveleth Play Six Periods To Scoreless Tie." Halsey Hall was there for the *Pioneer Press* and followed the headline with this bit of poetry:

> With hearts that were staunch and sturdy and a spirit that invited battle, encased in bodies that could stand the strain no longer, the St. Paul Athletic Club hockey team held the fast and heavy Eveleth ice locomotive to a scoreless tie at the Hippodrome Monday night after three extra periods of breathtaking hockey.

Babe Elliott would get his third shutout of the season, making thirty-six stops to eighteen for Monette in the Eveleth nets. The reporting of saves was now becoming more common in game stories. The visitors would have the shot advantage in all periods and the overall edge in play, but neither side could put the game away.

The violence of the first two games was gone, though Seaborn did exchange unpleasantries with a St. Paul fan, which came to nothing. Interest was as intense in Eveleth as in St. Paul as one thousand fans waited at the local Western Union office for results and the *Pioneer Press* received numerous calls from the Hill Top city and other Iron Range communities for game updates. After the third overtime, the two teams and the referees agreed to let the tie stand and to replay the contest on Wednesday after the Tuesday game.

Another excellent crowd, this one a bit under five thousand, was back for game four and would see the AC's get away only eight shots to Eveleth's twenty-three, but two of those got past Monette. Garrett and Conroy would score in the first and second periods, and that would prove enough as the visitors could get only one on "Ching" Johnson's shot with two minutes to go. The 2–1 victory gave St. Paul a 7–6 edge in goals, and the team now needed only one more the next night while keeping Eveleth scoreless to get to the national finals.

They wouldn't get that "one more," but neither would the "Red Rangers," as the visitors were occasionally referred to—the teams would battle to another scoreless tie at the packed Hippodrome. Goheen would abandon his headgear and protect himself with a strip of tape over his forehead. Elmer would need attention to his leg and only George Conroy would be available as a spare. Despite the overall feeling of weariness, the AC's battled through to win the right to face the Boston Westminsters. Eveleth's shot margin narrowed to 17–14 and Garrett came closest to scoring, but Johnson hooked him late in the first period, taking the "good" penalty. Halsey Hall described the game's aftermath for the *Pioneer Press*, March 9, 1922:

> After the final bell had sounded two things occurred that topped off the evening in a manner to be pleasantly remembered. The huge crowd which packed the build-

ing did not crash the exits as is so often the case, but waited to make sure of their favorites' triumph and with Manager Weidenborner's announcement, a cheer that shook the structure, resounded throughout the Hippodrome.

> Last, but not least, Captain Nicklin of the Rangers, walking into the St. Paul dressing room, congratulated the Saints and made a subtle plea for his city [alluding to the two games in Eveleth] by remarking, "Well, we're not roughnecks, are we?"

A day later the *Pioneer Press*, in column notes perhaps written by Hall, summed up the semifinals:

> Eveleth has departed, sadder but wiser. The boys who swung their sticks so carelessly on the Range played a gentler tune with them here and proved to be good hockey players when they played the puck instead of the man. The spectators behaved fairly well, getting some unnecessary but healthy "boos" out of their system occasionally and 'tis said that Eveleth resented this. Some people surely are sensitive.

## Here Come the Westies

The AC's were now in a truly national finals series for the Fellowes Cup. While they had won the regional MacNaughton Cup in 1915–16 and shared it with American Soo in 1919–20, this was as big as it got for hockey in the United States at this time. Cleveland had defeated Eveleth a year earlier in the USAHA's first season, and now it would appear that the Boston Westminsters had the opponent they wanted if the *Evening Transcript*'s Linde Fowler is to be believed. They were champions of Group One with a 6–2 slate and had a strong non-league record, but they departed for St. Paul with some injury concerns. On March 6 they had lost to Group One second-place finisher Pere Marquette 2–1 in a

Winsor Cup game that saw defenseman Irving Small suffer a dislocated shoulder and wing Wilfred Veno receive a cut over the eye that required two stitches.

Small, along with Captain Frank Downing, were the Americans on the team, hailing from Winchester and Somerville, Massachusetts, respectively. Veno and his brother Stan, known as "Shorty" and also a wing, were from Chatham, New Brunswick. Wing Norman Shay was from Hunstville, Ontario; defenseman "Ag" Smith came from Jarvis, Ontario; and goaltender Herb Rheaume came from Mason, Quebec. Spare Phil Rudolph hailed from Halifax, Nova Scotia. Ed Powers was behind the bench. Both Shay and Rheaume would go on to brief NHL careers, Shay with the Boston Bruins and Toronto St. Pats, and Rheaume with the Montreal Canadiens.

The final series was originally scheduled to open on Friday and Saturday, March 10 and 11, at the Hippodrome, but with the Eveleth series finishing up on March 8, the games were moved ahead by one day. The first game would be played on Saturday, March 11, and would be quickly followed by a Sunday afternoon contest. The teams would then go east to finish the series in Boston the following weekend. The quick turnaround in St. Paul appears to have been based on concerns for the quality of ice due to the warming trend previously noted. Weidenborner expressed great confidence that the ice would be in good shape, and the *Pioneer Press*, March 10, 1922, added:

The handlers of the surface are to be congratulated on the condition of the Saint's home rink in the Eveleth series. Despite a protracted spell of warm weather, the ice was far from slushy and even the heavy Rangers couldn't spoil it sufficiently to ruin a St. Paul score.

The Westminsters lodged at the St. Paul Hotel and worked out at the Hippodrome on March 9 and 10. The *Pioneer Press* continued:

The Easterners are a rangy lot and handle themselves well, giving all the appearance of champions. Their record proves them to be formidable foes and a dash of overconfidence on the part of the Saints might prove disastrous when the local favorites mingle with the boys from the Hub.

While the visitors readied themselves on the ice, the AC's rested from the rigors of the Eveleth series. "Doc" Wildermuth, the team trainer, attended to various ailments. Virtually all of the players had some nagging injury: Goheen's eye/head, Elmer's knee, Conroy's legs, Elliott's cold, and Johannesson's lingering shoulder pain, as well as Garrett's overall fatigue. None of these things, along with only two-plus days of rest, were viewed as preventing success. The *Pioneer Press*, March 11, 1922, beneath a headline reading "City Is All Agog Over St. Paul–Boston Hockey Series Opening Tonight," said: "St. Paul has evidently passed the crisis of its 1922 career as far as physical fitness and strenuous foreign battles are concerned." The neighboring *Minneapolis Tribune*, March 11, 1922, was far more positive:

Despite the excellent record boasted by the Eastern six, the Saints are generally picked as the winners of the four game series. The rest since Wednesday night has done the downriver players a world of good and they are expected to step onto the ice tonight in excellent shape.

On March 11, ticket sales were reported as brisk for the two games, but seating was still available and there would be special street car service to the Hippodrome. The Westies had toured Minneapolis's flour mills the day before and on this day would tour St. Paul, after being hosted at a special lunch at the Athletic Club's facilities. Then at 8:15 that night, it was time to play hockey for the national championship.

It became evident that there had been false

optimism about ice conditions, and the softness of the surface would be cited as a factor in St. Paul's 3–0 defeat. The visitors reportedly thrived under these circumstances, but another evaluation might simply put the loss on that bugaboo of all hockey teams, the hot goaltender. The AC's outshot Boston 21–14, with ten of those shots coming in the first period as Herb Rheaume held off the home team. Thereafter, the ice probably became a greater factor, although the *Pioneer Press's* Halsey Hall, on March 12, 1922, would cite overconfidence and even "staleness" as other reasons for the loss. The latter would seem to be unlikely since the team had just played three days earlier—perhaps fatigue was a more likely factor.

In any event, despite Stan Veno's goal on a pass from Frank Downing at the twelve-minute mark, Hall saw the first period this way:

> The Easterners were outplayed by the A. C. men in that first session ... [Wallie] Elmer, skating easier than at any time during the Eveleth series, penetrated the Boston defense often, but never to score, while the usually brilliant work of Tony Conroy and his forward mates, Goheen and Garrett, failed to produce a marker.

Irving Small would make it 2–0 for the Westies in the second period as the St. Paul attack slowed except for Johannesson's rushes. Small, whose name belied his stature, had been unable to play on the 1920 U.S. Olympic Team, a situation he would reverse in 1924. On this goal he beat Elliott in a one-on-one confrontation after some clever stickhandling. There would be another one on one in the third period after Stan Veno scored at the seven-minute mark on a Goheen-like rink-length dash. It would be Goheen, who had had some first-period opportunities, who was beaten when Rheaume came out of the nets to block his shot. Halsey Hall summed up the game:

> Clad in sky-colored jerseys ... [i]t is a fast skating, clever checking aggregation that has come out of the East to take the Saints down a notch in their bid for Uncle Sam's hockey supremacy. Playing before a crowd that numbered 5,300 paid admissions ... the men from the Hub City clearly earned their victory and won the admiration of the spectators with their clean play.

Ice conditions were no better the next day as the crowd dropped to thirty-seven hundred for game two. The start of the game was delayed as crews removed water from the rink's surface, but even then puddles remained. Phil Rudolph had to step in for "Ag" Smith on the Boston defense—the latter had dislocated his shoulder. For the AC's, no one had to sit out, but it was evident that Goheen was not on his game. The *Pioneer Press*, March 13, 1922, would comment that "the Moose deserves worlds of credit for playing in his present condition."

One minute into the game Stan Veno continued his heroics from the night before with another rink-length dash and shot that beat Elliott from close in. Ten minutes later, St. Paul countered when Goheen picked up a loose puck at mid-ice and passed to Garrett, who fired on Rheaume. The big Westie goaltender made the initial stop, but Conroy was there for the rebound. Playing conditions worsened in the second period due to the soft ice, and there were numerous tumbles by players and officials alike. With Cassin and George Conroy as the spares, Fitzgerald sent Cassin into the game with the hope his "bulletlike drives would pierce the Westminster defense" (*Pioneer Press*, March 13, 1922).

Neither Cassin nor any other local would find the Boston net over the next two periods as the ice again deteriorated. Then, with five minutes to go in the game, the slushy surface would contribute to the visitors' victory. The *Pioneer Press*, March 13, 1922, reported that

Irving Small, giant defensive star . . . who plays with his cap pulled rakishly over one eye and an air of assurance . . . had taken the puck up the ice unassisted for a close-in shot at Elliott which [was] . . . blocked . . . Babe stepped out to beat Small to the rebound, but . . . barely reached the puck and it twisted and rolled into the St. Paul goal, a thing it would not have done on decent ice.

The 2–1 victory sent the Westminsters back to Boston with a commanding two-games-to-none lead. One more game would take the series, but if St. Paul were to rally to win both games, then total goals would be the deciding factor. A tie in goals would necessitate one more contest. The teams were feted at a postgame banquet at the St. Francis Hotel. The AC's were entertained at dinner on Monday night at Harry Simon's residence. They boarded the Tuesday night train east, as their failure to win one game at home was pondered by various critical observers. Halsey Hall of the *Pioneer Press* on March 13, 1922, suggested that both the effects of the Eveleth series and the ice conditions were factors. Charles Adams, director of the Boston Arena, where the series would continue, had seen the St. Paul games and concurred on both counts. He felt the Westminsters were better rested and that the watery surface severely hampered the passing of the AC's, allowing the visitors to more easily break up rushes. Conversely, the Westies' offense was more individually oriented and therefore less affected by the conditions.

Just how bad were those conditions? Linde Fowler, reporting for the *Evening Transcript*, March 15, 1922, reported:

Two inches of slush and soft ice were removed for the first game and as much for the second. Before the second game was over the surface was so covered with slush and water that when a player stopped suddenly, a stream of water shot out far enough at times to cover the twenty foot space between the ice and the spectators' seats.

The two games had drawn an attendance of slightly more than ten thousand, with ninety-two hundred of that figure as paid admissions. The balance was accounted for by passes or "comps" in today's jargon. While the game results were disappointing to local fans, most everyone was impressed with the Westminsters. Typical was this comment by Ed Shave of the *St. Paul Daily News*, March 13, 1922:

Boston's Westminster team has gone, but it left a record for sportsmanship and clean playing which will long be remembered by local fans. They were a real hockey team, good in all departments. They showed that a team can play the cleanest of hockey and win.

They were continually applauded during the two games. St. Paul wanted St. Paul to win, but if such is not to be we are glad to have such a team as the Westminsters capture the championship.

Obviously "Minnesota Nice" was alive and well in 1922.

The AC's arrived in Boston at midday on March 16 amid observations by both the *Boston Globe* and the *Evening Transcript* that the team would do better on the artificial ice surface of the Boston Arena. In addition it was believed that St. Paul would be further rested from the rigors of the previous two games and the Eveleth series. The special correspondent for the *Pioneer Press* (most likely a Boston resident) went so far as to install the visitors as 10 to 7 favorites. No consideration seems to have been given to the effects of the long train trip from Minnesota.

The Boston Arena, where the games would

be held on March 17 and 18, had opened in 1910, only to be damaged by a major fire in 1918. Renovated, it played host to much early Boston hockey, including the NHL Bruins before the Boston Garden debuted in 1928. The facility, with an ice surface of 220 feet by 90 feet, had a capacity of approximately seven thousand, and there were close to that number for both contests.

The games would be followed closely from St. Paul, but since radio was in its infancy, telegraph would report the results home to both St. Paul newspapers from specially hired local correspondents. The telegraph would also send words of encouragement to team captain Tony Conroy from the AC fans:

> Knock them for a row[.] We are all back
> of you[.] It won't be long now till the big
> party[,] will it[?] We are having a mild
> [wild?] one tonight[.] . . . Regards to Fitz[,]
> Moose[,] Emmy[,] Babe and all the boys.
> Moran[,] Coleman[,] and McCarthy

Frank S. Rogers sent this greeting: "The bunch wish you all the best of luck," while on the other side, the *Globe*, March 17, 1922, would admonish, "Now, Westminsters live up to your St. Paul reputation." The resumption of the series again brought hockey to the front page of the *Pioneer Press* on March 18, 1922, when St. Paul residents awoke to read the headline "St. Paul and Boston in Scoreless Tie." The two teams had battled through three fifteen-minute periods and three ten-minute overtimes (with the usual change of ends at the five-minute mark) to arrive at no decision. "Ag" Smith was back in the Westies line-up, playing in spite of his dislocated shoulder, as the teams moved cautiously during regulation play—Boston being given the nod on overall scoring chances. In the first period, Elliott beat both Veno and Downing on breakaways, and Rheaume did the same to Conroy.

The AC's stepped up their physical game early in the second period, hoping to force turnovers with hard body checking, and got one good

*The Boston Arena, circa early 1920s*

chance, but Rheaume stopped Garrett. Thereafter the home team had the better opportunities, but they came to nothing—as when Downing could not convert Shay's pass right in front of Elliott, the latter subsequently thwarting Small, and then Small getting in the way of a chance by Shay. In the third period, Conroy's long, hard shot was headed for a corner of the net, but Rheaume was there for that save and two other key stops as St. Paul pressed the attack.

The tempo picked up in the first overtime as Veno and Shay had "a first-class scoring opening in the first five minutes . . . and Garrett . . . nearly won the game . . . on a long shot which Rheaume did not see until the puck was almost at his feet" (*Evening Transcript,* March 18, 1922). Small took a hard check, which appeared to injure his left shoulder, but he continued playing. The Westies missed a sure goal in the second overtime when Veno's pass to Downing was off target with Elliott out of position. The latter again came up big on Downing early in the third overtime, and Smith and Small combined on the classic give and go. Getting behind the AC defense, Small was about to shoot when he was apparently tripped from behind. While no penalty was called, the tumble was enough to force the Boston star from the game, which was then declared a tie. The *Evening Transcript,* March 18, 1922, declared:

> When they called [it] quits there seemed little likelihood that either team could score except on a fluke, no matter how long they kept at it, and they did play until the hour was so late [11:30] that those who depended on trains for out-of-town either had to leave before the final whistle or, in some instances, caught the last train by running for the last car down the station platform.

While the Boston press paid due tribute to their own stars, most notably Small and Rheaume, they were generous to St. Paul. Typi-cal was John J. Hallahan's comments in the *Evening Transcript,* March 18, 1922:

> As individuals . . . the . . . St. Paul forwards showed numerous brilliant stunts, especially Goheen, who hooked the puck away from an opponent about as often and as cleverly as any player who has appeared in the Arena, who "jumped" with astonishing speed for so large a man and whose weight and strength helped greatly in some of his dashes. He also had a wicked shot, as to speed, but last night it was off on direction. All of the visitors were inclined to wildness in their shooting, though they [did not get] some that were labeled goals only for the superb stops by Herbert Rheaume. Garrett has a great shot and proved himself to be an exceptionally fine player.

When the format for the play-off series was established by the USAHA there was no thought given to dealing with tie games. Now that one had been played and not resolved within what was regarded as reasonable overtime, what to do was left to the league's executive committee. Headed by President W. S. Haddock, it consisted of Secretary Roy Schooley along with Tom Kanaly, Boston Athletic Association; R. L. Von Bernuth, St. Nicholas Hockey Club of New York; and Frank Weidenborner. The committee's decision was to award half a game to each team, which effectively gave the championship to the Westminsters. Even with a victory in the March 18 game, the AC's could not win the series. Nonetheless the game was played and both teams competed just as if it really counted. There was still pride at stake for St. Paul in avoiding a sweep—for Boston three-and-a-half games to one-half sounded a lot better than two-and-a-half to one-and-a-half.

The series had been officiated by Canadian referees Fred Mitchell, Winnipeg, and D. Munro, Montreal, and up to the final game they had handed out few penalties. There were those who

*The Westminster Hockey Club of Boston, USAHA Champions, 1921–22*

thought they had let too many things go in game three and in the early stages of game four. They more than made up for their earlier perceived deficiencies by sending three players from each team to the box in the final period. By this time the Westies had a 2–0 lead, which stood up until the end. St. Paul had started strongly when Goheen nearly scored on Rheaume, but Boston soon gained the momentum and went ahead at the 7:19 mark of the first period. Downing, after taking a pass from Stan Veno, fed "Ag" Smith, whose shot deflected off an AC defenseman past Elliott.

In the second period, Smith played a role in the Westies' second goal when Shay took his pass and wound up with the puck in the St. Paul net. Conroy, as the captain of the AC's, disputed the goal and requested that goal judge Willie Gezzie be removed. It was within the authority of team captains to change what we now call off-ice officials, so Gezzie went, but the goal counted. Play roughened in the final period and the penalties followed, but there was no further scoring.

The Boston victory had come without the in-

jured Small, whose place was taken by Rudolph—but it was Smith and Rheaume on whom the Boston press heaped praise, while once again singling out Goheen as the outstanding St. Paul player. This time it was the *Globe*, March 19, 1922, paying tribute:

> He excelled his mates and it was not because of any fault of his that the Saints went down. He carried the puck in amazing style and several times had excellent chances to score, but because of being alone and forced to shoot while off balance[,] he could not lodge the rubber in the net . . . Conroy and Elliott were the other players who did well for St. Paul.

When the game was over the victors were visited by Ralph Winsor, the coach who had put Harvard on the college hockey map in the early years of the twentieth century. Winsor had not only had great success on the ice but was regarded as an innovator in both equipment and tactics. He is credited with computing and adopting the official radii for skates, known as the "Harvard Radius," as well as with developing the concept of back-checking and the side-by-side pairing of defensemen. He would go on to coach the United States to a silver medal at the 1932 Winter Olympics and find a place among the charter enshrinees of the United States Hockey Hall of Fame. The great coach congratulated the Westies, and the team responded with three cheers for the Massachusetts native.

Both teams were then honored at a dinner at the Boston Athletic Association hosted by Boston Arena director Charles Adams. Adams would lead Boston into the NHL in 1924, an act that spelled eventual doom for high-level amateur hockey in the United States. Although the national championship was lost, Weidenborner was not satisfied to end the season with a dinner when there was still the possibility of playing more hockey on the way home. The AC's moved on to Pittsburgh for a two-game series on March 21 and 22 with their Group Two rivals. The two teams had split four earlier games, and that trend would continue.

St. Paul jumped out to a quick 2–0 first-period lead on goals by Garrett and Conroy and made it 5–2 after two with a pair by Garrett and another by Goheen. The home team's Ray Bonney, the former AC goaltender in the MacNaughton Cup year, was under constant siege by his former teammates, who now found the net that had eluded them in the national title series. The local fans became so incensed at his play that they literally hooted him off the ice. Bonney refused to play the third period and was replaced by a local goaltender named Montgomery. The newcomer blanked the visitors the rest of the way as the locals made it a bit closer at 5–4.

Montgomery was back the next night as Pittsburgh took a 3–1 first-period lead with Conroy getting St. Paul's goal. The team "did not display the same dash they showed last night . . . the players appeared to be stale . . . Their play at times was listless," the *Pioneer Press,* March

23, 1922, reported. The home team made it 5–1 before Garrett and Goheen brought the AC's closer at 5–4. When Garrett got another goal midway through the third period to make it 5–4, it looked as if the momentum was swinging their way, only to have old teammate Herb Drury put it away 6–4 at the 11:42 mark.

The team, minus Elmer, who returned to his Kingston, Ontario, home from Pittsburgh, was back in St. Paul on March 24. Weidenborner had detoured to Milwaukee to see the new artificial ice rink there and to speak with local interests about entering a team in the USAHA the next season. When he got back home on March 25, he was high in his praise for everything Boston: opponents, hospitality, rink, and fans. He denied that the games were overly rough—though certainly the fourth could be described that way—according to the *Daily News,* March 25, 1922: "We just played good hard hockey and naturally the harder you play the rougher the game will be. Any fouls that were committed were unintentional."

The St. Paul manager could look back at a season that was the most successful to date from a financial standpoint and close to that description on the ice. The two MacNaughton Cup titles had been won in fewer games and against less talented opposition. On the other hand, while the USAHA Group Two championship did not lead to another Cup, in this case the Fellowes, it did put St. Paul on the national hockey map. There were more games, the opposition was tougher, and the AC's were competitive. A cartoon that ran in the *Pioneer Press* on April 10, 1922, aptly showed Weidenborner painting St. Paul on a "United States Hockey Map."

Slightly more than fifty-three thousand fans had come to the Hippodrome for the seventeen home games. This broke out to twelve thousand each for the Cleveland, Eveleth, and Boston series, while Duluth drew eight thousand, Pittsburgh five thousand, and the non-league games forty-two hundred. Gate receipts from these games amounted to about $30,000. Savoring these numbers, the *Daily News*, March 26, 1922, looked forward to the next season:

> Frank Weidenborner . . . is busy making plans for next year. He is negotiating with several good stick handlers who signified their desire to play with the St. Paul team.
>
> The A. C. may obtain the services of one good Eveleth player.
>
> Plans are under way to reorganize the league. Though nothing is definitely settled, it is proposed to get Minneapolis, Milwaukee and probably Chicago into the circuit.

Ed Shave, also writing in the *Daily News*, March 19, 1922, decried the lack of additional spares and advised: "St. Paul needs a good goal-shooting center, a wing and a man able to spare at wing or defense. They can be secured and those who handle the reins for the six should at once commence to angle for such performers for the coming season." *The ACE*, March 1922, reviewed the season in some detail, lauding Fitzgerald and his players while concluding somewhat wistfully:

> The St. Paul Athletic Club hockey team, that gallant aggregation of knights of the stick and skates . . . there has been no set of players that have labored so diligently and earnestly to put the Athletic Club and St. Paul before the public, as the 1922 hockeyists.
>
> But the local season has passed, passed into the hall of events that used to be and welcome Summer is on her way. Through her sunny months, however, and into the golden autumn, will linger memories of the 1922 hockey season with perhaps a touch of longing for the coming of 1923 and the victories it will bring.

# 7

# 1922-1923

## *Winning the West II*

"St. Paul this year flashed its greatest hockey team in history
on the ice of five rivals and at the Hippodrome. Many declare it
to be the greatest the country ever saw."

*Halsey Hall*, St. Paul Pioneer Press, *March 4, 1923*

Frank Weidenborner had taken on a new role for the 1922–23 season. Rather than manage the AC's as he had for the past three years, he would confine his interest in the sport to reports for the Athletic Club's monthly publication, *The ACE,* and continuing to serve on the USAHA's executive committee. He had resigned in the spring of 1922, citing the usual business conflicts. "Fitz" would now be both coach and manager in what would later be seen as a halcyon season. In the November 1922 *ACE,* the former manager would preview the season ahead:

We had a good team last season, but
we lacked good spare men [a familiar
theme] . . . The first thing Fitz did was to
secure more strength . . . [Johannesson] and
Elmer . . . will not be seen in a local uniform.
The former . . . will play for the [Milwaukee]
Athletic Club hockey team there . . . It is not
known where Elmer will play.

[Among] the new men are Joseph
W. McCormick, a former Captain of the
Pittsburgh Hockey Club, and also Cap-
tain of the 1920 Olympic hockey team.
McCormick plays right wing and shoots
from the right side. He has a splendid

record and there is not much need to
comment on his ability, as most of us have
read about him, if we were not fortunate to
see him play.

George [Clark], formerly of Winnipeg,
Man., plays center ice; comes here with
a good record as a goal-getter . . . Dennis
Breen, right wing or defense, played with
Eveleth last season, and local fans have
seen him with the "Red Rangers" and know
that he is an addition to any club.

Clarence Abel, another new defense
man, has played with our old American
Soo friends for the past two years. He is a
big boy and weighs close to 200 pounds
and is fast on his feet.

With these four new men, together
with the sterling "Babe" [Elliott] in front
of the nets, Frank Goheen, the Conroy
and Garrett Brothers, Charles Cassin, C.
Weidenborner, R. Rothschild, our Club
should be well represented.

George Clark would prove to be the most noteworthy of the new acquisitions—he would lead the team in goal scoring, picking up the slack for both Tony Conroy and Emmy Garrett, whose

*The 1922–23 AC's*

scoring decreased from the previous season. Garrett's new role as captain, succeeding Conroy, may have affected his production. The burdens of leading by example and serving as team spokesman may have proven too much for Garrett. Joe McCormick would have a productive season, but it would not quite match his Pittsburgh years. The Michigan-developed Abel and Breen proved to be more than adequate replacements on defense for both Johannesson and Elmer, and Abel provided a bit more offense. George Conroy would see limited action, Cassin and Bill Garrett somewhat less, and Weidenborner and Rothschild would not appear in a game.

The USAHA restructured itself for 1922–23, with all but Eveleth of the Group Three teams dropping out of the competition. Eveleth would join the formerly named Group One, now called

the Western Group, while the new Milwaukee club that Johannesson had joined became the Group's sixth member. The newly named Eastern Group (formerly Group One) would consist of the Boston Athletic Association, the Boston Hockey Club, the Canadian Hockey Club (New York), the New Haven Westminsters (formerly Boston), the St. Nicholas Hockey Club (New York), and the Victorias (Boston-based.)

League competition in the Western Group would increase from twelve to twenty games in the new season, with the champions of the two groups playing off for the Fellowes Cup. The increase in league games reduced those outside the regular schedule for the AC's from six to only two in the new season. Those two would be against Niagara Falls, Ontario, at the Hippodrome on December 18 and 19, before the AC's started league play in Milwaukee on December 21 and 22.

Fitzgerald had conducted indoor training during November and had the team on the ice at Lake Como on December 3 for an informal two-hour workout, with all but Elliott and Abel present. (These two were visiting family.) Five days later everyone but Abel would hit the Hippodrome ice for the squad's first regular practice as Fitzgerald assembled sixteen players to allow for scrimmaging. The two Georges, newcomer Clark and spare Conroy, were first on the ice as the coach divided the players and periodically shook up the combinations. The session lasted more than two hours. Workouts continued nightly leading up to the Niagara Falls series and were highlighted by the arrival of the team's new jerseys on December 13.

Replacing the black-and-white stripes of the previous season was a gold jersey with black shoulder stripes accented by black and gold pinstripes on the sleeves. The words "St. Paul A. C." were on the front with the "St. Paul" above the "A. C." The socks were also black and gold but of a shade slightly darker than the jersey. There would be more changes at the Hippodrome than in the team uniform. A portion of the gallery would now be set aside for reserved seating, allowing fans to purchase tickets downtown and thus avoid long lines at the ticket windows. On the ice Fitzgerald would restore the twenty feet removed from behind each net the year before, so that the rink would now be 240 feet by 119 feet. This would supposedly speed up the games, the exact rationale given to reducing the surface a year earlier.

On the eve of this new season that would follow the club's great 1922 run, Frank Weidenborner concluded his survey of league opponents (*The ACE,* December 1922) with this bit of optimism:

> Your club has some wonderful talent lined up for this year's hockey team, and barring unforeseen misfortunes, should finish one-two in the league race. Last season the local fans supported the boys in a wonderful way; give the boys your support again this year, and you can look for them to repeat.

Fitzgerald had been fortunate to schedule Niagara Falls—they were in Duluth for two games before coming to St. Paul. Without these tune-ups, the AC's would have gone into the regular season without any game action. After being routed by Duluth 7–0, Niagara Falls had come back to win the second game 2–1. The momentum of that victory carried over into the first St. Paul contest, and the AC's had to settle for a 2–2 tie because they ran into the proverbial "hot" goaltender. Fitzgerald had started McCormick at right wing, with Conroy on the left and Garrett centering. Goheen was at right defense and Abel debuted on the left. Elliott was, of course, in goal. St. Paul led into the second period on goals by Conroy and Garrett, but the visitors forced overtime by the end of regulation play. The

*The AC's appear to have changed jersey styles almost annually. Here is the 1922–23 version.*

ten-minute overtime settled nothing as Mayo, the Niagara Falls goalie, kept the AC's at bay.

Halsey Hall, in the *St. Paul Pioneer Press,* December 19, 1922, described Mayo as "king of the Ontario goalguards," but the king would be ruthlessly dethroned the next night as St. Paul put eleven goals behind him and Elliott got his first shutout of the season. It would be the team's most one-sided victory of the season, with Clark scoring three goals, Goheen and Breen two each, and Garrett, McCormick, and the two Conroys each having one. The next day Hall would declare of the AC's in the *Pioneer Press:*

> In passing the laurels to the St. Paul stars, the team as a whole deserves them. They are now ready for Milwaukee, ready as a team can be that tried its mettle against a respected foe and found itself strong. Milwaukee has a powerful aggregation . . . and boasts some individual stars, but win or lose A. C. fans are satisfied that it will be a wonder sextet that takes the title from their favorites.

Hall's description of Milwaukee as a "powerful aggregation" proved to be an overly optimistic evaluation of the new expansion team—they would win only four games in their only year in the league. However, the first of those four would come in their league opener against St. Paul in the new Castle Garden rink that Frank Weidenborner had visited the previous spring. Bill Boyd, who would eventually have his name on the Stanley Cup as a member of the 1927–28 New York Rangers, beat Elliott at the thirteen-minute mark of the last period to give the newcomers the 1–0 victory.

It had been an evenly fought battle, impressive for a first-year team against the national runners-up, with the saves being nearly even for each goalie. "Dinty" Moore, Milwaukee's netminder, had been injured after his team went ahead, but following a ten-minute respite

to repair the damages, he returned with thirty seconds remaining. With former AC teammate Johannesson helping, Moore held off McCormick's final efforts at the end to secure the win. Moore was almost as impressive the next night, when, after two first-period goals by Clark and Goheen, he blanked the AC's the rest of the way while sustaining another injury when Abel's shot hit him beneath the eye in the second period. After quick repairs, he was back in action, but his teammates could not beat Elliott, and St. Paul had its first league victory.

## Home Sweet Home

Duluth, with some new faces in the lineup, was due to inaugurate the home season at the Hippodrome on December 26 and 27. Fitzgerald ran the team through a 9 A.M. Christmas Day workout, minus Joe McCormick. The new wing had returned to Pittsburgh for a holiday visit but was due back in time for the first game. However, when the puck was dropped for the season's opener, McCormick was nowhere in sight. For whatever reason, the Olympic veteran did not return until the second game, and his absence was felt—Duluth's two first-period goals were enough to ruin St. Paul's opener.

The scoreboard at the east end of the rink reflected the 2–0 win for the visitors and was an upgrade from the previous season. In addition to showing the score, it was of such a size that it contained the lineups for both teams, including player numbers and the referee's name. It replaced a board that was not only old but frequently obscured by smoke and poor lighting.

The new scoreboard looked considerably better the next night when George Clark showed why he was lured from Winnipeg by scoring in each period, which was all the AC's needed—Elliott let the visitors have nothing. The goalie's great play would continue to be a key to St. Paul's success. What one of the visitors did get was some apparent crowd interference. According to Ed Shave, *St. Paul Daily News,* December 28, 1922:

Play was stopped for a time during the second period when some overly enthusiastic spectator, leaning over the railing on the north side of the rink, is alleged to have swung at Seaborn. [Jim Seaborn, like Breen, was a former Eveleth player who had been lured to a new team.]

Police were called to eject the guilty one from the rink but he was not discovered.

Seaborn was booed continually during the games. He is playing [a] clean . . . game . . . and the fans should forget the trouble last year during the series at Eveleth.

McCormick's return was immediately felt, raising the team's energy level, with improved passing, stickhandling, and defense. Clark profited considerably by getting to the front of the net, where McCormick and Goheen found him for two of his three goals.

Abel had taken a puck to the mouth in the third period, cutting his lips and severely bruising his face, but he soon returned to the game and was ready for the first series of the new year against Eveleth on January 2 and 3. The "Red Rangers" had split with Milwaukee and, like Duluth, had some new players to replace Breen and Seaborn. Memories of the epic play-off series of the last season were no doubt still in the minds of the crowds that came out to see both games. The first night Hippodrome attendance was estimated at about five thousand, and the fans would witness a scoreless struggle until late in the game.

George Clark beat Eveleth's new goalie Bernie McTeigue in heavy traffic with two minutes to go, providing the locals with the only goal they would need. The visitors had come close to taking the lead in the second period, but "Babe" Elliott thwarted them. Halsey Hall wrote in the *Pioneer Press,* January 3, 1923:

The big red ice machine . . . swept down the rink. Past the usually impregnable A. C. defense . . . Then, in the twinkling of an eye, Davis, only a spare with little chance for glory, came face to face with his grand moment . . . Up he skated but the gold of his opportunity must have blinded him, for he went too far before attempting to shoot. With a leap, Babe Elliot was upon him. He shot, but falling to the ice, Elliott blocked the progress of the puck . . . Black and Gold skaters rushed to the rescue as 5,000 fans gave vent to a thunderous cheer of relief.

Eveleth would play the second game without Bob Armstrong, one of their newcomers from what is now Thunder Bay, Ontario. Armstrong had collided with Goheen the night before, and while "Moose" was back at it, "Armstrong . . . was sorely handicapped by his Tuesday injuries and drank the defeat from a seat on the bench" (Halsey Hall, *Pioneer Press,* January 4, 1923).

The defeat was another 1–0 victory for St. Paul as Elliott came up with a second shutout. This time it was Captain Emmy Garrett with the game winner, which came six minutes into the second period when he picked up Breen's rebound and put it past McTeigue. The AC's had gotten the better of the play in the first two periods, but Eveleth fought furiously to avoid the sweep. As described by Lynn Fredenburgh, *Daily News,* January 4, 1923:

With the Saints leading and the end drawing near, the Eveleth players streaked up and down the rink battling like a bunch of tigers in front of the St. Paul net . . . Back and forth the tide of battle raged, with the Saints putting up a defense that time and again hurled the rangers back toward the other end of the ice after it seemed they would penetrate the Saints' inner works. Elliott played a great game, several times saving victory . . . by wonderful stops.

Fredenburgh had begun his column with the question: "Hockey popular in St. Paul? The ayes have it. More than 6,000 persons jammed their way into the Hippodrome." While Fredenburgh would not suggest that the Hippodrome was inadequate, *Pioneer Press* columnist L. S. McKenna would do exactly that, on January 15, 1923:

> If St. Paul is to continue in the United States loop and is to be represented by first-class aggregations as it has been in the past, larger quarters will have to be sought to handle the crowds. The Hippodrome, although it will hold 6,000 fans, is not adequate.
>
> In the last game with Eveleth it was packed to capacity and tonight will find it just as full. Hundreds of others would like to attend, but they will not be able to gain admission. It looks as if the only solution to the problem is the erection of a large artificial ice rink.

McKenna's concerns were eventually resolved nine years later in downtown St. Paul, but the AC's and the minor league pros that followed them would continue to use the Hippodrome for the foreseeable future. The more immediate future concerned the series with Pittsburgh on January 15 and 16. St. Paul had come out of the Eveleth games with minimal injury problems. Abel's facial bruises were healing and Goheen had weathered his collision with Armstrong quite well. The physical problems that developed during the nearly two-week layoff before Pittsburgh's arrival were colds and related symptoms, which afflicted Abel, Breen, Clark, Garrett, and McCormick. Fitzgerald had considered bringing in a Winnipeg team during the lull, but elected to go with rest and light workouts before resuming league play.

It proved to be the right decision—the AC's were rested and hardly stale for the first game. Fitzgerald had stepped up the pace of the last practice on January 12 and then gave the team two days off before the series' opener. St. Paul was tied with Duluth and Cleveland for first place with a 4–2 record, and Pittsburgh trailed behind at 3–3. Joe McCormick would be facing his old team for the first time, and he made the best of that situation. Following a scoreless first period, Abel had given the locals a 1–0 lead ten minutes into the second stanza when McCormick made it 2–0 just as time was running out. His old team protested that the gong had ended the period, but the goal stood. Garrett got a third marker in the last period on a pass from Goheen from the left side of the net. The AC's had their fifth league win, seventh overall, and Elliott his fourth consecutive shutout and six for the season.

He would not score or collect any assists, but it would also be a good night for Tony Conroy. Goheen had been feted two years earlier and now it was Conroy's turn. The St. Paul native was honored between the first and second periods by the Knights of Columbus for his service to the sport. The Catholic fraternal order presented him with a gold watch, chain, and charm. The *Daily News,* January 7, 1923, would say of him:

> Tony has been accumulating battle scars, but not one of them ever kept him out of play, or even held up the game.
>
> It has seldom been Tony's lot to bring the fans to their feet through sensational work. Primarily he is a combination player who foregoes the thrill of glory for the betterment of team play. He is . . . a fast skater, a clever stickhandler and a hard man to stop. Defensively he has always been a bulwark, despite his rather diminutive proportions.

Looking on were USAHA president William Haddock and secretary Roy Schooley, who were in town for a league meeting the next day. They would both be seeing the AC's play on their home ice for the first time. Also taking place between the two games was a luncheon sponsored by the Knights of Columbus for both teams at the St. Paul Hotel. Then it was back to the ice for what turned out to be the marathon game of the season.

Another five-thousand-plus crowd was on hand to watch six periods of hockey, three regular and three overtime, totaling seventy-five minutes, before Pittsburgh's Harold Darragh settled matters with two minutes to go in the third overtime period. Darragh would later move on to a 308-game NHL career with Pittsburgh, Philadelphia, Boston, and Toronto and live to age ninety-one. With the latter team he would win a Stanley Cup in 1931–32. On this night, he was a twenty-two-year-old "rangy lad with curly hair [who] streaked up the right side of the rink; glided by frantic defense men and burned the puck into the net past the burly Babe" (Halsey Hall, *Pioneer Press,* January 16, 1923).

It was a tough loss, made tougher by the fact that the AC's thought they had scored what would have been the winning goal in the second period when Abel's shot went through the net and was ruled no goal. It was the closest they would come to scoring, and the loss put an end to Elliott's shutout streak. The split allowed idle Duluth to take undisputed possession of first place as Cleveland also split their series with Eveleth. But the disappointment would be short-lived. Good news! Milwaukee was coming to town.

After an auspicious beginning that saw them split series with both St. Paul and Cleveland, the new franchise had run into the injury bug and tumbled into the basement never to escape. The medical problems were now over, and the Brewers, as the sportswriters liked to call them on occasion, played better than expected. The AC's had allowed only four goals and blanked the opposition in nineteen periods of league play, but tonight would be different. Leading only 1–0 on George Clark's first-period goal, Goheen made it 2–0 on a pass from Clark early in the third period. Milwaukee quickly got that back from future NHL'er Bill Boyd, only to have Breen set up Conroy for St. Paul's third goal. The visitors continued to press hard, and they got their second score one minute from the end of the period.

Some four thousand fans had witnessed the unexpectedly competitive 3–2 victory over the tailenders on January 22. A similar crowd was on hand the next night as the team and Babe Elliott returned to form with an easy 5–0 blanking. Clark, McCormick (two), Garrett, and Cassin, making one of his few appearances of the season, had the goals. The sweep had moved the AC's into first place, and now they would face more severe tests in northeastern Minnesota.

## Trouble in Duluth and Eveleth

Neither Halsey Hall nor Ed Shave, the beat writers for the two St. Paul newspapers, were assigned to games normally outside the Twin Cities, but both were on hand for the series in Duluth on January 25 and 26 and in Eveleth on February 9 and 10. The in-state rivalries were intense, as past seasons reflected, and sports editors wanted their own writers covering, as opposed to the stringers they used in Cleveland, Pittsburgh, and Boston. Perhaps not mentally prepared after the easy Milwaukee series, St. Paul played their worst period of the year in the opening session of the first game in Duluth. The AC's dominated the first five minutes, but the home team took control and scored four goals, two by star Mike Goodman, to take what proved to be an insurmountable lead. Halsey Hall, *Pioneer Press,* January 23, 1923, described it this way:

> The opening session was one that probably will not occur in the lives of the Saints during the remainder of the season, but while it lasted it was powerful and at its close the Black and Gold trooped to their dressing rooms, hurled sticks madly on the floor and sat down to take stock of what had happened. Then they went on the ice, shook off the superiority which Goodman and his speeding [crew] had established and looked like the Saints of old battling, but battling in vain.

St. Paul would return to form for the remainder of the game as Elliott surrendered only one more goal, but two incidents would mar the evening and put the packed Duluth crowd into a foul mood. In the second period, Abel's hard check on Seaborn took him out of the game and put his status for the next night in doubt, and Goheen's hit on Wilfred Peltier in the third period resulted in an unconscious player and a broken wrist for the Duluth import from Winnipeg. While Hall described the hit as "legitimate in any hockey family," Sandy McDonald, *Duluth Herald*, January 26, 1923, saw things differently:

> Previous to permanently crippling [untrue] Peltier, Goheen had been acting like a mad man ... For five minutes before he maimed Peltier, Goheen had been slashing, clubbing, and bodychecking players who did not have the puck.
>
> When he was sent to the boards he was booed from every quarter of the big rink and many over excited fans used some right loud talk.

Despite their 5–0 win over the Western Group leaders, the Seaborn and Peltier injuries had incensed the "righteously angry fans," as McDonald described them. Continuing, he put an understandable hometown twist on what happened afterward:

> Fired by repeated bodily attacks made on local players by the visitors, the fans were raving when the contest was concluded ... Several hundred fans [twenty-five hundred attended the game] waited in the smoking room of the [Duluth Curling] club for the St. Paul players to come out and when the latter put in an appearance the fans threatened an attack, which was stopped by the police. Seven husky gendarmes sandwiched themselves among the Apostles, with first a cop and then a player ... escorted ... to their bus. Two policemen accompanied the players to their hotel.

McDonald went on to describe the AC's as "so many wildcats ... trying to save themselves from the disgrace of a whitewash ... Goheen ... became more vicious ... it would be for the betterment of hockey if Goheen were forever barred from the amateur ranks." Hall, of course, disagreed, writing in the *Pioneer Press*, January 26, 1923:

> But bigger than any of his slanderous critics, Goheen stands out as the courageous hockey player that the St. Paul fans have always known him to be. He merely says, "I shall be out there playing my best tonight." Frank is naturally sorry that Peltier's injury resulted from a check inflicted by him but such things happen in hockey games.

Reading these quotes some eighty years later, one is struck by the fact that the belligerent nature of the sport has been there a long time and is "as much a part of the culture of the game as sticks and skates and pucks" (Jim Kelley, ESPN.com, March 11, 2004).

St. Paul fans had accompanied the team to Duluth, and Hall took note of them in his "Notes of the Battle on the Duluth Sector" following his January 26 story:

> The band of St. Paul rooters who grouped themselves back of the A. C. bench certainly made themselves heard. They answered hoot with howl and cheer with cheer and kept their spirits up even during that tempestuous first period. Tonight more are expected to be on hand and a royal hockey evening is promised.

"Royal" might be a bit more expressive term than needed, but the AC supporters got more of what they expected the next evening when their team rallied from a 2–1 deficit to score three third-period goals for a 4–2 win. Jim Seaborn was able to play for the home team, but Peltier had to watch from the bench when George Clark tied the game at the 1:20 mark. McCormick got the game winner at 3:30, and Clark added the clincher at 4:50. Abel had scored the earlier St. Paul goal in the second period on a pass from Clark, who enjoyed a three-point game. Hall viewed the win as justice done, writing in the *Pioneer Press,* January 27, 1923:

> The scoring of the victory by the Saints was only the trend of true Duluth retribution of its right course. The A. C. undaunted played clean, heads-up hockey from start to finish and there were many open admissions by fair-minded members of the audience that these visitors of black and gold had been shamefully treated as a result of Thursday's game.

Goheen had been understandably the target of the Duluth boo birds during the second game and, although not scoring, had played an outstanding game. While Hall paid homage to him in his game story, perhaps the greater tribute in an age when sportswriters were far more openly biased, would come from Louis Gollop of the *Duluth News Tribune,* January 27, 1923:

> "Moose" Goheen was the individual star for St. Paul. With the howling, jeering, and hooting of 2,500 fans at every move he made, this athlete did wonders on the ice last night. He played as though the hostile crowd was miles away and played clean hockey as well. He also took numerous bumps.

The team returned to St. Paul right after the game, but the Goheen controversy came with them. Ed Shave, *Daily News,* January 30, 1923, took issue with McDonald's comments:

Sandy is very wrathy . . . I do not think that Goheen deserves such a razzing.

In his long athletic career he has never been accused of anything that smacked of rowdyism.

He has been criticized in hockey. Frank does not use his stick illegally. When he is body checked carrying the puck, usually the man checking him goes down. When Frank is on defense and body checks, his opponent goes down.

Frank checked Peltier . . . and the latter fell upon his wrist. Frank did not hit him on the wrist or step upon it. It was an accident.

Last year Goheen was cut under the eye in the series in Duluth. "Doc" Wildermuth took four or five stitches in it. He was also cut on the side . . . and . . . back of the head. Two of those cuts were not made by body checking.

Last year in the four games at Duluth and at Eveleth Goheen was penalized once . . . If Frank is as bad as Sandy thinks, it's strange he's not on the [penalty] bench more.

The team would be idle until the trip to Eveleth, but Fitzgerald occupied them with practices while keeping an eye on their future opponents' series in Pittsburgh and Cleveland's two home games against Milwaukee. Sweeps by the hosting teams would put the Western Group race into a three-way tie. As things played out, that is exactly what happened—Eveleth unexpectedly dropped both games in the Steel City.

Fitzgerald conducted his last practice on February 7, and the team left at noon the next day for Duluth, where they would sleep over before taking another train to Eveleth on game day, Friday, February 9. They would not leave Duluth until 3:50 P.M. and expected to dine on the train and then nap for an hour before the puck was dropped—not quite the schedule that any contemporary professional or college team would follow. Prior to departure Fitzgerald had asked

that two outside officials handle the Eveleth series, but USAHA president Haddock turned down
the request. Two referees from the league staff,
Jacoby and Munro, were assigned to the games.
Perhaps "Fitz" was anticipating trouble in Eveleth
and thought he'd do better with non-league officials since Munro had worked the contentious
Duluth series.

It was apparent from the start that Goheen
would be a target of the home team. At the
twelve-minute mark of the first period, he came
down the left side, went around the defensemen,
jumping over one of them, Percy Nicklin, and
then drew Eveleth goaltender Bernie McTeigue
to one side and put the puck behind him. That
bit of skill did not sit well with the locals. Halsey
Hall, *Pioneer Press,* February 10, 1923, reported:

> In the first period Goheen was beset by
> two Rangers and, beside himself, showed
> signs of fight. Three Eveleth players
> started for him and backed him against
> the boards. Down from the stand sprang
> half-a-dozen plainsclothes men from the
> Oliver Mining Company, and three men
> in uniform. It looked for a while that battle
> scenes would be flashed on the silver sheet,
> but the disturbance was finally quieted.

St. Paul made it 2–0 early in the second period
when Breen carried the puck in deep and got
it to Conroy, who then passed to McCormick.
He put it through what we now call the five
hole. (The five hole is the space between the
goaltender's leg pads. It is notorious for being
the most vulnerable spot for a goaltender because it is nearly impossible to cover all of the
time.) Between periods Fitzgerald had urged
his players to "go out and get together. You can
do it. Then the game is safe" (Ed Shave, *Daily
News,* February 10, 1923). Following his coach's
instructions to a tee, two minutes into the
third period Goheen passed out to Clark from
behind the Eveleth net, and the team's lead-

ing scorer made it 3–0. The home team's Ade
Johnson had taken three penalties in an effort to
"get" Goheen, and even with the game winding
down Manager King had shouted to his players,
"There's three minutes left, go out and get some-
body" (Halsey Hall, *Pioneer Press,* February 10,
1923). No one got anyone, and the AC's were
looking ahead to a sweep.

February 10 dawned at 26 degrees below
zero as the team came down to breakfast. All
were quite ready for a renewal of action that
proved to be a bit more subdued than the previous night's play. Some twenty-five St. Paul fans
had made the trip to support their heroes, and
they were delighted when Abel made it 1–0
three minutes into the game. Playing like a forward, he traded the puck three times with Clark
before scoring. The lead held into the third period when, with Breen in the penalty box, Eveleth
tied the game when Bob Armstrong's long shot
eluded Elliott. The first half of the overtime period went scoreless and then, according to the
*Eveleth News,* February 15, 1923,

> the mighty Goheen took the puck from
> near his own net and started a terrific
> rush down the ice. He passed Armstrong
> and Gailbraith in the forward line and by
> the time he reached Ching Johnson and
> Nicklin he was going so fast nothing could
> stop him. With a terrific shot he crashed
> past the defense right into the net for the
> winning goal.

Two minutes later Abel got his second goal
on another pass from Clark, this time coming
from behind the net, to end things at 3–1. The
sweep restored St. Paul's Western Group leadership at 10–4, with Cleveland and Pittsburgh
tied for second at 8–4. The next challenge for
the AC's would be Cleveland, who came to
the Hippodrome on February 19 and 20, after a visit to Milwaukee. Similarly, Pittsburgh
would visit Eveleth at the same time, and both

had the potential to challenge St. Paul's lead. Much of that lead could be credited to Babe Elliott's superb goaltending, which had to this point resulted in an incredible nine shutouts in sixteen total games. The figures for league play were eight in fourteen games. Although he would be cited in individual game stories for his play, as in the recent Eveleth series where he had made thirty and thirty-three saves, respectively, to his opponent's thirteen and nineteen, there would be no glowing tributes such as the one given Joe McCormick. Returning from the Iron Range, Halsey Hall wrote of the prototype Lady Byng player in the *Pioneer Press*, February 12, 1923 (the Lady Byng Memorial Trophy is given to that player in the NHL who combines a high standard of playing ability with sportsmanship and gentlemanly conduct—McCormick might have won this award if he had ever played in the NHL):

> Joe McCormick is bursting again into the limelight through his remarkable record for clean playing ... The graceful Joe, a favorite in every city on the circuit regardless of the heat of battle, has been penalized only five times in the last seven years ... In these days of games when penalties are altogether too numerous, McCormick has presented a brand of play that delights those who revel in clean, speedy and skillful hockey. Joe remarked ... that he could almost name the specific instances when he was penalized ... McCormick ... is always in the best of condition.

While the St. Paul beat writers would not give that kind of praise to Elliott, he would get his due from Frank Weidenborner, whose brother he had replaced. Writing in *The ACE*, January 1923, the former manager said, "It is hard to say much more about Babe Elliott ... I don't see how he could improve on his last sea-sons play, yet he does seem a little more agile, and he is helping his defense with his advice."

## Home Briefly Before Moving East

Both Cleveland and Pittsburgh could not gain ground on the AC's, as the former split with Milwaukee and the latter dropped both games in Eveleth. Cleveland's failure to sweep in Wisconsin left them a game behind St. Paul as the series opened on February 19. Cleveland needed to take both games in St. Paul to gain the Western Group lead, while a Pittsburgh sweep in Duluth at the same time would put them back in contention.

Eddie Fitzgerald's skaters, with help from Duluth, made sure the scenario that played out was one that virtually clinched the group title for the AC's. Before sixty-seven hundred fans, "who jammed every nook and corner of the mammoth Hippodrome," according to Halsey Hall, *Pioneer Press*, February 20, 1923, the first two periods were as competitive as expected. George Clark, who was challenging Cleveland's Nels Stewart for the Western Group scoring title, got a goal in each period to give the home team a 2–0 edge heading into the last canto. Then, to the delight of the Hippodrome fandom, the locals pumped in five straight goals between the second- and thirteen-minute mark to wrap up a 7–0 drubbing of their closest rivals. Clark got the first two, followed by Breen, Goheen, and Garrett. While St. Paul had beaten non-league competition by wider margins, this win was the most decisive over a USAHA opponent. Halsey Hall, *Pioneer Press*, February 20, 1923, wrote:

> In many respects the third period was the most remarkable ever seen at the Hippodrome, for it found the Saints running roughshod over one of the best aggregations in the country ... the Indians are mad clear through. They hark back to last year ... as proof of the fact that they can come back.

The truth was that they would not come back. The week's rest after the Eveleth series had obviously done the AC's a world of good. Though the score after the first two periods was close, they had held Cleveland to only nine shots on goal, ten for the game, before conducting their third-period shooting gallery. The momentum continued the next night when they took a 2–0 lead after one period. Clark would get the first, his fifth of the series, but it was Goheen's that Halsey Hall described most vividly, in the *Pioneer Press,* February 21, 1923:

> The puck had been knocked from the stick of some aspiring Clevelander by a St. Paul poke when Goheen, skating free and wide, picked it up. Like a flash he was off. Stewart, sensing impending danger, motioned frantically to Winters to stop Moose on the boards and he himself moved over to center to cut off Goheen's dash there. Over on the right waited Debernardi.
>
> But Goheen did not stop. With a fantastic leap [*sic*] he was over Winter's stick. A Thorpe-like [football star Jim Thorpe] twist and his bulky frame had eluded the long armed Stewart. Debernardi skating from the side, was far from the speeding Moose. As the safety man in a football game, Moose Jamieson blocked the way, but with a final glorious maneuver Goheen swept by like a whirlwind and climaxed . . . with a shot that smoked as it lined past the bewildered Turner.

Cleveland rallied in the second period when Stewart added to his goal total by putting one by Elliott on a long shot from mid-rink, but that was as close as the visitors would get. Goheen scored the clincher five minutes into the last period on an unassisted dash from center ice. The 3–1 victory would be the last at home until the final play-offs, which now seemed assured. Duluth had upset Pittsburgh twice, effectively ending their title hopes, but St. Paul would need success in its March 2 and 3 series in Pittsburgh before the team could claim first place and the right to advance to the Fellowes Cup championship series.

Cleveland could still win the group by sweeping Duluth and the AC's in its last home series on March 9 and 10, but St. Paul would also have to lose both of its games to Pittsburgh. It was a remote possibility and one that Fitzgerald hardly thought likely. Arriving in the Steel City on March 1, he told the stringer for the *Pioneer Press,* March 1, 1923:

> We expect to have the pennant sewed up before we leave here. It is going to be a hot series but as the team is playing well now we expect to split even at least. I realize that we will have our hands full as the Pittsburgh team has been encountering some hard luck, but they always play their best hockey against St. Paul. No matter what they do against any other team, they are playing at top speed against us.

The games would be a homecoming for Joe McCormick, who had spent much of his career in Pittsburgh, and it was McCormick who set up the first game's only goal in the last period. Moving up ice with Clark abreast, McCormick drew Pittsburgh goalie Ray Bonney out of position, allowing Clark a virtual open net after taking McCormick's pass. It was an easy goal, but the first two periods were hard fought as Babe Elliott made twenty-eight saves to Bonney's sixteen. Pittsburgh's best scoring chance came late in the first period when Elliott came out fifteen feet to block a Paddy Manners shot, only to have Herb Drury pick up the rebound. Fortunately Goheen got back to cover the net until the AC netminder recovered.

The win assured the visitors of a tie for first place as Cleveland staved off elimination with a victory against Duluth. St. Paul would have to wait until the next night before it could come up with the clincher, and it was Goheen, with two first-period goals, who did the job. The AC's played without McCormick, who had injured his wrist in a collision the night before but had continued to play hurt. Also playing hurt, but in the second game, was Tony Conroy, who had taken a stick to the eye in the middle period. Bandaged up, he returned to finish the game. Once ahead by two goals, Fitzgerald directed a defensive game as St. Paul mustered a total of only nine shots to Pittsburgh's twenty-one. One of the latter eluded Elliott near the middle of the last period to make the final 2–1. "There was rejoicing among the St. Paul players as it was the finish of a stubborn fight, but they cannot afford to ease up before they go into the series with the winners in the Eastern section," according to the *Pioneer Press,* March 4, 1923.

There were still two games in Cleveland before the finals could begin, and the AC's moved on to what was then called the Forest City. Fitzgerald had originally hoped to play exhibition games in the East between the Pittsburgh and Cleveland series, but those contests were cancelled. The logistics of such games would have been difficult, and with the team in Cleveland at season's end, it was still positioned to either move east or return home depending on the schedule of the Fellowes Cup finals.

Going into Cleveland, St. Paul could look back on a seven-game winning streak, which included three series sweeps and fifteen periods of shutout hockey. But the team would come out of Cleveland with the winning streak ended at eight and the shutout periods concluded at eighteen. McCormick and Abel would sit out both Cleveland games, the latter having come up with a sprain in the last Pittsburgh game. Tony Conroy, despite two stitches below his left eye, continued to play. His brother, George, also known as "Shifty," took Abel's place on defense, and Goheen moved up to fill in for McCormick.

The changes had no effect on the continued success of the AC's, as Clark scored in the first and third periods while Garrett got one in the middle session of game one. Elliott pitched his eleventh and final shutout of the season, turning aside eighteen shots in the 3–0 win. Things did not go nearly as well the next night in the final game of the regular season. Elliott's magic ended when he gave up two goals each in the first and second periods as St. Paul went down 4–2. The AC's got their two goals in the second period from Tony Conroy and Goheen, but they never got closer than one goal.

As the team left the Elysium Rink ice, the *Pioneer Press,* March 11, 1923, reported: "The Saints received a great ovation after the game, and many of the fans personally extended their best wishes to the St. Paul icers for their success in the coming series with Boston for the world championship."

The *Pioneer Press* stringer's use of the word "world" is, of course, indicative of the American tendency to regard purely national championships as somehow "world" events, a practice that started with baseball and continues to this day. "World" it was not, but national it certainly was, and the manner in which the finals would be played was now set.

### A New Boston Challenger

The defending champion Boston Westminsters had relocated to New Haven, Connecticut, during the Eastern Group regular season but could not repeat their success of 1922. The new Eastern champion was the Boston Athletic Association, a more American team than the Westies, with two players who had been in the finals the previous year with the former Boston team—American Irving Small and Canadian Ag Smith. Both defensemen, Small and Smith were joined by Ajax Campbell on the back line and Albert "Frenchy" Lacroix in goal. The center was Gerry Geran, and the wings were Edward Enright, John Lyons, Justin McCarthy, and Willard Rice. Besides Small, Lacroix (Newton), Geran (Holyoke), McCarthy (Arlington), and Rice (Newton) were all Massachusetts natives. They would join Taffy

Abel on the 1924 United States Olympic Team, and Lacroix and Geran would also join him in the NHL. The coach was Fred Rocque. The team was popularly referred to as the BAA or by their nickname, the Unicorns. They had won the Eastern Group title with a 9–1 record, compared to a 15–5 mark for St. Paul, but they had also compiled a 9–2–1 non-league record.

On the eve of the St. Paul–Cleveland series, USAHA president Haddock announced plans for the Fellowes Cup series. Unlike 1922, when a point was awarded for a victory and a half-point for a tie, the finals would be a best-of-five format. All games would be played to a finish, and if the series was tied at two games each, Haddock would determine the place and date of the deciding contest. The association's representatives for games in the West would be Frank Weidenborner, St. Paul, and Gordon Hegardt, Duluth. R. L. "Pop" Von Bernuth, New York, and Tom Kanaly, Boston, would do the same in the East. Haddock would name the referees and review the recommendations for goal umpires (judges) and timekeepers. There was the sticky question of the availability of ice in St. Paul, and the league would make that determination shortly.

It soon became evident that the warm-weather plague of a year earlier would not be repeated, and the first two games were scheduled for St. Paul on March 13 and 14 (*Pioneer Press*, March 12, 1923):

The ice was pronounced Sunday [March 11] to be in fine shape for the series. The surface was so good that skating was permitted on it Saturday night and Sunday. It was flooded Sunday night and is expected to be hard and fast for the opening game. The officials of the local hockey squad are praying for a siege of cold weather until after the series.

The games would then resume in Boston on March 22 and 24. This schedule did not sit well with the BAA—they would be playing their last game on March 10 and then would have to entrain immediately after the game in order to arrive forty-eight hours later in St. Paul on the Monday night before the Tuesday night start of the series. Kanaly, who was the Unicorns' manager, felt the schedule put his team at a disadvantage in adjusting to local conditions. League secretary Roy Schooley told Kanaly his concerns would be considered. They were, and there would be no change in the schedule. Despite his earlier worries about orientation, Kanaly elected to stop in Chicago on Monday, March 12, and arrived in St. Paul early on game day, March 13. There was still time for a practice session at the Hippodrome.

Halsey Hall and his columnist colleague L. S. McKenna at the *Pioneer Press*, March 13, 1923, were confident that this would be St. Paul's year. Hall wrote:

The Saints should win. They are fully 25 per cent stronger than last year with Abel and Breen offering a defensive wall against which the hopes of many star forward lines have been crushed. The Unicorns are reported stronger than the Westminsters but it was a battle weakened and futilely fighting St. Paul team that saw its passing game flounder in the slush last year.

McKenna concurred:

Veteran hockey fans . . . declare St. Paul the best balanced machine ever developed in the Northwest . . . Fitzgerald has surrounded himself with nine high grade puck carriers who have succeeded in coping with the opposition at every turn.

Twin Cities fans will know the real strength of the champion Saints after the two games here with Boston and there is a feeling that the locals will surprise the hockey world by downing the Eastern champs with ease.

McCormick and Abel would be ready for the 8:15 P.M. puck drop on Tuesday night, but there would be no "downing the Eastern champs with ease." Sixty-five hundred fans were on hand and would be treated to extra between-periods entertainment featuring comedian Heine Brock, women pair skaters McNamara and Lipsin, and a saxophone quartet. All reserved seats had been previously sold, while general admission tickets were available on the night of the games.

The BAA would take the lead at the six-minute mark when McCarthy, who was also the visitors' captain, got control of the puck from three AC defenders and beat Elliott. The lead held for four minutes, at which point the crowd was treated to some vintage Goheen. Ed Shave, *Daily News,* March 14, 1923, described the scene:

> Frank Goheen tied the score and sent the mammoth crowd into hysterics. Frank, who time after time carried the puck clear through the Boston team, dashed down the right side of the rink. Three defense men forced him clear to the boards. He ducked one, hurdled the stick of the other, dashed around the third (Irving Small) and while going at top speed shot. Although from a side angle[,] the rubber hurtled into the goal with the guard never touching it.

But the joy lasted only three minutes. Ed Enright got the lead back for the Unicorns when his long shot from the left hopped and eluded Elliott's grasping hand for what would be the winning goal. The *Boston Evening Transcript,* March 14, 1923, described the last two periods:

> That would be the last scoring of the evening, although not the last action by a considerable margin. Time and again, the big Hippodrome rocked with [the] enthusiasm of spectators as the teams put on stirring offensives, only to jump back to the defensive in time to prevent the success

of a counter-attack. During the second period especially, Lacroix gave a wonderful exhibition. In the third period, as was quite natural, the Bostonians played a strictly defensive game. Smith, Small, and Lacroix being reinforced at times by a mate as they barred the way to the Unicorn's cage.

The third period had highlights other than defense. Five minutes into the period St. Paul scored the tying goal, but it was disallowed because of a forward pass, the latter not yet permitted by the rules. Then, with twenty-five seconds to play, Goheen took a cut over the eye from a stick and was carried from the ice. No worries. He'd be back the next night to try to help make Ed Fitzgerald's prediction come true. The *Daily News,* March 14, 1923, projected: "We will win tonight. I think we played as well as Boston, but they got two by 'Babe' Elliott, while we slipped only one past Lacroix."

The AC's had actually played well enough to win, but Lacroix had performed superbly, and he would be even better in game two. The home team sent twenty shots his way, while the BAA could put only five on Elliott, two in the first period and three in the third. It mattered not, as the game was lost late in the second period when Gerry Geran, often described as a slow skater but great stickhandler and playmaker, shot from center ice and the puck went through Elliott's legs for the game's only goal. This came after St. Paul had nearly scored on three different occasions earlier in the period. According to Halsey Hall, *Pioneer Press,* March 15, 1923:

> Clark, alert as ever for an opening, seized a rebound and made a worthy stab. But Lacroix was agile and blocked it. On another occasion Taffy Abel charged the full length of the rink, only to be partially halted by Smith and see his shot go wild. Again Joe McCormick, heeding not the pain that throbbed in his right wrist, [wove] in and out through a maze of Boston sticks and

maneuvered to a position directly in front of the net, where he let a backhand shot fly. It met the same fate as the others—repulsion at the hands of Lacroix.

As the game wore down late in the third period, St. Paul would have two more good opportunities to send the game into overtime. With a minute left, Garrett fired what is now called a "one timer," which missed the corner of the net by inches. Thirty seconds later, Lacroix was drawn out of position, but his defense quickly covered for him and the BAA had a 1–0 victory and 2–0 lead in games.

Once again the home team had played well enough to win, with Goheen wearing a heavy bandage and McCormick and Abel turning in notable efforts. Abel had taken three penalties, but the Unicorns failed to capitalize, depending on their defense and "the blond iceberg," as Halsey Hall described Lacroix in the *Pioneer Press*, March 15, 1923. Those factors proved to be enough to protect Geran's one-goal lead and send sixty-five hundred fans home wondering how their team could be down two games to none for the second year in a row on home ice.

This year's schedule allowed for a full week before the series would resume in Boston, as opposed to the preceding year's five days. The additional time would help with injuries—Conroy and Garrett were also recovering from previous hurts. There would be no injury scratches as the team headed east on the overnight train on March 19. Trainer Doc Wildermuth and backup goaltender Cy Weidenborner, who had not seen game action since the 1920–21 season, would not make the trip. The daunting task of taking three games in a row in order to bring the Fellowes Cup west caused Halsey Hall to present a brave face to his readers in the *Pioneer Press* on March 19, 1923:

There is no down-heartedness evident among the St. Paul representatives . . . Rather their attitude is one of determination to wipe away [the] memory of the local defeats with a great comeback. Followers of the game believe they stand a better chance at Boston where the smaller rink will not permit the B. A. A. [defense] such a scope for the exploitation of its prowess. McCormick always shines away from home and the road record (7–3) of the Saints this year is such that their chances are mighty good to make Boston do considerable worrying.

Caution was the word with the BAA as Fred Rocque put his charges through their final workout at the Boston Arena on March 20. Rocque had been impressed with the defensive pairing of Abel and Breen. The BAA players had taken a fancy to Breen, who at 220 pounds was huge for the time. His stickhandling and shiftiness—we would now use the term "deke"—were admired. While they thought Goheen was big, fast, and a good stickhandler, they regarded McCormick and Abel as shiftier. Rocque had McCarthy shadow Goheen and felt he had contained him to some extent in the second game. McCormick was viewed as the fastest skater for the AC's and Elliott as "one of the nation's greatest goaltenders" (*Pioneer Press*, March 22, 1923).

The Unicorns were in better physical shape than their opponents, although McCarthy was suffering from a cold and Small had gotten the worst of a practice collision with Campbell. St. Paul arrived in Boston on March 21 with no one worse off than at the start of the trip, with the exception of Clark, who had come down with an ulcerated tooth, which was quickly remedied. On detraining, Fitzgerald was predictable in his comments (*Pioneer Press*, March 22, 1923): "Certainly we're going to reverse things. We didn't get a break out there at the Hippodrome. That can't last. Something must come our way in these games here. They were nip and tuck battles too, but I think we have a great chance to overhaul Boston."

The luggage of the AC's did not keep pace

with their trip east and caused their scheduled afternoon practice to be pushed ahead into the early evening. At the practice, the team so reflected Fitzgerald's confidence that they gave observers the impression that it was they, not the BAA, who had the two-game lead (*Pioneer Press*, March 22, 1923):

> The B. A. A. players seem to take some stock in that same assertion ... They believe that the Gophers [AC's] will be more dangerous here than they were on the Hippodrome surface. They point out that on the larger playing surface ... the speed of Captain Jerry (Justin) McCarthy, Geran and Eddie Enright had full play in checking back. When McCormick, Abel, or Goheen rescued the puck from a B. A. A. attack they had a lot of space to cover on their way back to Boston territory and this gave the Boston speed boys a chance to dash back and perhaps break up the attack from behind.
>
> Here, the playing surface is smaller and consequently the Bostonians believe that their job is going to be more difficult.

Game three on March 22 bore a similarity to the first encounter in the series in that all the goals would come in the same period. But in this case it would be the last instead of the first, and the outcome would be an amazing comeback win for St. Paul. The BAA stepped up their attack considerably from the games in Minnesota, but the visitors still led in shots, twenty to thirteen, after two sessions. In the first period, Rice's two consecutive chances on Elliott went for naught, and Abel, Goheen, and McCormick all missed opportunities. There was more of the same in the middle canto as Rice, who seemed to be able to gain open ice better than his teammates, drove the rubber hard at Elliott, who gathered it into his pads. Later, with Goheen and Small off for roughing, Geran missed a key pass from Rice and, still later,

another from McCarthy. Both were scoring chances in today's hockey-speak. The AC's had their own failures, most notably when Garrett's near breakaway was thwarted by McCarthy's alert backchecking.

Geran would redeem himself close to three minutes into the last period when, after a long, slow skate from his own end, he went around both Abel and Breen. Babe Elliott came out to meet him, but the Dartmouth grad sidestepped him and scored. The seven thousand Boston Arena fans "cheered to the echo," wrote John J. Hallahan in the *Boston Globe*, March 23, 1923. Sensing an opportunity to get the clinching goal, the Unicorns pressed the attack. Rice came close once and Elliott repulsed two other attempts as play moved into the last two minutes. Two more minutes to a sweep and the Fellowes Cup, but three minutes earlier Ed Enright had relieved Willard Rice at left wing. The substitution proved crucial when Enright went off for hooking Goheen, putting the BAA's on the power play (again, a term not then in use). John J. Hallahan in the *Boston Globe*, March 23, 1923, described the scene:

> The B.A.A. men charged toward the St. Paul goal. Leo Hughes [a late addition from Boston College] ... was at right wing. He lost the puck. Goheen poked it away and the Back Bay men were well scattered.
>
> Goheen rushed along and evaded Ag Smith, as Denny Breen was racing down the right lane. Goheen went right up to the mouth of the cage. La Croix tried to stop him, but instead of shooting[,] passed to Breen and the latter scored. There was but a minute and six seconds to play. The St. Paul players tossed their sticks in the air and Abel, the big husky defenseman, like a schoolboy, threw his gloves high and yelled with ... glee.

Linde Fowler, covering for the *Boston Evening Transcript*, March 23, 1923, described the goal as

a "fine piece of work" and then reported that the arena fans gave the AC's "a hearty cheer," a reflection of "how fair the Boston crowds are." Then, as "everybody more or less settled back … for a tie score in the regular three periods and an overtime," the improbable happened.

On the face-off after the goal, Garrett won the draw and got the puck to Goheen on left wing. Goheen would recall for the *Minneapolis Morning Tribune*, December 28, 1953, what happened next:

> My biggest [thrill] came one night in Boston against a great Boston A. A. team. They always seemed to have a jinx on us. This game was 2–2 [actually, it was 1–1] with 40 seconds [actually 66 seconds] to go and I got a break and went down the left side. Two defense men closed on that side, but I thought I might as well let'er go.
>
> LaCroix was in goal. I didn't dream that shot was good, but it went in. I'll never forget little Alec [Harold] Mitchell, the referee. He said, "Moose, I knew it would go in the way your stick was bending."

The goals, both on the power play—the rules of the day did not call for a penalized player to return after the first goal—were scored within three seconds of each other. Amazingly, it was not until January 21, 2004, that such a short time period between two goals by one team was recorded in the NHL. The Minnesota Wild performed the feat late in the third period of a 4–2 home victory over the Chicago Blackhawks on goals by Jim Dowd and Richard Park. The previous NHL record was four seconds, held by a number of clubs. Interestingly enough, eighty-one years had passed between the two occurrences and both were accomplished by Minnesota teams calling St. Paul home.

The dramatic 2–1 comeback victory with only a minute and six seconds left in the game brought critical comment down on Unicorn coach Fred Rocque, who was taken to task by both the *Evening Transcript's* Linde Fowler and the special correspondent for the *Pioneer Press*. Both felt he should have left the more experienced McCarthy and Rice on the ice late in the last period instead of substituting Enright and Hughes. Linde Fowler, *Evening Transcript*, March 23, 1923, wrote: "Somehow it seems as if one of the two regular wings should have been in the lineup at that stage of the game with B. A. A. a goal to the good."

There would be a day between games—unlike in St. Paul where it was necessary to play on successive nights because of the tenuous nature of natural ice—providing a welcome rest after Thursday's emotionally draining game. Fowler felt the momentum was now with the visitors, adding dramatically in the March 23, 1923, edition: "To have the cup of victory up to the lips and then have it dashed away practically in the last minute of play, its contents untasted, must have been bitter." The special correspondent for the *Pioneer Press* and the columnist L. S. McKenna had optimistic outlooks. On March 24, 1923, the special correspondent wrote:

> In Boston there is a feeling that the Saints have at last found themselves … Today the betting was even money … Manager Ed Fitzgerald of the visitors is confident that his squad will emerge from tonight's struggle a victor. The St. Paul manager declares that every man on the team has a feeling that the breaks have at last swayed to St. Paul's side …

McKenna agreed:

> Thursday night's last minute victory has renewed the belief of local puck enthusiasts that the Saints have a fighting chance to cop the title. The two counters in a minute's time … was the first break the locals have enjoyed in the series. The victory is certain to spur Fitzgerald's crew on to greater things and with just a little break

# ST PAUL BEATS B. A. A. IN GREAT SPURT ALMOST AT THE END, 2-1

## Crowd of 7000 Sees Visitors Tie and Then Win On Goheen's Goal—Series Stands Two to One In Boston's Favor

*The* Boston Globe *commemorates St. Paul's win over the BAA.*

in luck the Saints have an excellent chance of tying up the series tonight.

While these two scribes may have been optimistic, the headline writers were not so inclined. Where game three of the 1921–22 series made front-page news in the *Pioneer Press,* St. Paul's victory in the same game of the current series was relegated to its usual sports' page location. Unfortunately, as events played out, there would be no reason to change that position for game four—the great comeback victory would prove to be the high-water mark for post-1920 major league hockey in St. Paul. The AC's were never able to come as close to a national championship as they were before play got under way on March 24, 1923, in front of another packed arena throng.

As in the first game, all the scoring would take place in the opening period. The Unicorns would draw first blood at 5:26 when Gerry Geran picked up the puck at mid-ice, got by the St. Paul defense, and feinted Elliott out of position for the 1–0 lead. Earlier Goheen had a near-breakaway, but McCarthy got back to prevent the possible goal. Unfortunately, no one could stop him six minutes later (*Pioneer Press,* March 25, 1923):

> "Moose" Goheen's goal . . . came as a result of a similar play [to Geran's], although a bit less spectacular. Garrett was in for Clark at center. Goheen, after having been down several times, broke through the Hub defense, drew LaCroix a bit out of the net and the puck nestled in the curtains.

"Nestled in the curtains" is a descriptive phrase of sheer beauty that one won't find in any contemporary game stories. It is an example of writing that is long gone but captures the charm of this era so well. Not so charming was the cut Breen would shortly take on his hand through the flimsy gloves of the times, but he stayed in the game and was on the ice when Geran struck again. Rice took the puck in his own end and

passed to the BAA's star at mid-ice. With Abel and Breen looming in front of him, Geran shot, the puck going between the two defensemen, who apparently screened Elliott as the disk went through his legs for a 2–1 lead.

The AC's stepped up the attack in the last two periods in a desperate attempt to force overtime. In the second session, Clark, Goheen, and McCormick all had great chances, but Lacroix was there to make the key stop. The Unicorns dropped back to form a defensive triangle of Geran, Rice, and Campbell. They successfully thwarted Breen and Garrett in the third period as St. Paul threw all five skaters into the attack. The *Pioneer Press,* March 25, 1923, picks up the action:

> A big crowd of 7500 persons rocked with excitement. It was hockey's greatest period of the season here and St. Paul was doing all the rushing. Garrett, Breen, and Goheen were making wonderful bids.
>
> It was eight minutes after the start of the final period before . . . Rice . . . took the puck into St. Paul territory, but it didn't stay there long . . . Breen checked Rice . . . and Breen was chased to the penalty box. Rice followed him a moment later . . . and the St. Paul attack was unceasing. But Lacroix had vowed that this time there would be no last minute pucks sneaking past him.
>
> The Unicorn cage was a fortified citadel under his guardianship in that final period. Just as he knocked down a vicious drive, the whistle blew.

The 2–1 lead had held up for the decisive victory and the retention of the Fellowes Cup in Boston, albeit with a new holder. BAA had won largely on the strength of Lacroix's goaltending. "Frenchy" had held the AC's to four goals and turned in one shutout while thwarting St. Paul's leading goal scorer, George Clark. Nonetheless, the *Christian Science Monitor,* March 26, 1923, would conclude:

Geran should be classed as the outstanding player of the series chiefly because it was through his sole effort that two games were won for the Boston team. The second game in St. Paul resulted in a 1–0 victory for Boston, the goal being scored by Geran and in the final game . . . the two goals by him were the cause of the victory.

Goheen had scored three of the AC's goals, and Elliott had been almost as impressive as Lacroix, allowing only six. In his season-ending article in *The ACE,* March 1923, Frank Weidenborner would tell the membership:

> As the only star, Frank Goheen demonstrated that he is without question the greatest American hockey player in the country today. Frank's work has been on the sensational order in every game. He sacrificed his . . . individual work many times for the team . . . which is so necessary to win a game. The Club is proud of Frank and knows that his untiring efforts were mainly responsible for the fighting spirit of the team.

Weidenborner then moved on to the goaltender:

> Babe Elliott, who has proven again that he is one of the greatest goal tenders ever placed between the nets, is another important man of the team. Babe's work saved many a game, and his conscientious efforts were certainly rewarded.

The rest of the team followed:

> Joe McCormick, a new man with the Club this year, has won his way to the hearts of all fans and proved that he is the highest ranking right wing in hockey. His accurate low shots have time and time again proved the means by which our centerman has got goals. We are proud of Joe. Breen and Abel,

the new defense men, played good hockey at all times, and were the most feared defense of any in the League . . . Emmy Garrett and George Clark played center position very creditab[ly]. Tony and George Conroy and Charles Cassin played good hockey and were valuable cogs in the machine.

The former manager reflects a noticeable, but understandable, bias toward Goheen, while giving Elliott the credit he seemed to not often get during the season. It is difficult to understand his cavalier dismissal of George Clark as merely playing creditably at center, when the Winnipeg native finished tied for second to Nels Stewart in the Western Group goal-scoring race, with fifteen to Stewart's twenty-two. There is even a hint that Clark picked up his goals off of McCormick's rebounds. Nonetheless, everyone comes in for praise of some sort, and Weidenborner concludes that "this has been a brilliant hockey season and we look forward to another year in the hopes that we can be as well represented again as in the past season."

The team left Boston on Sunday night for New York, where they laid over until Tuesday, taking in the sights of the big city before returning in increments to St. Paul. The vanguard, consisting of Fitzgerald, Breen, Garrett, and Goheen, reached home on Wednesday morning, with the others expected in the next two days. Fitzgerald would not comment on the future but said the team had been well treated in Boston. Some BAA fans actually felt the AC's had the better team but that the Unicorn defense managed to keep them at bay while Geran and Lacroix came up with key games. The manager had been offered the opportunity to extend the season, as had occurred the previous year with the final contests at Pittsburgh. There were chances for games with various Boston colleges, the Hamilton Tigers, and the Winnipeg Falcons, but Fitzgerald preferred to close out the season with the national championship series. Years later Goheen would look back fondly on those days. Interviewed in the *Minneapolis Star,* circa 1958, he said: "It's hard to put a finger on any best night. One that gave me great satisfaction came in Boston against the BAA club. I scored the winning goal in the closing seconds. Trouble is . . . we lost the championship playoffs."

## All-Star Selections

Well before the season was over, newspapers in Duluth and St. Paul had named All-Star teams. Louis Gollop, writing for the *Duluth News Tribune,* February 26, 1923, selected three teams. He named Elliott, Goheen, and McCormick to the first team, Clark and Conroy to the second, and Breen to the third. Goheen was selected as a defenseman, although he also played up front, and Clark, Conroy, and Breen were named as spares to their teams. A total of nine players were chosen to each team, six at goal, defense, and forward, along with three spares. Of Elliott, Gollop would say, "In our opinion Elliott is the best of the lot . . . a steady player, keeps his head, and always has control of himself." Goheen was linked with Eveleth's "Ching" Johnson as a "pair of the greatest scoring defense men in the world. On defense they have no equal." McCormick was described as "a great stick handler and a deadly shot."

Not to be outdone, Halsey Hall of the *Pioneer Press,* March 4, 1923, named first and second teams, as well as an honor roll. While no AC'ers made the latter, Elliott, Abel, Goheen (as a forward), and McCormick were on the first squad. Breen and Clark got the nod for the second group. Each team consisted of a goaltender, three defensemen, and four forwards. In handing out the accolades, Hall described the St. Paul selections:

Elliott last year put himself on the throne of goal guards and this year built a wall around his throne. Supreme at stopping long and short ones and a master at knowing when to leave the net to attack a foe . . . Taffy Abel, in many ways, was the spirit of the St. Paul team. Always full of enthusiasm, this huge youngster early won his way to the hearts of the fans and stayed there. Besides being neat on the defense he was a hard-going rusher . . . Goheen was the greatest and most outstanding player of the year, and for that reason and because of his indomitable courage he is made captain of the mythical octet. Goheen can do everything and do it well . . . Joe McCormick is an antelope on skates. Graceful of stroke and body, he glides along, a back-checking menace and also an offensive one. He was the best right wing in the league . . . At defense is our own Dennis Breen, whom Manager Fitzgerald says is the best body checker in the league . . . George Clark . . . scorer par excellence, is worthy of center . . . Clark was always there in a pinch to paste the puck in the net, and he was clever at checking on the forward line, besides fitting neatly into team play.

As expected, Cleveland's Nels Stewart would make both Gollop's and Hall's first teams. The only other American-developed players besides Abel, Goheen, and Conroy named to either squad were Gollop's first-team selection of Duluth's Gus Olson and third-team pick of Eveleth's Vic DesJardins.

Elliott, as the USAHA Western Group's leading goaltender, and Clark, the second leading goal snipper in the loop, would get their just rewards.

The big prize, a national championship, had eluded the AC's for the second year running, but if one believed in the popular notion that good things run in threes, then surely 1923–24 would be their year. If only it was to be true.

# 8

# 1923-1924

## *Play-Off Problems*

"St. Paul had great prospects at the start of the season . . . incidents combined to make the road one to be traveled only by the greatest of teams. This the Saints proved to be, but their spirit was greater than their physical ability."

St. Paul Pioneer Press, *March 16, 1924*

When Ed Fitzgerald assembled the AC's at the Hippodrome on December 14 for their first practice, he had some concerns for the 1923–24 season. The coming year was an Olympic one, with the Winter games scheduled for Chamonix, France beginning on January 27. The USAHA was responsible for the United States team and fully expected that Frank Goheen and "Taffy" Abel would participate. Their absence would hurt the defending Western Group (formerly Group Two) champions, as had the defection of Joe McCormick to Edmonton of the professional Western Canada Hockey League three days earlier. Seen off at Union Station by Tony Conroy, Emmy Garrett, and newcomer Wilfred Peltier, McCormick's last words were: "Go to it boys and win the National championship this year"(*St. Paul Pioneer Press*, December 11, 1923).

One could only imagine Fitzgerald's reaction when McCormick's good wishes were passed on to him as he contemplated a third of the previous year's team being lost for most or all of the new campaign. Added to those personnel woes were the 42-to-52-degree temperatures that had been plaguing the state. St. Paul had been scheduled to open the season at Duluth on December 20 and 21, followed by a series

*Winnipeg native Wilf Peltier played two seasons for the AC's, 1923–24 and 1924–25.*

against the new Minneapolis Rockets, who had replaced Milwaukee, on December 26 and 27 at the Hippodrome. The team would then head to Eveleth for two games on January 2 and 3. However, conditions were such that there was no ice in either Duluth or St. Paul. This raised havoc with both the schedule and practice times, causing the Duluth and Minneapolis series as well as some proposed non-league clashes to be postponed or cancelled and curtailing practice periods.

Fitzgerald had thirteen players for his first workout on less than perfect ice as two players made their debuts with the team. Peltier, it will be recalled, had been with Duluth the prior season and was involved in the encounter with Goheen. He had been knocked unconscious and came away with a broken wrist. Now they would be teammates, as would Bill Broadfoot, from Regina, Saskatchewan, where he had played for both the Regina "Pats" and the university. He was now a student at the University of Minnesota's Agricultural College. Both were forwards who could at least partially compensate for the projected losses. All the others would return, including George Nichols, who had seen only limited action in the 1922–23 season. Charles Cassin and Bill Garrett would not return, but neither had played much the year before.

Fitzgerald had to move his next practice to Lake Como the following day. The goal nets were hauled out to the lake, and he ran the team through a two-hour workout. The ice was rough in places, but the coach was pleased with the practice. After the session, the team chose Goheen as their captain, a position he had previously held and was prepared to assume, as it had become clear that Goheen would not be joining the Olympic team.

USAHA president Haddock warned that if players refused to join the American team, they would face suspension from their club team unless a "legitimate" excuse could be provided. Both Goheen and Abel had begged off

because of business concerns, but Haddock applied pressure, as reported in the *Pioneer Press,* December 14, 1923:

Some of the clubs are looking at the matter from a selfish point of view and instead of insisting upon their players going are really encouraging them to stay at home in order to give their clubs a better chance for the National Cup competition this year. The Association is responsible to the American Olympic Committee for providing creditable representation for this country in the Olympic Games.

I think from now on instead of issuing invitations to certain players we will draft them and any that refuse to obey the call, unless their excuse is extraordinarily good, will be considered outside the pale of our organization.

We must have another high class defense man, and our selection is [Clarence] Abel of St. Paul. We need another right-handed shot on the forward line and have called on [Gus] Olson of Duluth. Goheen of St. Paul really should have accompanied the team but he, too, thought more of local interests than he did of national honor.

It was a hardnosed shot at Goheen's patriotism, directed at a man who had served in the U.S. Army in France during World War I and had played for the 1920 Olympic team. In the end, the new captain, now married, convinced Haddock that he had "legitimate" reasons to be excused. Abel was apparently unable to be as convincing and reluctantly agreed to go, fearing the loss of his playing card with St. Paul. Besides Olson, Haddock also wanted the naturalized "Ching" Johnson and Harvard's George Owen, but they all managed to be officially excused. In the end, the 1924 Olympic team was essentially the Fellowes Cup championship BAA team supplemented by Abel, Pittsburgh's Herb

Drury, former BAA player Frank Synott, and Art Langley, a Melrose, Massachusetts, native. Gerry Geran was forced to withdraw before the tournament began because he was unable to arrange his business affairs.

The Olympic team was instructed to assemble in Boston on December 27, but Abel was late in joining and did not participate in the team's first pre-Olympic game against the Boston Hockey Club on January 2. The Olympians won 2–0 but lost the second game 3–1. Abel had the only goal. Two days later the U.S. team lost 2–0 to Minneapolis in Boston and then came back to take the second contest 3–2.

The Olympics had been of great concern to Fitzgerald in 1920 when he was a player, but now his focus was on the USAHA season at hand. He had hoped to get back on the ice on Christmas Day or shortly thereafter, but it was not until December 29 that the AC's were able to work out again. The practice, originally scheduled for Lake Como, took place at the Hippodrome and was followed by another the next day. Much practice time had been lost to the weather, and the coach had to make up for lost ground in preparation for the opening series in Eveleth. The team staged its final workout early on New Year's Day before departing on the late train for Duluth and then the trip to the Iron Range.

The AC's had taken five of the last six encounters with Eveleth, but the opener would go to the hosts, who had had two weeks of practice and had played two prior games. Despite that advantage, St. Paul took a 1–0 first-period lead when Goheen converted Clark's pass. Eveleth had lost "Ching" Johnson to Minneapolis but had acquired center Eddie Rodden, who had been with the Toronto Granites the previous year and was a newcomer at center. Rodden would go on to play for four different NHL teams. The locals launched fifteen shots at Elliott in the second period—two would get by him for the ultimate 2–1 win. If there was a moral victory, this would be it. Halsey Hall, having apparently moved on to other beats, was not in Eve-

leth, but a stringer was there to summarize the visitors' efforts (*Pioneer Press*, January 3, 1924):

> The AC stickers did their stuff so efficiently that they outplayed a team with two weeks' practice and two games . . . Billy Broadfoot . . . was going all the time while he was on the ice. Clark gave great promise of being better than last season and Breen was capable on offense and defense, and Elliott was in no way to blame for the defeat. McCormick was not missed and as several of the players remarked, "a defeat is better than a victory if it proves a successful experiment and shows up what we have been unable to find out in practice."

St. Paul had pressed the attack in the final period, but without success as they reversed the second-period shot total in their favor. During a particularly heated flurry, Eveleth's Billy Hill had thrown his stick at Goheen's shot, a situation that today would draw a penalty shot but got him only two minutes.

With Abel playing on the Olympic team, Fitzgerald chose to start George Conroy on defense, rather than moving Goheen back. However, the next night the coach switched to Conroy's brother Tony. This time the 2–1 score would be reversed, with Eveleth scoring in the first period while Bill Broadfoot got St. Paul's two goals in the second period. Both scores were from in front of the net, as the newcomer "picked up the loose ones," as he told the *Pioneer Press*, January 4, 1924. The third period was also a mirror of the previous night, with Elliott making far more saves than Eveleth's McTeigue.

## Home Stand

The team was back in the capital on January 4, preparing for Pittsburgh's invasion on January 7 and 8. Pittsburgh and Cleveland had thrown a scare into the USAHA leadership back in

December by suggesting that they both be moved to the Eastern Group because the four other Western Group teams "have brought matters to a crisis by refusing to abide by certain decisions of the association's officers" (*Pioneer Press*, December 22, 1923). The "decisions" were never specified in the press, and Fitzgerald professed to have no idea why the two teams wanted to switch. The crisis passed, and St. Paul prepared for the series with practices on January 4 and 5.

Pittsburgh was off to a fast start with home series sweeps over Duluth and Minneapolis. They had done so with a largely revamped lineup from the year before, which featured, most notably, future NHL Hall of Famers defenseman Lionel Conacher and goaltender Roy Worters. The AC's had come out of the Eveleth series in good shape, with George Conroy no worse for wear from a skate cut and Emmy Garrett, who had not made the trip, suffering from a cold.

"Times were hard by 1924. The depressed economy discouraged both working people and small businessmen," wrote Mary L. Wingerd in *Claiming the City*, a history of St. Paul. Those conditions were not so overt as to discourage an all-time-high eight thousand fans from jamming the Hippodrome for the series opener. The game would be scoreless after three periods, when Pittsburgh's "Texas" White beat Elliott at the 9:20 mark of the overtime period. Fitzgerald had kept Tony Conroy on defense, and he responded with several rushes, as did his partner Breen. Clark, Broadfoot, and Goheen all had chances, but Worters held sway. The visitors picked up the tempo in the overtime, outshooting the AC's 7–4 before White "found the corner of the mesh with a fiery thrust" (*Pioneer Press*, January 8, 1924).

The St. Paul Co-Operative Club hosted the Pittsburgh team at a luncheon the following day at the Athletic Club's headquarters on Cedar Street. Some of the luncheon guests were no doubt among the six thousand fans on hand that evening when things went better for the home team. Clark opened the scoring ten minutes into the opening period when he stickhandled his way through the Pittsburgh defense and beat Worters. But just before the end of the session the visitors scored. Midway through the second period, Peltier converted Clark's rebound, and soon after Breen made it 3–1 after a long dash up the ice. Pittsburgh applied considerable pressure in the last period, as Elliott came up with eleven saves to Worters's two. One got by him at 10:10, but the home team held on for the win.

The game had been chippy throughout, and when St. Paul was shorthanded in the last period, the *St. Paul Daily News*, January 9, 1924, commented upon what we now call penalty killing:

> Frank "Moose" Goheen was again a star. His wonderful stick handling and ability to keep the puck from the Pittsburgh players when his mates were serving time on the bench in the final period, practically won the game for the Saints . . . At one time during the final session, Referee Steve Vair faced the puck off at the goal line when the Saints stalled behind their own net.

The AC's had six days to ready themselves for the Cleveland series on January 14 and 16, but even though the team was idle, it was still in the news. Frank Weidenborner was no longer writing his monthly column for *The ACE*—the reason for that was no doubt found in the *Pioneer Press*, January 12, 1924:

> Weidenborner started suit against Warren and Ordway [Athletic Club members] to obtain membership [ownership] of the hockey team, on the ground[s] that the organization belongs to him and that Warren and Ordway merely were members of a committee to obtain public support of the team . . . and that he was entitled to the profits of the games played . . . in the winter of 1922–23 [which] amounted to $15,000.

Warren and Ordway denied that the team was owned by Weidenborner . . . and that the profits were more than a nominal amount, and asked that the action be dismissed . . . the defendants engaged in the enterprise only from the standpoint of public spirit, and not for any pecuniary profit.

The outcome of this action is unclear, but what is known is that Weidenborner would leave St. Paul later in the year to continue his insurance career in New York. While his departure was not under the most pleasant circumstances, a case can certainly be made for him as a significant early force in the development of the sport in "the State of Hockey."

Breen, Clark, and Conroy came out of the Pittsburgh series suffering from various ailments, but none that would keep them from playing. Cleveland arrived with a familiar face in its lineup, former AC'er Jeff Quesnelle. The visitors, like Pittsburgh before them, arrived with a clean 4–0 slate but would leave with considerably less. The first game would bring memories of the epic struggle with Eveleth two years earlier that had ended in a scoreless tie. This game would also extend into three overtimes as the teams were locked in a 1–1 draw after regulation play. They had traded first-period tallies, with St. Paul's goal coming when Clark scored off of Garrett's pass. Both teams had opportunities to win in regulation and overtime when the issue was finally settled. The *Pioneer Press*, January 15, 1924, reported that

far into the third extra period the battle [raged] . . . Then the rush which was destined to win for the Saints formed and they came down three abreast. Tony Conroy on the left, drew the defense . . . over and shot to Garrett, with a clear field ahead. Emmy maneuvered Turner from his citadel and plunked the rubber into the mesh to a thunderous roar [of] accompaniment.

The Co-Operative Club would hold another luncheon on the day following the first game, but, in a break with normal scheduling, this series would not resume until the following night. The day of rest was welcome after the grueling seventy-five minutes of hockey played in the first game, during which Goheen had taken a stick cut near his left eye and Clark had received a bloody nose. "The night was bitterly cold but the play warmed up from the first period on and kept the 6,000 fans on anxious seats," reported the *Pioneer Press*, January 17, 1924, in its game two story. There would be no scoring in the first period, but each team registered a goal in the second. For thirty-year-old Goheen, it would be another big night in a career of big nights, as he picked up the opening goal ten minutes into the middle session when he finished a pretty line rush that started when Peltier stripped the puck from the visitors' Mickey McQuire at center ice and stickhandled through two backcheckers before passing to Garrett. Then Garrett was confronted by another "Moose," Cleveland's Jamieson, but he slipped the puck to his own "Moose" on the left side and Frank took care of the rest.

Cleveland came back three minutes later on a Nels Stewart goal, but Goheen wrapped things up midway through the third period, as described in the *Pioneer Press*, January 17, 1924:

The Moose [Goheen] staged a copyrighted rush down the right side of the rink and banged the puck into the net. It quickly bounced out and lay on the ice, few realizing that the goal had been made until Referee Sproul faced the puck in the center. This goal came while Breen . . . [was] sprawling on the ice in his own territory as the result of a tumble. Denny took time out for nearly three minutes while Doc Wildermuth put him in condition.

The sweep put St. Paul in a tie for the Western lead with a .667 percentage, shared with

*The Cleveland Hockey Club, 1923–24. Quesnelle and Wilkie, the first two players from the left, also played for the AC's. "Coddy" Winters, ninth from the left, was a Duluth native who was later enshrined in the United States Hockey Hall of Fame. Nels Stewart is at the very end.*

Pittsburgh, though the latter had played more games. The AC's would have a great opportunity to take the lead outright—their schedule for the remainder of the month, reshuffled because of the earlier weather problems, consisted of three games with the winless Minneapolis team. The new entry, coached by Fred Rocque of BAA fame, had gotten off to a rocky start, despite luring "Ching" Johnson and his brother Ade from Eveleth to go along with some of the former Milwaukee players. The games would be played at the Hippodrome, which was now home to both USAHA Twin Cities entries.

Minneapolis's games had not drawn particularly well up to this point, but the prospect of a renewal of the traditional rivalry between the cities at the highest level brought out the kind of crowd that the AC's now regarded as routine. The first game on January 21 was closely contested, with Minneapolis dominating the first period and taking a 1–0 lead on "Ching" Johnson's unassisted tally at 3:10. St. Paul took control of the last two periods, outshooting

their neighbors 13–4, as Peltier in the second session and Clark in the last got the tying and winning goals.

The team would have a week off before resuming the series on January 28 and 29. Rest was always welcome—invariably someone was nursing an injury. Clark and Breen had not been at their best for the first Minneapolis game. They would be ready for this series, but Bill Broadfoot would not. The rookie wing had injured his foot in the January 21 game and would sit out these two games. Taking his place would be George Nichols, out of St. Paul Central High School, who had played one game the prior season.

Minneapolis had upset Cleveland 2–0 in their last outing, but they could not convert that momentum into success against the AC's. "The ice was soft and sticky and the puck behaved queerly, but it did not keep the Saints from scoring," said the *Pioneer Press*, January 29, 1924. That scoring would come from Goheen three minutes into the game and George Conroy, cracking the lineup after playing in the first game at Eveleth. The 2–0 first-period lead blossomed to 5–0 after two sessions, as Goheen got number two, Clark another, and Tony Conroy, still on defense, his first of the season. Rocque pressed the attack in the third period, but the shots largely went wide, and Elliott had a 5–0 shutout, his first of the year.

He would get his second of five for the season the next night, but the game would be far closer than the cakewalk of the night before. It started out in a manner suggesting that it just might be another easy win when Goheen scored at fifty-one seconds into the game. Clark had taken the puck from a scrum right after the opening face-off, stickhandled his way to the left of the Minneapolis defensive pair, and then passed to Goheen who put it away. That was all the scoring there would be. The AC's had a 14–10 advantage in shots, but the overall play was ragged, characterized by many missed passes.

It may not have been pretty, but it was a win, and it put St. Paul on top of the Western Group with a 7–2 record, good for a .778 percentage. Pittsburgh was behind at 8–4 and .667 as play moved into February. The late start had compressed the schedule so that February would be St. Paul's busiest month. The team would play thirteen games over a twenty-day period, an intensity level greater than many modern-day pro teams endure. (Contrast that pace with the present-day Minnesota Wild, who played eleven games during the entire month of February 2004.)

## Busy, Busy, Busy

Fitzgerald and company left St. Paul on January 30 for a twelve-day road trip that would take them to Cleveland for games on February 1 and 2, Boston on February 5 and 6, and Pittsburgh on February 8 and 9. Broadfoot made the trip, although his foot still bothered him. A train change occurred in Chicago, permitting the team to proceed to Cleveland during the day and allowing a full night's hotel rest before the

opening game. The importance of this series and others was emphasized by the *Pioneer Press*'s Cleveland stringer on February 1, 1924:

> St. Paul comes here with a powerful all-around team that has a commanding lead . . . To stay in the race, Cleveland must stop the victorious march of the Saints, although Cleveland will have a chance to work into the championship round if Pittsburgh takes two from Eveleth . . . the general opinion is that the Blues will be counted out of the running unless they annex at least one of the games with the Saints.

"Championship round" refers to the new method for determining the winner of the USAHA's Western Group. Rather than having the group winner advance directly to play the Eastern champion as in 1922–23, the top three teams in the West would now engage in a playoff round-robin. Each team would play two two-game home-and-away series with the others, and the team emerging with the best record would be the West's representative.

All that was still a month away. Now there were two immediate games at hand, and third-place Cleveland would snap St. Paul's six-game winning streak with a decisive 4–2 triumph in the first. Stewart gave the home team a 1–0 first-period lead, but not before Elliott demonstrated why he was the best goaltender in the Western Group (*Daily News*, February 2, 1924):

> Moose Jamieson took the rubber down the ice then passed it to Stewart, who slammed a furious shot at the cage only to have it blocked by Elliott with his pad.
>
> Stewart got at it for another whang as it reposed near the cage after this stop, but again Elliott took a desperate chance and stopped it with his hand.
>
> Debernardi was on top of it immediately and got it on the rebound, but Elliott had him headed off from a shot, so he

passed it to Stewart on the other side of the cage, and Stewart put it into the corner for the first goal, although Elliott threw himself at full length on the ice in a frantic effort to stop it for the third time.

Cleveland would get another goal in the second period and two more in the third before Peltier and Clark both connected with less than two minutes to go in the game to make the final a respectable 4–2.

Respectable wouldn't be enough if St. Paul was to maintain its lead, and the team came back the next night to cop a 3–1 win in a game that wasn't settled until the second overtime. Smarting from the first game's slow start, the visitors struck early when Peltier scored within the first three minutes of the game. The home team countered late in the second period, and it was 1–1 at the end of regulation. After a scoreless first overtime, the AC's got goals from Breen and the clincher from Peltier when he got behind the Cleveland attackers in his own end and went the distance to deke out Cleveland's netminder Vern Turner.

The AC's kept their lead, and now it was off to Boston for a reunion with the BAA after an opening game with the Boston Hockey Club. Before those games would take place, word was received that Canada had defeated the United States 6–1 for the Olympic Gold Medal at Chamonix, France. Both countries had overwhelmed the opposition in the preliminary and medal rounds. In getting to the medal game, the Americans had defeated Belgium 19–0, France 22–0, Great Britain 11–0, and Sweden 20–0, but they were clearly outplayed by the Toronto Granites, representing Canada. This revived a discussion in the press concerning the wisdom of sending all-star teams to represent the country as opposed to the Canadian policy of using a particular team, at this time the Allan Cup winner. After criticizing the U.S. approach, the *Pioneer Press,* on February 4, 1924, had some interesting comments concerning two AC players:

Consider the case of Taffy Abel. When he came to St. Paul he was a great hockey player but the fans didn't find it out . . . because he was not great in his new setting until he had accustomed himself to St. Paul's style of play.

Consider also Wilfred Peltier. He, too, was a good player when he left the Duluth team but he appeared to be a total loss during his first games here. He didn't look like any kind of loss in the last Minneapolis game, and reports from the East indicate he has been starring there. It took him that long to fit into St. Paul's play.

Abel had played well in the Olympics, in addition to carrying the U.S. flag in the opening ceremony. He had scored fifteen goals, and along with Drury and Small was regarded as one of the American team's top three players in the medal game. Fitzgerald would welcome his return for the regular season and the play-offs.

As to the larger issue concerning the U.S. representative to the Olympics, the reality at the time was that the available talent pool was spread over a number of teams. It would have been difficult to have adopted the Canadian practice, but the 1924 team came close, with seven of the ten players coming from the BAA. One can only speculate what the outcome at Chamonix might have been if Goheen, Geran, and George Owen had been able to play for the United States.

The St. Paul players spent a day sightseeing in New York before heading to Boston, where George Owen would be in the lineup for the Boston Hockey Club. Fitzgerald had announced that Goheen would see little action in the two Boston games, allowing him to rest up for the subsequent league games in Pittsburgh. Though both Boston teams were in the Eastern Group of the USAHA, the two contests would not count in the standings. Bill Broadfoot, George Conroy, and George Nichols were tapped to see more action. But in reality, when the puck was dropped at the Boston Arena, Goheen was on the ice, and it was good that he was there.

The first two periods were played at a fast pace, and "the arena was jammed to the rafters with a yelling mob of hockey fans who showed their appreciation of keen play" (*Pioneer Press*, February 6, 1924). The AC's had three one-on-one's with Boston goaltender Browne in the first period, but he made the stop each time. The one he did not make occurred early in the final canto when Goheen—who else—connected after a mad scramble in front of the net. The home team took the offensive after the goal, but it stood up until the end.

It was reunion time the next night as St. Paul met with their BAA opponents from the Fellowes Cup series of the prior season. Old "friends" Gerry Geran and Ag Smith were on hand to greet them, but the core of the team was still in Europe following the Olympics. Despite their depleted ranks, the home team played well and almost took the early lead when Smith and Geran found clear ice, but Elliott came up with the big save. Peltier was similarly denied on a brilliant stop by the BAA goalie. The AC's finally broke through at 6:20 of the third period (*Pioneer Press*, February 7, 1924):

> Peltier, [Clark], and Goheen carried the puck near the B. A. A. cage. Goheen tried to shoot the rubber in but [Nicklin] blocked it. The B. A. A. goalie was so nervous that he started to follow the puck and knock it out of danger. Peltier saw his chance, secured the puck, and shot it home before [Nicklin] could get in position.

It was a bad error in judgment that Geran, who had been a thorn in St. Paul's side in the 1923 finals, remedied a little under six minutes later. Starting behind his own net, he wove up the ice, deked Elliott out of position, and put the tying goal behind him. Then came an interesting turn of events, as reported in the *Pioneer Press*, February 7, 1924:

When the third period closed with the score one all, the St. Paul players hustled to the showers to get the eleven P.M. train . . . so as to be in shape for their games in Pittsburgh Friday and Saturday. Manager Brown of the Arena . . . induced them to return to the ice and play a sudden death period, first team to score to win.

Hall . . . clinched the game for the B. A. A. when he tallied the winning goal in 3 minutes, 49 seconds after the sudden death period started.

This is the first instance of sudden death involving the AC's since the team was founded in December 1914. Up to this point, overtime had been played to a conclusion, allowing the team scored upon to rally to tie or win the game in the remaining minutes of the overtime period. Sudden death was in practice in the NHL from the league's founding in 1917 through the 1927–28 season. After 1928, the practice of playing to a conclusion was resumed until November 1942. At that time, overtime was suspended because of World War II restraints on train travel. It would not be reinstated until the 1983–84 season.

Fitzgerald had not quite kept his promise to give Broadfoot, George Conroy, and Nichols extensive action, but all did appear in the BAA game. The AC's finally made it to their train and arrived in Pittsburgh with an 8–3 record and .727 percentage, compared to the record of their hosts at 10–4 and .714. It was a slim lead, and St. Paul would be content if they could leave still in first place, according to the *Pioneer Press*, February 8, 1924:

> The Saints said today that they would be satisfied with an even break in the series. This would retain their lead by a fraction of a game and would send them home from their eastern invasion in first place with five of their remaining games scheduled . . . against the weaker teams in the league.

The team worked out at Duquesne Garden on Friday afternoon, February 8, before the 8:30 P.M. drop of the puck. Herb Drury was still with the Olympic team, but Pittsburgh hardly missed him, because the toll of four road games in six days showed in St. Paul's performance. Defenseman Lionel Conacher, "The Big Train" as he was known—he would later be named Canada's Athlete of the Half-Century—put on a Bobby Orr–type performance with three of the locals' five goals. The first was thirty-eight seconds into the first period of game one when he intercepted Goheen's shot on goal and went all the way back to put one past Elliott. Pittsburgh got its second goal before the end of the period, and, although Goheen made it closer early in the middle period, Conacher added two more goals.

The weary AC's fought back early in the final period on Tony Conroy's two goals to make it close at 4–3, but the home team got the clincher halfway through the period when White broke through St. Paul's attacking five and faked out Elliott to finish it off at 5–3. It had been a gritty performance by a tired team that had simply "run out of gas," in today's parlance. That situation would continue the next night when the hosts grabbed a decisive 3–0 first-period lead, added a fourth goal early in the second, and then continued to shut down the AC's for the rest of the game. Goheen had been roughly handled by the locals in both this and the first game, but the brawl that erupted in the second period when the scoring was over did not involve him—he was in the penalty box for tripping. The *Pioneer Press*, February 10, 1924, described the scene:

> McCurry, the local wing man[,] made a pass at Tony Conroy, who had blocked his shot in front of the St. Paul net. Conroy struck back and this was the signal for a free-for-all fight.
>
> Soon the players from both teams became entangled in the brawl without any serious damage being done. Police reserves rushed out on the ice and brought about an armistice among the belligerents.
>
> When the fighting started, George Conroy went to his brother's assistance and he was in the thick of the fray ... [bringing] him a ten-minute rest on the penalty bench. McCurry was also ruled off for a similar penalty and there was almost a resumption of the fight when McCurry and Conroy got together on the bench.

## Back Home, but Still Busy

The road trip had been quite disappointing—the team returned to Minnesota with a 2–4 record for their efforts. A case could be made that the two Boston games, which were played intensely though they did not count, had taken too much energy from the AC's, leaving them vulnerable to the sweep at Pittsburgh. As a result of losing those games, the St. Paul team now found itself in second place, with an 8–5 record to Pittsburgh's 12–4 mark. The good news was that they were home to face the bottom clubs in the Western Group, with Duluth due February 12 and 13, Minneapolis on February 15, and Eveleth on February 18 and 19. The regular season would end with a trip to Duluth on February 22 and 23. In the injury department, the swing east had resulted in only a cut over George Clark's right eye. Fitzgerald could look forward to winnable games with a healthy lineup and "Taffy" Abel's return from the Olympics.

Abel was due in New York on February 12 on the ocean liner *Berengaria,* and it was hoped he could be back in St. Paul in time for the Minneapolis game. Until his return, Tony Conroy remained on defense, and the locals returned to form with an easy 4–1 win in the first Duluth contest. After an opening scoreless period, Clark put in his own rebound off of Duluth goalie Ivor Anderson early in the second period. Breen made it 2–0 at 2:28 of the third before the visitors made it superficially close a bit more than ten minutes later. Then Breen came back again, followed by Goheen just before the end. Duluth had been hampered by the absence of star Mike Goodman, who was nursing an eye injury from an earlier game. Without him, the Zenith City skaters could muster only four shots on goal to St. Paul's twenty-four. Babe Elliott never had it easier.

The disappointing road trip probably contributed to a drop in the AC's usual six-thousand-plus attendance, with the crowds dropping to the four-thousand level, but the spectators would see a more competitive game the following evening. While Goodman was still out, Duluth changed goaltenders and went with Tallion, who allowed only two goals and turned aside twenty St. Paul shots. Those two goals came midway in the first period within a minute of each other. First Tony Conroy and then Goheen connected. It was all the home team would need as the visitors could pick up only one of their own in the second period. The two victories were just what was needed to restore confidence but not enough to pull ahead of Pittsburgh.

Abel was still missing when the AC's took the ice against Minneapolis, and despite the intense intercity rivalry, only three thousand fans showed up. They would see a game in which Minneapolis got the better of the play in the last two periods, but St. Paul still came away with the victory, scoring a goal in each period. Wilfred Peltier, sometimes known as "the Fox" or "the Frenchman," would have a great game, setting up George Clark in the first period and Emmy Garrett in the second. George Conroy would get the final goal two minutes before the end, taking a pass from Garrett. The AC's had taken fifteen shots on goal and had three of those go in, while Minneapolis had kept Elliott busy with twenty, but he kept them all out for his fourth shutout.

As the team looked ahead to the Eveleth series, the *Pioneer Press*, February 17, 1924, chose to profile Tony Conroy and made some observations on his recent play:

When Abel joined the Olympic forces, Fitzgerald tried Tony at defense . . . and since . . . teamed with Dennis Breen, [he] has played stellar hockey in a position which, until this season, he never dreamed of filling. He is the champion all-around position player of the league.

With the return of Abel, Tony is now available for both forward and defense duty, and according to his own advice, he likes the bumps that come to a defense man. Breen and others . . . are outspoken in their praise of Tony's work this year.

However, the fact was that Abel had not returned. The *Pioneer Press*, February 18, 1924, posed the question, "Where is Abel?"

Fitzgerald . . . manager and worrier . . . is still hoping that Taffy Abel will report in time to start in the first game with Eveleth tonight. Abel was at Sault Ste Marie, Canada, at latest reports and was said to be tending toward St. Paul by slow degrees.

Innumerable wires have been sent in his general direction, but each of them has arrived at its destination a few moments after the departure of Mr. Abel. New York, Boston . . . have been communicated with, but Taffy has pursued his casual way, ignoring all communications. It is assumed that he will reach St. Paul, but no one is bold enough to guess at the exact time.

The "exact time" had still not arrived as play got under way for the first game of the Eveleth series. The set was particularly crucial to the Iron Range team because they had a clear shot at finishing ahead of Cleveland and making the postseason round-robin. The visitors showed their intensity by dominating the first period but failed to score the all-important first goal that might have provided the "jump" for a win. The home team also failed to score but more than made up for things in the middle period when Goheen, Breen, and Conroy provided a 3–0 lead that went to a final 4–0 count when Clark got the last goal early in the third period. St. Paul had been outshot by their opponents for the second game in a row but still came away with a victory, and Elliott had his second straight shutout.

Game two would provide more offense from the AC's, particularly from Clark, but his four-goal performance and the 5–2 triumph was overshadowed by Abel's return, as reported in the *Pioneer Press*, on February 20, 1924:

> One of the biggest attractions, taken literally and figuratively, was Taffy Abel. Looking as robust as ever, Abel skated on the ice with his mates before the game to receive a deafening ovation which was even greater when he entered the contest as a spare for Breen in the first period . . . Taffy played altogether about ten minutes . . . Once or twice he staged the rushes that St. Paul fans know so well . . . [He] missed a goal by a hair's [breadth] after a neat bit of combination work with Clark.

The big man was back, but it was George Clark who returned Eveleth home with nothing to show for their efforts. Clark got his first on a pass from Goheen, but the visitors got that one back with less than a minute to go in the opening period as Elliott gave up his first goal in seven periods on a screened skate deflection. A mere seventeen seconds into the second period, Peltier converted another Goheen setup, and Clark followed with two more. Eveleth's DesJardins brought the visitors closer before the period's end when he skated through the entire St. Paul team and deked Elliott out of position. The "Red Rangers" could not close the gap, and Clark got his final goal early in the third period to end things at 5–2.

The AC's were now back on track with a five-game winning streak as they headed to Duluth for the season-ending series. The set had been originally scheduled for before Christmas, but the statewide thaw had caused its cancellation. A sweep at the head of the lakes coupled with Pittsburgh losses would send St. Paul into the round-robin with considerable momentum. It would be homecoming for Wilfred Peltier, "a Duluth castoff," as the *Pioneer Press*, February 23, 1924, described him, and he would have his best game of the season. Unfortunately, his effort wasn't good enough to keep the winning streak alive, despite the presence of a large group of cheering AC fans up from St. Paul for the state curling bonspiel (tournament). Peltier started things off at 5:11 in the first period from a scramble in front of the Duluth net. The lead quickly evaporated as first Gus Olson and a now healthy Mike Goodman gave the locals the lead. "The Fox" got two second-period tallies, and the visitors took the lead into the third period. They couldn't hold it as Bob Neuton got two goals within the first 2:30 to give the home team the 4–3 win.

It had been a great effort by Peltier, and he would continue it a day later as St. Paul rebounded with a delightful 7–3 romp. Abel started things off with his first of the year at 2:42 of the opening period, and that was soon followed by goals from Peltier, Conroy, and Breen. Peltier got his second, fifth in two games, to start the second session before the locals finally beat Elliott. Clark made it 6–1 at the end of two, but Duluth rallied for two third-period scores before Broadfoot got the visitors' last goal, thirty-seven seconds from the end. Elliott had been struck on the head and knocked unconscious late in the game but resumed his position once revived.

## The Round-Robin

The win left St. Paul with a 14–6 league record, 15–7 overall, which was good enough for second place in the Western Group. Pittsburgh continued to win and finished at 15–5. Cleveland managed to edge out Eveleth with a 10–10 mark for third place so that the three play-off contenders were set. It was now a question as to the how the play-offs would be conducted. The answer arrived when on February 24 USAHA secretary-treasurer Roy Schooley announced the schedule from his Pittsburgh offices:

March 3–5: Cleveland at St. Paul
March 7–8: Pittsburgh at St. Paul
March 11–13: St. Paul at Cleveland
March 15–17: St. Paul at Pittsburgh
March 20–22: Pittsburgh at Cleveland
March 27–29: Cleveland at Pittsburgh

The winner of the play-offs would then advance to face the Eastern Group champion.

In announcing the playing dates, Schooley emphasized two points: one, all teams would get a week's rest before beginning play, and, two, it was necessary to start the first two series in St. Paul because of the Hippodrome's reliance on natural ice. Both Cleveland and Pittsburgh had artificial ice plants. Fitzgerald was not pleased with the USAHA plan and reacted angrily, as reported in the *Pioneer Press,* February 25, 1924:

I shall certainly not accept that schedule. It could not possibly have been made more unfair to St. Paul.

We must play in all of the first eight games, playing our full schedule . . . in fourteen days. We play Cleveland here first and then Pittsburgh and while we are playing [at] Pittsburgh[,] Cleveland is at home resting for us while we must get on the train after we finish with the Pirates and get to Cleveland just in time to play again.

Nothing doing on this one.

The Schooley plan gave Pittsburgh and Cleveland rest periods after their games in St. Paul, but the AC's would always be either playing or traveling. They would oppose rested teams in all their series while their opponents would not face a more rested team. They would play each other in the two final sets when presumably the fatigue factor would be equal. Fitzgerald wired Schooley a suggested revision:

February 29–March 1: Cleveland at St. Paul
March 4–5: Pittsburgh at St. Paul
March 8–10: Pittsburgh at Cleveland
March 14–15: St. Paul at Cleveland
March 18–19: St. Paul at Pittsburgh
March 28–29: Cleveland at Pittsburgh

The proposed revision would still keep the first two series in St. Paul, hopefully precluding any ice problems, but at the same time addressing St. Paul's concerns about always coming up against fresh competition. Schooley's response was prompt but did little to placate Fitzgerald. The most significant change was moving the dates of the Cleveland-at-Pittsburgh series back to March 21–22 from 27–29. This was required in order to start the Fellowes Cup series in Boston before the seasonal closing of the arena on March 29. That change was made possible by eliminating one of the two rest days between series and removing the off-day from the St.-Paul-at-Cleveland series. The USAHA officer felt he could not start the play-offs any earlier because St. Paul had requested Cleveland as their first opponent but that team needed time to recuperate from injuries. He never addressed Fitzgerald's concerns about the scheduling sequence for his team and for both the Cleveland and Pittsburgh series.

Although Fitzgerald had strongly suggested that he might consider not participating in the play-offs if his concerns were not addressed, things progressed according to the revised schedule. Having second thoughts about his decision to face Cleveland first, the St. Paul manager told the *Pioneer Press* on February 26, 1924: "I only wish I could get Pittsburgh Tuesday. I think the boys would sweep the series in their present condition."

That would seem to be an overly optimistic

prediction, but perhaps "Fitz" was encouraged by the team's late run and most recent rout of Duluth. The AC's had won the season series over Cleveland three games to one, though one of the victories was in overtime. The visitors had arrived in St. Paul on Sunday night, March 2, after an all-day train ride from Chicago. This would allow for a good night's rest before game one the next evening. Both teams were in good physical shape, despite Schooley's earlier worries about Cleveland, but there were concerns over the ice conditions at the Hippodrome. The *Pioneer Press* on March 1, 1924, felt the home team might have an edge:

> The Hippodrome ice sheet measures about eighteen inches thick and can stand a vast amount of shaving before the bottom is touched. That the ice may be slow and sticky is highly probable and that this will work to the advantage of St. Paul is certain.
>
> With Goheen, Breen and [Abel], all huge gentlemen of supreme stability who can go through by sheer weight when speed is checked by slow ice and can stand their ground on defense all the better if speedy opponents find the footing insecure, there is no fear that slush will prove sticky for St. Paul and sleek and slippery for an enemy.

The team had their last workout on March 1 and awaited a Cleveland team described by the *Pioneer Press* on March 2, 1924:

> [This] veteran and brainy aggregation loves to meet a team that plays a rushing game[,] for the Indians have a set style of lying back, checking with three men strung on the forward line in their own territory closely in front of the defense. The Indians play this style and wait for the breaks and when the breaks come they are pounced upon with alacrity by Nelson Stewart and his mates.

It was 1922 all over again as fears about slushy ice were realized when play got under way in game one. The Westminsters had thrived on the conditions, and it was Cleveland's turn, despite getting only eight shots on goal. Three of those eluded Elliott, two of them by Stewart, and these would be enough to win a tightly contested game. The crowd, somewhere between fifty-five hundred and seven thousand, depending on which newspaper source, roared their approval when Peltier appeared to give the home team a 1–0 lead at the ten-minute mark of the first period. Referee Steve Vair disallowed the goal because it came off a forward pass, something not yet allowed by the rules. Two minutes later, it was the visitors with the lead when Stewart set up McQuire.

"Old Poison," as Stewart would eventually become known, spewed his venom in the second period, scoring two unassisted goals within fifteen seconds of each other to put Cleveland ahead 3–0 after two sessions. Fast goals were a skill that Stewart would later hone in the NHL, scoring two in four seconds for the Montreal Maroons against the rival Canadiens on January 3, 1931. It is a record that stood alone until American player Deron Quint duplicated it on December 15, 1995, for Winnipeg in a 9–4 victory over Edmonton.

It would not, however, be a perfect day for the Cleveland center when, after Peltier's early third-period shot was blocked by goalie Vern Turner, Stewart picked up the rebound only to have Goheen take it away from him. Goheen then went behind the net and fed Peltier out front for the first goal for the AC's. Three minutes later, Breen grabbed Tony Conroy's rebound and St. Paul trailed by only a goal. The rally would fall short, but not before some local fans tried to help. According to the *Pioneer Press*, March 4, 1924:

> Not a soul in the Hipp . . . would have been willing to pay his income tax twice on the chances of St. Paul to tie the score, but it was not to be. The Indians played

back, let their sticks lie carelessly on the ice to thwart speeding Saints and upon gaining frequent possession of the puck, shot it far down the ice, many precious seconds being wasted while Babe Elliott helped retrieve it for some frantic St. Paul skater. The crowd grew so wild that spectators put their legs over the side of the rail to obstruct the puck sliding down the rink and brought discredit upon itself by booing the work [of the officials].

The visitors could use such game-delaying tactics because the icing rule (prohibiting the shooting of the puck the length of the ice) had not yet been introduced to the sport and would not be adopted by the NHL until 1937.

The AC's now had a day off, the only one in the play-off schedule, to recover from their 3–2 defeat and hoped that better ice conditions might turn things around. That was exactly what happened. The ice was better—and so was St. Paul, as the scoring pattern of the first game was exactly reversed in the home team's favor and without a third-period rally. Not only was it reversed, but George Clark matched Nels Stewart's opening game performance. Clark went down the center of the ice just after the three-minute mark of the first period and beat Turner when the visiting goalie failed to control the rebound on Clark's first shot.

The 1–0 lead became 2–0 midway through the second period when Clark completed a rush with Goheen and Peltier. Thirty seconds later, Goheen got the third goal for the AC's and a solid 3–0 lead. Elliott had shut down Cleveland to this point and he continued to do so for the rest of the game, making key saves on Stewart and Holman in the last period. He had a better effort from his defensemen. The *Pioneer Press,* March 6, 1924, reported:

> The work of the defense was better than on the first night, Breen and Abel falling into their stride of 1923. Dennis pulled two

body-checks that showed why he is ranked a past-master at this art while Abel was giving evidence of a back to form movement with individual rushes galore and frequent defense bits of starring.

The 3–0 victory was savored throughout the city, but in no greater way than at the Athletic Club itself. In a special arrangement with the *Pioneer Press,* results of the play-offs were forwarded to the club rooms, where newspaper readers could telephone to see how the locals had done. While the series was now split at a game apiece, St. Paul held a 5–3 edge in goals, which could be a determining factor in the event of ties in games won and lost. The next challenge would be Pittsburgh, a team that had won three out of four from the AC's, the last two rather handily.

Readers of the *Pioneer Press* on March 7, 1924, would awake to read that the Pittsburgh team members had arrived on Thursday night and were

> in fit condition for the battle they expect. Their long rest has cured minor hurts of the regular season and has enabled them to get beneficial practice with Herb Drury in the lineup. [Drury had just returned from the Olympics.] Drury will not start the game but may be used as a spare on defense or both for this versatile gentleman is at home in any position.
>
> The drop in temperature assures perfect ice for the game tonight. A fast surface suits both teams but suits the spectators most of all.

Those spectators would again number in the sixty-five hundred range, and they would see another shutout—but unfortunately not by Babe Elliott. In a tightly played game in which the shots were almost equal, Roy Worters would keep the AC's out of his net while Harold "Baldy" Cotton would find the back of Babe Elliott's. It

A GOOD PLACE
TO BUY YOUR
SPORTSWEAR

MAURICE L
ROTHSCHILD & CO
*Palace Clothing House*
Robert at 7th

MINNEAPOLIS        ST. PAUL        CHICAGO

*Hockey skates and equipment were available at
this downtown St. Paul sporting goods store.*

would be the game's only goal and come unassisted at 1:33 into the second period. Cotton
was another Pittsburgh player who would go
on to an NHL career, mainly with Toronto, but
tonight he was the Steel City's hero. The home
team came right back at the visitors, as the
*Pioneer Press* on March 8, 1924, described:

> That set the match to the St. Paul offensive
> fuse and the Saints hammered away. Time
> and again Goheen and Abel, the three
> forwards [Goheen was being used as a
> forward], or Denny Breen and a teammate
> came down the ice to meet the baffling

Rodger Smith, Lionel Conacher, and Roy
Worters whenever the backchecking
forwards were eluded. Once the Saints
crashed in on Worters[,] the goalie and
Smith went to the ice in a mad sprawl
to block the madding throng of St. Paul
skaters.

The one-goal loss kept the AC's ahead on
total goals at 5–4, but a victory in game two was
needed. The *Pioneer Press,* March 8, 1924, laid it
on the line:

> The 1924 hockey fire will burn for the last
> time at the Hippodrome tonight unless
> unforeseen developments arise, and the St.
> Paul A. C. hockey players are determined
> that in the flame will be written victory.
> Unless victory . . . is achieved the Saints
> will depart for Eastern soil decidedly down
> in the race.

Denny Breen had taken a stick cut to the nose
in game one, but that would hardly keep him out
the next night, when the teams would battle until
after midnight. The term "epic" is overused, but
there is no better word to describe this game.
Both goalies would come out of it with shutouts
as they turned back all shots in ninety-five minutes of hockey played in three regular fifteen-
minute periods and five ten-minute overtime
sessions. In a fierce attempt to keep the hockey
fire burning for the *Pioneer Press,* St. Paul would
get forty-six shots on Worters, while Elliott would
handle a relatively few twenty-four. The close
calls would be many.

Worters lost sight of Tony Conroy's first
period rebound, but Conacher won his battle
with Abel to clear it away. Elliott stopped Smith
in the same period when the latter got behind
the AC defense. Both Garrett and Tony Conroy
forced Worters to make exceptional saves in the
middle stanza, and Goheen had his chances in
the third period. The home team nearly got the

win just before the end of regulation when Clark shot Peltier's rebound just over the net. After an even first overtime, Worters came up with another big stop on Abel in the second overtime and did the same to Clark in the third. Cotton nearly won it for the visitors in this overtime, but Elliott was there to deny him.

At this point Roy Schooley, the USAHA official in charge because President Haddock had not yet returned from the Olympics, was wired at a Pittsburgh newspaper office where he was getting updates on the game and asked how long this should go on. Schooley ruled that two more periods be played. If the tie still stood, the game would only be replayed if necessary to determine a champion.

So the game moved into the fourth overtime, and Peltier had the best opportunity to send the seven thousand fans home happy. Taking the puck behind his own net, he evaded the backchecking Pittsburgh forwards, and when Lionel Conacher loomed ahead, launched a long shot that hit the post and bounded away. Another overtime could settle nothing, and finally it was over. The *Pioneer Press*, March 9, 1924, concurred in Schooley's ruling:

To prolong the game would have been useless since both teams were so worn and weary that the chances of breaking the deadlock were becoming more and more remote with each passing minute. [It had lasted over four hours when it was halted.]

The determination to score was there [but] the skates would not propel their owners with the drive necessary to pierce the solid defense thrown up by either team.

Before Pittsburgh boarded their train at Union Station later on Sunday morning, Fitzgerald conferred with Schooley by phone concerning the status of the tie. He could have insisted that the game be replayed but agreed that

that would upset the established schedule and further delay the play-offs. It should be recalled that all play-off action had to be completed before the ice went out in Boston on March 29. The ruling that the tie would only be replayed if required to determine a champion stood.

St. Paul left that same night from Union Station for Cleveland and the next round beginning on March 11. The squad was in reasonable physical shape considering the overtime ordeal, but Goheen's shoulder was bothering him from a fall during the long game. They arrived in the Ohio city to face a team that was comparatively rested with no greater concern than objecting to the officials. Steve Vair and George Hiller had handled the St. Paul games, and, apparently because of the protest, John Dwan would replace Hiller. Fitzgerald was happy with anyone as long as he got equal treatment.

Cleveland's Elysium Rink had been sold out the previous week, and those ticket buyers were rewarded with an opening goal by Austin Wilkie. The AC's were playing two men short as a result of penalties to Breen and Goheen. Breen had been sent off for tossing his stick, and "Moose" had gotten into a near fistic encounter with Nels Stewart, but only Goheen went to the penalty box. The *Pioneer Press*, March 12, 1924, reported other problems for the St. Paul star:

Goheen was singled out for the large share of booing and for some unknown reason the crowd "rode" him before he exchanged hot words with Stewart. The climax came when the giant Saint collided with Stewart in a rushing body check which sent Goheen hurtling through the air to land on his back on the ice.

Stewart helped the locals increase their lead to 2–0 when he set up Jamieson at the 8:10 mark of the second period and then got the clincher in the last session after taking Debernardi's pass. The AC's had fired fifteen shots at Turner but

*Union Station, St. Paul*

could get nothing by him as Elliott handled twenty of twenty-three attempts.

St. Paul could justifiably blame the loss on fatigue combined with facing a rested team, a situation that Fitzgerald had feared from the beginning. However, no one could have imagined that fatigue would be so intensified by playing what amounted to another full game in the Pittsburgh series. The next night, "weary and devoid of the fighting spirit for which they are noted, the Saints struggled through three furious periods before they cracked under the strain," according to the *Pioneer Press,* March 13, 1924.

The scoreless tie came to an end at 4:50 of the first overtime period when Debernardi came down the side of the rink, drew Elliott out of position, and sent the puck home for Cleveland's second straight win. In the middle period, Debernardi had almost helped give the locals the lead. The *Pioneer Press,* March 13, 1924, described it this way:

Debernardi passed the disc to Stewart who shot it with lightning speed toward the Saints' net . . . Elliott had been drawn to one side by Debernardi . . . The Saint star leaped toward the corner of the net, lost his balance and while sprawled upon the ice drove the disc back to the center of the rink.

Unfortunately Elliott couldn't repeat his athleticism in the overtime, and the result was elimination from the play-offs. The team had lost the Cleveland series three games to one, trailed Pittsburgh one game to none, but had only been outscored eight to five, thanks to the kind of goaltending described above. Even a sweep over Pittsburgh would leave them at 3–4 for the play-offs, while a sweep by either Cleveland or Pittsburgh in their head-to-head series would leave the swept team with the same record, while the winner would win the West with a 7–0 record.

Nonetheless the AC's moved on to Pittsburgh to close out the season. It is logical to ask why the team even played these final two games. The answer seems to lie in the fact that the Pittsburgh management, which controlled Duquesne Garden, where the teams played, had fully expected that the series would draw great crowds. They had added one thousand extra seats, and the games had been sold out for a week. No one could have projected the goal-scoring drought that hit St. Paul, forcing early elimination. The games would be played, and hopefully the AC's could at least salvage some pride.

Pride would have to wait for the last game as the weary Minnesotans could only keep the first game competitive through two periods. Leading 2–0 entering the third period, Pittsburgh overwhelmed them as McKinnon, Conacher, and Drury each got goals to jack up the final to 5–0. The *Pioneer Press*, March 15, 1924, described St. Paul as:

> lacking their usual dash in their play . . .
> They also appeared to be stale. They
> were tired and weary from their strenu-
> ous schedule and this was reflected in
> their play. St. Paul had the worst end of
> the schedule in the semi-final series . . .
> Goheen was suffering from a bad shoul-
> der and he had to retire from the ice at
> frequent intervals.

Besides Goheen's shoulder problems, the team lost Breen in the final period when he threw himself in front of Elliott to help prevent a goal. He was carried from the ice and appeared only as a spare in the final game. That game reflected the AC's pride, as reported by the *Daily News*, March 16, 1924:

> St. Paul came suddenly to life. It may have
> been the nearness of St. Patrick's day that
> brought forth the talent[ed] spirit of those
> scrappy Irish—Goheen, the Conroys,

Breen and Garrett. Just how their rehabilitation was effected no one can tell. But 5,000 wild-eyed Steel City rooters will inform the world that the Gopher state crew was in to win.

After Pittsburgh's "Duke" McCurry scored within the first thirty-four seconds, the AC's did come to life as Peltier tied the game just before the six-minute mark. They were perhaps energized when Conacher's spearing of Abel went without penalty, but the big defenseman went to the box for roughing. It would be one of nine penalties handed out by the officials, with none resulting in any goals. The teams fought on through the end of regulation as Goheen, despite his injured shoulder, kept the AC's hopes alive with his stick-handling magic. Though "the Gopher state crew was in to win," it was not to be. McCurry got the game winner when he took Cotton's wide shot against the boards and beat Elliott on his unprotected side. Sudden death was still not the norm, but the visitors could not even things up in the remaining eight-plus minutes.

It had been a creditable showing by a team that might have simply given up. While the 2–4 road trip in early February cost them first place, they could have redeemed themselves in the play-offs. Granted St. Paul had the worst of the schedule, but that does not excuse twenty-one periods of scoreless hockey. The club's top scorers of Clark, Goheen, and Peltier were simply shut down—Cleveland's Vern Turner and Pittsburgh's Roy Worters played superb goal.

Cleveland and Pittsburgh wound up splitting their remaining four games, each winning one at home and one away. However, it was Pittsburgh that advanced to the finals on a 5–2 play-off record and 8–3 total-goals advantage in head-to-head competition with the Ohio team, which had a 5–3 record in the round-robin. There was some discussion about playing off the earlier St. Paul–Pittsburgh tie, but the resulting scheduling complications made that option impractical.

The Boston Athletic Association repeated as the Eastern Group winner for the second consecutive year, but this time the Fellowes Cup would go west. Pittsburgh won two of three closely contested games in Boston and then took the final two back home with a decisive 6–1 win in the last game. The series was played on the basis of the best four of six capturing the title.

## All-Star Selections

The AC's failure to win the West resulted in some changes when it came time to select All-Star teams. Louis Gollop of the *Duluth News Tribune* named Goheen and Peltier to the first team, Elliott and Breen to the second, and Clark to the third. This was one fewer player than the year before. Goheen had held his first-team position, and Elliott was dropped to the second.

Clark went from second to third and Breen reversed that selection. Peltier made his first appearance, and Tony Conroy was dropped entirely. Unlike the year before, no spares were chosen.

The *Pioneer Press* changed format from two teams and an honor roll to simply one team of nine players, "on the theory that a hockey team needs nine to be a smooth running organization" (March 16, 1924). Here the biggest change from the prior year occurred, with Breen, Clark, and Goheen making it, as opposed to the six who were named to either the first or second team in 1923. Abel, Elliott, and McCormick (who did not play) were dropped. Goheen was the only American-developed player named to either the Duluth or St. Paul teams, while Nels Stewart continued to make both teams. There was no indication that Halsey Hall was involved in the selections. Clark would again finish second to Stewart in the Western Group goal-scoring race, with thirteen to the Cleveland center's twenty-one.

# 9

# 1924-1925

## *Injury Woes*

"The Moose ... did well at the start and it was only when illness took a temporary toll from his powerful frame ... that he slumped to become only a ghost of his real self."

St. Paul Pioneer Press, *March 25, 1925*

The new season would bring some major changes to the USAHA. The schedule doubled to forty games for the Western Group, evenly split into twenty home and twenty away, and further split into first and second half. Teams would now play each other eight times, with the winners of each half playing off for the right to meet the Eastern Group titlist. The number of games played actually exceeded by ten the number scheduled for each team in the NHL. The pro league, which had been in existence for seven years in Canada, had admitted Boston as its first American-based franchise in 1924, and that move was just a prelude to more such teams and the ultimate demise of the USAHA and major-league amateur hockey.

But that was still in the future, and Ed Fitzgerald had to be concerned with the present and how he was going to play even more games without one of his key stars, George Clark. The team had been competitive since the league began, but the past season had seen the club outclassed in the play-offs, with only one victory on six goals to show for its efforts. Clark could not be admitted to the United States from Canada because of immigration issues apparently unique to him. His loss was significant—he had provided a

good part of the team's scoring punch during his two-year stay. Clark had the scoring touch like other imports before him, and now the manager/coach would have to hope that the reacquisition of Jeff Quesnelle, who had been with the team three years earlier, and Regina, Saskatchewan, product Harvey Naismith would help take up the slack.

Preseason games had been declining in recent seasons and this year would be no different, despite the doubling of the regular-season schedule. What would be different is that, rather than hosting games, the AC's would travel to Winnipeg for a two-game set against the Winnipeg Tiger-Falcons and Selkirk, Manitoba, teams on November 21 and 22. St. Paul would see some familiar faces in their opponents' lineups. On defense for the Tiger-Falcons would be Connie Johannesson, a veteran of St. Paul's 1921–22 club, and none other than George Clark would suit up for Selkirk. In the nets for the latter team was Charlie Gardiner, a future Hall of Famer with the Chicago Blackhawks, who would die prematurely after leading Chicago to the Stanley Cup in 1934.

Harvey McNair would assume Frank Weidenborner's duties for the new season both as hockey reporter for *The ACE* and as the club's hockey chairman. Hockey stories in *The ACE* had been rare in 1923–24, but McNair would revive them. Writing before the season began, in the December 1924 issue he previewed the team that would prepare for the new campaign in Winnipeg:

> This year's plans call for all the old favorites to be with us again. These include Frank Goheen, Tony Conroy, Emmy Garrett, Wilfred Peltier, W. B. [Babe] Elliott ... Clarence Abel, D. M. Breen, Cy Weiden-borner [who had not played since 1921], George Conroy, and George Nichols. In addition to these boys ... there have been added ... [Jeff] Quesnelle ... on the forward line. We also have added ... Harvey Naismith, a forward ...
>
> This will give ... a better balanced team ... [W]e will have two complete forward lines and plenty of defense men as well as several who can be used in either place ... to escape the disastrous results of injuries and to keep fresh men on the ice at all times.

Before leaving for Winnipeg, Fitzgerald had been conducting workouts at the new artificial ice rink at the Minneapolis Arena (at the corner of 29th Street and Dupont Avenue). He would continue to use the arena until the Hippodrome could hold natural ice. In Winnipeg, St. Paul would start fast in both games and then fade. Against the Tiger-Falcons they would get two first-period goals and carry that lead into the last period, only to have the locals come back to gain a tie. No overtime was played. The next night they led 4–1 going into the final period but gave up two goals, one by George Clark, to hang on for the win.

The games were played in twenty-minute periods, as opposed to the USAHA's fifteen. This fact, combined with the reality that the players were not yet in full playing shape, could

**HOCKEY**

**Advance Sale of Season Seats**

Orders are now being received for season reserve seats.

Seats may be purchased for 10 games, or the first night of each series, or the second night of each series.

**One Season Reserve Seat, 20 Games - - - - $18**

**One Season Reserve Seat, 10 Games - - - - $10**

If seats are desired for ten games only your application should state whether you wish to attend the first or second game of each series. Applications should be made in writing to—

J. E. Fitzgerald, Manager,
St. Paul Hockey Club,
St. Paul Athletic Club,
St. Paul, Minnesota.

*Season ticket plans, 1924–25 style*

account for the late rallies by the home teams. In any event, Fitzgerald was able to play actual lines as McNair had described in his story. Quesnelle centered for Garrett and Tony Conroy, and George Conroy and Peltier were Naismith's wings. This marks the first time in AC history that three-man lines skating in contemporary shifts appear.

The squad would now get ready for the regular season opener in Cleveland on December 5 and 6 before going to Pittsburgh on December 12 and 13. St. Paul would play most of December on the road and reverse that process in January. Much was made by local observers of the advantage that the new Minneapolis artificial ice surface would give the club in the coming season. According to the *St. Paul Pioneer Press*, November 30, 1924:

> Usually ... the team has started the ... race under the handicap of lack of practice.

Mild weather has prevented ice at the Hippodrome . . . and the only practice the team could obtain was short, insufficient workouts at nearby lakes and ponds. [With] a month's practice on suitable ice . . . Coach Fitzgerald has been able to develop more team play . . . In past years . . . [m]ore attention was paid to getting . . . back to normal speed on skates and bettering . . . endurance than in perfecting combination play.

The team left on December 3 for the opener without any injuries of note, and there was more than cautious optimism in the air, as reported in the *Pioneer Press*, December 4, 1924:

The Saints have not been behind . . . in finding new strength and they feel that [they] have advanced enough to make up for the superiority Pittsburgh showed . . . They would be a little more confident had not Clark . . . [been] lost to the squad but, even without Clark, they enter the race rated as one of the strong teams of the league and accorded, by observers about the circuit, a good chance of fighting it out for the western championship.

Cleveland was back with Nels Stewart and his supporting cast, and they were as competent as ever, although probably taken by surprise when their ex-teammate Jeff Quesnelle scored for St. Paul 0.13 seconds into the game. The locals quickly regained their composure and scored twice before the first intermission. That's all the goals they needed—despite AC offensive domination in the last two periods the St. Paul team couldn't get one by goaltender Turner. Nor could they get any by him the next night, when the hosts got all four of their goals in the second period. This was more than enough, as the Breen and Abel defensive combination was victimized for two of the tallies. Goheen took a hard check to the ice but was not seriously hurt.

Fitzgerald had hoped to play two games against Princeton and then return west for the Pittsburgh series, but the on-campus (Hobey) Baker Memorial Rink did not have ice. St. Paul arrived in the Steel City on the Wednesday before the series started. The coach put the team through a lengthy workout emphasizing team play and defense. Afterward he gave a long interview to the *Pioneer Press*, December 12, 1924:

Naturally we were disappointed at the reversals we encountered in Cleveland, but we will be hitting our stride soon[;] we were handicapped in not getting the kind of practice that Cleveland and the Yellowjackets [Pittsburgh] had.

After paying tribute to the national champions, who had further strengthened themselves through the acquisition of future NHL'ers Harold Darragh and Hib Milks, Fitzgerald expressed satisfaction with Naismith's performance in Cleveland and indicated that Quesnelle would be a good spare for Goheen. After praising Peltier, he concluded: "We have a good team and we will make some trouble for the leaders once we hit our stride." The "stride" was still to come. Herb Drury scored first for Pittsburgh, but Goheen, who was continually harassed, evened things up before the period ended when he stole the puck from McCurry and fired a long shot from the right side. The second period was scoreless, as was much of the third, but at the 10:26 mark Drury scored the game winner with Garrett in the penalty box. Pittsburgh's Baldy Cotton got the clincher two minutes from the end. Pittsburgh had put twenty-nine shots on goal to St. Paul's meager thirteen. The 3–1 final would be repeated twenty-four hours later, once again in the home team's favor. This time it was Lionel Conacher getting the first marker, followed seconds later by Darragh. Just before the end of the opening session, Naismith got the AC goal on a pass from Breen.

Breen, a defenseman, would be involved in a fascinating second-period incident at a time when goaltenders had to serve their penalties. The *Pioneer Press*, December 14, 1924, described the situation:

> Elliott ... succeeded in grabbing a hold of the puck and skated to the side of the rink. At the same time he tucked Cotton's stick under his arm. He was sent to the bench for two minutes.
>
> Breen was to guard the cage and he performed yeoman service. Shot after shot was turned away. Goheen and Conroy ... succeeded in freezing [the puck], and prevented ... scoring until Elliott served his sentence.

This situation could also have occurred in the NHL of the time, but the practice of requiring goalies to serve penalties was discontinued after the 1948–49 season. Thereafter, goaltender penalties would be served by another member of the team who was on the ice at the time of the infraction. There would no second-period scoring, but Cotton repeated his first-game late goal.

The AC's would come back to Minnesota sporting an unusual 0–4 record and sharing the Western Group cellar with Eveleth. While they were back in the state only one series would be at the Hippodrome. The club had worked out at the Minneapolis Arena, but they would not play games there until December 19 and 20 against Minneapolis before going to Duluth on December 22 and 23. The year concluded with their first home series against Eveleth on December 29 and 30. Unfortunately they would play all those games without Frank Goheen.

It was now revealed that Goheen had contracted a cold en route to the two preseason games. He nursed it on the train ride to the opener, but it settled in his stomach. During both the Cleveland and Pittsburgh series, he was under a doctor's care and urged not to

play, but play he did. He saw action as a spare in two of the games and managed to score a goal in Pittsburgh. On the eve of the Minneapolis games, he was home in bed. This situation would have a major impact on the club. As Louis Gollop, now writing for the *St. Paul Daily News*, December 17, 1924, would put it: "Goheen is St. Paul's team. He makes the difference between a winning and losing team."

That difference would account for a 1–4–1 record over the six games, leaving the AC's with the worst start in their history. There was a solid core of St. Paul fans on hand for the first Minneapolis game, which ended in a 1–1 tie. The USAHA had now adopted a scoring system of two points for a win, minus two points for a loss, and one point for a tie, abandoning the old percentage system. Only one ten-minute overtime was required, but frequently more were played. In this particular game, two overtimes were played after Peltier fed Abel from behind the Minneapolis net and the big defenseman put it away with three minutes to go in regulation play.

The team had played well enough against Minneapolis without Goheen and had picked up a point. Minneapolis had won three earlier games, so there was hope that things were turning around. But it would be awhile before that happened. The AC's put on a creditable performance the next night before forty-five hundred fans, which was at the time the largest Minneapolis crowd that had ever seen a hockey game in the Mill City. The fans would see "Cooney" Weiland, a new face in their lineup, score a first-period goal. Weiland was another future Hall of Famer who would later go on to a college coaching career at Harvard. Quesnelle tied the game in the second period when he converted Garrett's rebound. A minute later, Boyd got the game winner for Minneapolis when his long shot skidded off Elliott's skate into the net.

Duluth also had some new faces in the lineup when St. Paul took to the ice at their new

rink. Most notably, Ivor Anderson was succeeded in goal by "Tiny" Thompson, and Herbie
Lewis would be at left wing. As with Weiland,
these two would also wind up in the Toronto
Hall of Fame. Breen had played the Minneapolis
games with a bad cold, but that would not keep
him from the trip north. On both nights the
AC's started strong, only to finish weak. In
game one, they put great first-period pressure
on Thompson and came away with the early
lead on Quesnelle's goal, but lost on second-
and third-period home-team goals, the last by
Lewis. Abel, attempting to fill the Goheen role,
made a number of Moose-type rushes, but
Thompson made the saves.

A day later St. Paul again took the early lead
on a goal by Breen, but once again the home
team got a marker in the second period and
two in the third for the win. It would not be a
merry Christmas for the team as they contemplated the Eveleth series. Their old rivals were
not in much better shape, having won only two
games, but they had *won*. The club had not been
blown out of any games, but Goheen was still
at home in White Bear Lake. The *Pioneer Press*,
December 28, 1924, pondered:

> Lack of condition, poor defensive work
> and other causes have contributed to the
> slow rounding . . . of the St. Paul team . . .
> and not the least has been the strong ele-
> ment of hard breaks, but now after a few
> practices on home ice, there is a growing
> feeling of confidence that the long awaited
> sun will rise. Victory is now in the nature
> of a necessity if a pennant chase is to grow.

A day later, the paper, perhaps alluding to the
"other causes," went to some length to point out
that the team had played all their games on the
road. There was also speculation that Goheen
might be able to play against Eveleth, but the
more likely scenario would see him return in
early January.

## Things Get Better

The slow start had obviously dulled the city's
enthusiasm for the sport and accounted for only
thirty-six hundred fans being on hand for the
opener on December 29. But those fans saw the
AC's finally get it together for their first victory,
a game in which they clearly outplayed Eveleth.
Only two minutes into the game, Abel picked
up the puck at mid-ice, got around the defense,
and scored on Eveleth's new goalie, Pat Byrne.
The visitors failed to register a shot on goal until
the second period, when Tony Conroy made it
2–0 halfway through that period. While the Red
Rangers would get a late-second-period goal
and outshoot their hosts in the final period, the
day was clearly St. Paul's. Naismith was impressive, though he failed to score. "Time after time
his elusive skating and clever stick handling en-
abled him to reach the Ranger net," the *Pioneer
Press* reported on December 30, 1924.

Neither Naismith nor his teammates could
follow up the victory in game two when Vic
DesJardins, Abel's old friend from American Soo,
produced a two-goal game while goalie Byrne
threw a shutout at the AC's. Adding a third goal,
the "Red Rangers" came out of St. Paul with a series split. The AC's would actually have a 20–15
shot advantage, but Byrne was always equal to
the task, and his teammates continued to press
the attack even with a healthy lead.

It had been a disappointing setback after the
performance of the night before, but there was
good news ahead: the "Moose" would be back.
Fitzgerald worked the team on New Year's Day
in preparation for the Minneapolis series on
January 2 and 3. The *Pioneer Press* on January 2,
1925, reported:

> After watching the St. Paul star [Goheen]
> in . . . practice . . . Fitzgerald decided he
> was ready for action and acquiesced to
> Frank's pleadings for a chance to play.
> Fitzgerald said . . . he would use

Goheen at center ice . . . Fitzgerald may stick to his usual plan of starting Conroy, Quesnelle, and Garrett, but Goheen won't be kept on the bench for long.

With Goheen back . . . and . . . [since] the players have so improved their condition and team play . . . Fitzgerald is confident the Saints will take both games.

Goheen's return brought out a good crowd of five thousand, although still short of the numbers that were common in the past three seasons. According to the *Pioneer Press,* January 3, 1925:

> Goheen . . . got into the game after the first five minutes of play and introduced himself with a spectacular advance . . . but his scoring effort was turned aside by Hurley.
>
> Goheen did noble work . . . but his body could not endure the strain he called upon it to give and he was not as effective as the Goheen of old. He is not yet ready for the grind.

Goheen was now thirty-one years old, in his ninth season with the AC's, and working as a storage accountant for Northern States Power.

Garrett gave the home team the first-period lead after stealing the puck from "Ching" Johnson at center ice, going around a defenseman, and deking out Hurley. Johnson's brother Ade tied things up early in the second canto, and the visitors then went ahead on a controversial goal at the ten-minute mark. Elliott thought he had made the stop on Yankowski's long drive, but the goal judge felt otherwise. After much carping, the goal stood, but the judge was replaced. Goal judges at this point were stationed right on the ice behind the cage. They were given small white flags by the home team and raised them when a goal was scored. It was all Minneapolis needed, as Hurley kicked out nine St. Paul shots in the last period to gain the 2–1 victory.

Another five thousand would see Garrett score again in a tied game two, after Minneapolis

had taken the lead on Ade Johnson's goal after six minutes of the opening period. Six minutes later, he would take Quesnelle's pass and feint Hurley out of position to even the count. Neither team would score again, although Garrett had a great opportunity to win when his last-minute shot on goal flew through the air while the bell sounded to end regulation play. Two overtimes were played, but no one broke the tie.

Fitzgerald had predicted a sweep, perhaps overly encouraged by the prospect of Goheen's return, but had to settle for considerably less. There would be a sweep in the team's near future, but for now the *Pioneer Press,* January 5, 1925, assessed their recent play:

> The Saints set a fast pace Saturday night and did not seem to tire as easily as . . . in prior games. Garrett, Conroy, Quesnelle, Peltier, and Naismith were in top form . . . and all . . . played good hockey.
>
> Abel and Breen . . . did admirably well . . . there was always one or two of the forwards to help stop the Miller attack . . . Quesnelle, Garrett, and Naismith did exceptionally good checking in mid ice.

Goheen was mentioned in this report, referring to his long illness and noting that he "showed signs of returning speed which should be his when the second half of the season starts." This is a somewhat backhanded compliment that prepared the public for the story that broke the next day. Goheen would not be going to Eveleth for the series on January 6 and 7. After observing his play against Minneapolis, Fitzgerald was convinced his star needed more rest before returning to action. Goheen would stay in St. Paul and skate on his own. When the team returned from the Iron Range, he would join them for the Duluth series on January 9 and 10.

The squad left for Eveleth on January 6, stopping in Duluth to catch a bus to the Hill Top city.

The ice was soft in the Eveleth Hippodrome, slowing the game's pace in the first two periods. When it looked as if the contest was heading for a scoreless tie, DesJardins, who had been the home team's hero in St. Paul, scored what appeared to be the game winner with only 2:40 left to play. Elliott claimed that something other than a stick was used—perhaps a hand—but to no avail. Then, with only fifteen seconds left on the clock, "Quesnelle got the rubber about center ice . . . and he dodged in and out among the Eveleth team. He was bodychecked and backchecked repeatedly [and] a few feet in front of the net and a little to the left he sent the puck bounding into the net for the most surprising play of the night," as described in the *Pioneer Press*, January 7, 1925. It was the kind of comeback that frequently gives the tying team the necessary adrenaline rush to take the game in the extra period. Eveleth peppered Elliott with five shots into overtime, but it was Naismith who would end it at 4:45. The improbable 2–1 victory led to another win the following evening when Tony Conroy's first-period tally stood up for the rest of the game. Fitzgerald had his sweep and he got it without Goheen. Perhaps the first half could be salvaged, but the AC's had dug themselves into such a hole that it would take more such sweeps to get back in the race. However, the next three series would be played at home and "the man" would be back. The problem facing the team was that all the opponents were formidable contenders.

## Splitsville

Following Duluth into the Hippodrome would be Pittsburgh on January 19 and 20 and Cleveland on January 26 and 27. Between the Duluth and Pittsburgh series would be a nine-day break, and there would be six days between Pittsburgh and Cleveland. These days would be a contrast with the earlier hectic pace of games and would provide more time for recuperation and practice.

Hopefully, the momentum provided by the improved play at Eveleth would continue, and even if first place was not possible, a good basis could be established for the second-half run. Fitzgerald would put out Quesnelle, Garrett, and Conroy to start the first Duluth game and then insert Goheen at center between Naismith and Peltier. They would be facing a team trailing a surprising Minneapolis by only a point in the race for first place. Abel set up Quesnelle for St. Paul's first score in the initial period, and they took the lead into the final period when Mike Goodman came up with the tying goal for Duluth. This time it would be Tony Conroy playing the hero's role with an unassisted effort less than two minutes after Goodman's score. It would be enough for the team's third win in a row. How did Goheen do? We read in the *Pioneer Press*, on January 10, 1925:

> Moose Goheen's playing on Friday convinced the fans that he is rounding into shape and will be an important part of the St. Paul team from now on. Moose thrilled the crowd with several sensational advances down the ice, and did some effective body checking that played no small part in the St. Paul victory.

Besides that good news, the "Inside Out" column in the *Pioneer Press*, January 10, 1925, also took heart in the win:

> The Saints should rise. Although they have suffered a succession of misfortunes that have prevented them from forming the team they wanted, they are assuredly stronger than the current standings place them [fifth]. They will make no end of trouble for aspiring teams later in the season.

But the streak would come to an end in game two as "Tiny" Thompson showed the form that would ultimately put him in a Boston Bruins uniform from 1928 through 1938 as he back stopped Duluth to a 1–0 win. Mike Goodman got his second goal of the set—this one a shot in overtime that Elliott never saw. The game almost went the other way, when just at the end Thompson stopped Abel right at his doorstep. The AC's had a scare when Breen cut his ankle in the third period, but he was back for the overtime.

St. Paul had needed both wins to have even a remote possibility of taking the first-half crown, and now they would face the first-place team. Pittsburgh had split at Eveleth, a series they should have swept, so they came to the Minnesota capital realizing that splits were not the best way to stay on top. In the week leading up to the set, Fitzgerald had put the squad through a number of good workouts. The pause gave Goheen, who had played largely at center this season, more time to regain his original form. He had checked particularly well in the Duluth series and would need to continue that, as well as stepping up on offense, if the AC's were to be competitive.

Competitive they would be when sixty-five hundred spectators came out to the Hippodrome to watch a game on slow ice that went to the visitors 1–0 on a second-period goal. The *Pioneer Press*, January 20, 1925, described the game:

> Herb Drury fooled around with the puck in front of the St Paul net for several seconds . . . and just when the St. Paul defense figured his tactics were of a negligible value he unleashed a swift shot, ankle high, and before Elliott had time to set himself to stop it, it whizzed passed him for the only goal of the game.

Worters turned aside nineteen shots for his shutout and stymied St. Paul's two best opportunities in the last period.

The Pittsburgh goalie would also play well in game two, but Babe Elliott would play better

and come away with his second shutout of the season. Abel nearly put the locals up 1–0 late in the first period when he missed a wide-open net that Worters had vacated. But he didn't miss fourteen minutes into the middle period when he came around the back of the Pittsburgh net and banked a shot off Worters's skate into the net. Conroy made it 2–0 three minutes into the last session, and that proved to be the clincher but not the end of interesting developments. Cotton had slashed Goheen across the hips, and when the latter tumbled to the ice, his stick hit Baldy's forehead. Cotton had to be carried from the ice and needed stitches. That brought a reaction from the visitors, as reported in the *Pioneer Press*, January 21, 1925:

> Lionel Conacher and other Pittsburgh players did some fast talking for a few moments and when Conacher insisted on playing center against Goheen . . . Fitzgerald withdrew Goheen and sent Quesnelle into the game. Thus foiled[,] Conacher withdrew to the confines of his defensive position.

Fitzgerald had used Quesnelle, Naismith, and Garrett together for the first time and was pleased with the result. Naismith had proven to be a workhorse, playing virtually the entire game when Breen's hip took him out of the match early, but Tony Conroy took over for him on defense.

Breen's status was doubtful for the final series of the first half, against Cleveland, but Fitzgerald had the flexibility of using either Conroy or Goheen with Abel. He did not have to use either, as the veteran defenseman returned to full service. Cleveland had not posed a serious challenge to Pittsburgh as had Duluth and, earlier, Minneapolis, but as long as Nels Stewart was around they were not to be taken lightly. Also still around was Duluth native "Coddy" Winters, the venerable defenseman still playing at age forty—he was at this point about ten years older than the average USAHA player.

The first Cleveland game would result in St. Paul's most decisive victory of the first half, but it is better remembered for an injury to Tony Conroy. With nothing at stake but pride, only twenty-three hundred fans showed up for the game, and they saw a Cleveland team content to play a passive game and wait for goal-scoring opportunities to develop. The AC's got the better of those and led 2–0 on Breen's and Quesnelle's goals midway through the last period. It was then that the visitors' Gus Wilkie checked Conroy into the left boards and Stewart followed with a vicious check from behind. In today's NHL, such an action would result in both major and game misconduct penalties. Conroy crashed into a steel girder and was knocked unconscious. The crowd became incensed at what it regarded as an unprovoked attack on one of its own, and there were soon three hundred fans on the ice. Once order was restored, it was Wilkie who got a five-minute penalty, while Stewart skated away with nothing.

The AC's took full advantage of the power-play opportunity when both Goheen and Abel scored to end things at 4–0. Conroy was taken to Midway Hospital to have three stitches taken over his left eye and three in his cheek. He was out of the next game but back in action for the second-half opener. The next game proved to be another three-period scoreless affair like the earlier Duluth game. It also ended badly when Stewart, the real villain of the previous night, scored in the second overtime for the Cleveland win. The visitors had continued their laid-back style, and this time it worked.

St. Paul finished the first half with a 6–12–2 mark, good for –10 points and only fifth place in the Western Group. Pittsburgh won it with 15–3–2 and 26 points. However, once the new year arrived, the team improved to 5–4–1 over its last ten games.

## A New Beginning

As the first half wore on, concern started to arise in league circles that the winner of both halves might end up being the same team. How would the Western Group representative to the Fellowes Cup finals in this case be determined? Some new variations were proposed, but Ed Fitzgerald had his mind made up. He told the *Pioneer Press*, Janaury 24, 1925:

> As long as we agreed to the split season, it is best to see it through, although the forty game schedule [without a split] and playoff would suit me. St. Paul is now in a position to challenge for the lead in the second half or drive to third [a playoff spot], but the fans expect the split affair. If the league votes otherwise, so be it.

The vote went to retain the split season, and Harvey McNair would now look with some optimism to the second half in *The ACE*, January 1925:

> The St. Paul hockey team has finally struck a stride which may not take it to the championship, but which will make it well worth watching for the rest of the season . . . The future . . . is brighter. The team is in good physical condition, it has regained its confidence. Goheen is the Moose of old. Harvey Naismith has found an important place in the forward line . . . the Saints are not stepping aside for any opponent in the Western Group. They expect to enter the second half with a fighting chance at the top and a certainty . . . they will not be far out.

February's second-half schedule would be just like January's, and except for a jaunt to Eveleth all other games would be at home. It gave the AC's a great opportunity to continue their improved play under optimum conditions and to see if there was truth to Fitzgerald's and McNair's forecasts.

The first three series would be February 2 and 3 at Minneapolis, February 5 and 6 at Eveleth, and February 9 and 10 at home against Duluth. Fitzgerald began the second half schedule with everyone available to play and four thousand fans anxious to see a victory over the arch-rival city. They got that victory on second- and third-period goals by Abel and Garrett, respectively, and Elliott, now team captain, picked up another shutout. The game was in doubt right up to the last minute because Garrett's clincher came with only thirty seconds left. Tony Conroy had worn a leather helmet for protection, which was an unusual practice for the time. Helmets were not required by the NHL until the 1979–80 season. But it was a different story in game two when Minneapolis made Russ Oatman's goal two minutes into the game stand up for the win. Garrett had two great scoring chances—the last at the end of the game when he faced an open net as the gong went off to end play before he could shoot.

Tony Conroy was unable to make the trip to Eveleth because he had aggravated his shoulder injury from the Stewart/Wilkie incident in the two Minneapolis games. The ligaments joining his collarbone, left arm, and back were torn loose, but it was hoped he would be ready for the Duluth series. Eveleth awaited the AC's, and the *Eveleth News*, February 5, 1925, commented on two of St. Paul's players:

> Goheen doesn't mean to be rough, but just . . . is, that's all. When he gets going down the ice, he just doesn't see anybody between him and the net and any obstacle like Cotton or some other player not wearing the Saint uniform, is bumped with more or less force.
>
> Babe Elliott is here too, and that Babe is some goalie himself. When the locals are not keeping Goheen from scoring, they'll have to be trying to get the pellet past Elliott . . . But they're all ready for them.

Ready they were as the home team put a temporary halt to any St. Paul resurgence, sending the visitors to their second 1–0 defeat in a row. The game was similar to the most recent loss to Minneapolis in that an early goal, this time by nemesis DesJardins, stood up until the end. The AC's got the better of the shots, 17 to 14, but Eveleth goalie Pat Byrne "parried many shots that looked like sure counters" (*Pioneer Press*, February 6, 1925). One he did not parry was an open-net miss by Abel late in the first period. Both DesJardins and Peltier were penalized in the middle period for "arguing," described in the game story as "quarreling" (a penalty you'll not find in the current NHL rule book). The *Pioneer Press* story added that "Goheen seemed tired from recent contests and was not at his best this evening."

That comment may explain why Fitzgerald gave "Moose" very little ice time in game two. The encounter started well enough for the AC's when Garrett and Quesnelle got first-period goals to Eveleth's one, but by the end of regulation the home team had tied up the game. DesJardins had another great game, scoring one goal and setting up two others. One of the latter came in overtime as Galbraith converted his pass for the game winner. It was early in the season, but Eveleth was in first place, and they would learn to like it there.

Fitzgerald returned to St. Paul with little to say about the two losses but quite a bit to say about the Hippodrome ice. A mid-winter thaw threatened to make the ice unplayable and force cancellation of the Duluth series. "Fitz" would have none of it. He told the *Pioneer Press*, February 9, 1925:

> Skaters have been kept off the . . . sheet since Friday, thereby saving the surface. We went on a tour of inspection Sunday morning and found that the ice was in fairly good shape. It is at least 50 per cent better right now than the rink we played Eveleth on last week and far better than the

ice on which we played the [Westminsters] of Boston a few years ago. The series will go on as scheduled.

George Conroy had appeared in the Eveleth games, filling in for his older brother, who was still out of action. He would play against Duluth and score the first St. Paul goal in the second period after the visitors had taken a 1–0 lead. The game winner for the locals came one minute into the third session, when Garrett took Naismith's pass and caught Thompson out of position. The broom that had swept against the AC's on the Iron Range continued to sweep in their favor the following night, and this time a 1–0 victory would go their way. Another three thousand fans were on hand, and they looked on in dismay when, early in the second period, Abel fell on Herbie Lewis's skate and took a three-inch cut along the side of his nose. Goheen took his place on defense, and soon after, Quesnelle put Garrett's rebound into the net. If the team could respond with two wins after the Eveleth defeats and Tony Conroy out of the lineup, what might they do if George Clark returned?

There appeared to be a possibility that Clark's immigration problems might be solved, allowing him to return for the balance of the season. The team certainly missed his touch around the net, but the speculation proved to be nothing more than that. St. Paul would have to go the rest of the way with its present lineup. There would be six days before Pittsburgh arrived for games on February 16 and 20. After that, Cleveland came in on February 23 and 24, followed by Eveleth on March 2 and 3. The three days between the Pittsburgh games allowed for the visitors to play Minneapolis twice.

The break was a welcome one—it provided enough time for Tony Conroy to finally make his way back into the lineup, as well as allowing Abel to recuperate. Added to that, while Goheen had played quite well back on defense, taking six of St. Paul's third-period shots in the second Duluth game, he had injured his ankle.

While expected to play, his effectiveness could be impaired. Injuries had played havoc with St. Paul's "franchise" player this season.

Pittsburgh arrived in St. Paul after losing two games in Duluth and with injuries to two key players, Drury and Smith. A third, "Doc" McCurry, had been taking dental school exams back in Pittsburgh but would arrive in time to play in game one. Despite these problems and with only one spare available to them, the visitors dominated the first ten minutes of play and kept the game close right to the end. St. Paul was only able to score with the man advantage in the second period when George Conroy put in Breen's rebound. The goal would stand up to give the AC's their third straight win and full possession of first place. Goheen had played defense, but Abel was back for the second game.

Tony Conroy showed he was ready for the rest of the season when he opened the scoring in game two, ten seconds after the puck dropped. Taking the disc from the opening face-off, he beat Worters from thirty feet when his shot hit the crossbar and fell into the net. The team got thirty-two shots on goal and generally dominated play but could score no more, while the weary Steel City skaters managed to get two by Elliott for the victory.

All six teams in the West were now tightly grouped in the standings, but Cleveland was at the bottom, and the *Pioneer Press*, February 22, 1925, viewed them as a surly lot:

> Cleveland has become the storm center of the league . . . Cleveland invariably participates in a game where penalties are frequent and where the referee becomes arm-weary from motioning blue and white clad athletes to rest in the penalty box to cool their passions.

Little did the writer know how insightful those words would be. With nine minutes gone in the opening period, three Cleveland players were sent to the penalty box for roughing, holding, and tripping. This gives true meaning to the then-unknown term "power play," as USAHA rules allowed for such a possibility. Today this would be viewed as a five-on-two, but then it was thought of as a six-on-three. Regardless, St. Paul failed to capitalize, and when everyone was back on the ice, Nels Stewart scored within a minute. The AC's countered with a masterly second period when Conroy, Naismith, and Garrett all found the net for a 3–1 lead. The visitors got a third-period goal, but the game was won. Victory would also come the next night, but in a most unusual way.

Goheen gave the locals a 1–0 lead at 7:57 of the opening frame after Cleveland had dominated the first six minutes. The ice deteriorated in the second period, slowing play, and there would be no further scoring until 5:19 of the last session. As reported in the *Pioneer Press*, February 25, 1925:

> Nelson Stewart sent a long shot from the side of the rink at Elliott. The puck cartwheeled its way to Babe's skate and the goal judge raised his hand. Then in [an] instant he said it was not in and there was a scramble in front of the net.

Referee Bill Keane was well behind the play and rushed to the net to get the goal judge's decision. The goal judge indicated he had raised his hand too soon and that there was no goal. Keane accepted the verdict only to face Cleveland's wrath:

> Stewart started a protest that nearly precipitated a fight on the ice. He skated over to where Shannon, coach, and Irvin, manager, were sitting and told them the decision was terrible and after a few minutes more talking Stewart waved the players off the ice.

Keane waited a couple of moments and then faced the puck off near the St. Paul net. Elliott, as captain, then skated the length of the ice with the rubber, shooting it in for the forfeit goal and the 2–0 victory. Things were not quite over. As the visitors were leaving the ice, they were showered by folded programs from the fans, and one of those fans, H. Kasten, made some understandably negative remarks. Then, according to the *Pioneer Press*, February 25:

> Kasten says that Stewart struck him with his fist and that before he knew what was happening, he saw three sticks coming at him. One of the sticks hit the top of his head and made a three-inch gash.
>
> A large crowd of fans stayed around the doors waiting for something to happen ... but police cleared the Hippodrome of spectators and the Cleveland players jumped in their chartered bus and were taken to their hotel.

The USAHA slapped a two-thousand-dollar fine on Cleveland for pulling their team off the ice, and warrants were issued for the arrest of Stewart and three of his teammates on a charge of assault and battery. The players were subsequently arrested and released on one-hundred-dollar bail bonds.

Forfeiture of hockey games is quite rare—the last incident in the NHL was in March 1955, when Montreal forfeited a game to Detroit following riots at the Montreal Forum relating to the suspension of Maurice Richard. Prior to that, the previous occurrence had been in 1933.

The two victories over Cleveland had put the AC's into a first-place tie with Eveleth at the midpoint of the second half of the season. With both clubs sporting 6–4 records, the two teams would now meet in a pivotal series. A sweep by either would result in a commanding lead and provide a buffer to absorb the pitfalls of the season-ending road series both teams faced. They had split their head-to-head games at three each, and both had rested a week. It was time to play, said the *Pioneer Press*, March 3, 1925:

For a game of sustained action, there has been nothing like it offered at the Hippodrome this season. From start to finish there wasn't a lull in the fierce play that was waged with first place at stake. At times it seemed the leg-weary players would drop from sheer exhaustion, but fatigue seemed only to spur them to greater efforts … Never once did they falter … [T]hey found Byrne playing the game of his career in the net.

St. Paul outshot the visitors 23–21, but only one got by Byrne when Goheen set up Naismith for a 1–0 first-period lead. Goheen played better than he had earlier in the year, but his efforts went for naught, thanks to the Eveleth netminder. The Iron Range skaters tied the game in the second period and won it in the last with two more tallies.

The exhausting pace of the first game showed itself the next night, when the *Pioneer Press*, March 4, 1925, reported that "both teams had shot their wad in the classic struggle of Monday night, for neither team displayed the form and cunning of the first game." While Goheen had returned to form, he played the role of unfortunate goat before the packed Hippodrome crowd:

In the closing minute of the second period Goheen recovered the rubber in back of his own goal. While nursing the puck out … he slipped to the ice and knocked the rubber ahead of him. Galbraith … and Elliott raced for the disc, and Galbraith won, batting the rubber past Elliott for the lone goal of the game.

It was a game breaker, and St. Paul could not get it back. While officially they had twelve shots on goal, they had a far greater number of what today would be called "scoring chances," but their shooting was frequently off target. The net result was Eveleth's move into first place. The AC's slipped back to third, behind Pittsburgh.

## Breaking Even: Not a Road to the Play-Offs

There was still time to recover, but the nut to crack would be a big one since all of the remaining series were on the road. Cleveland would be the first stop on March 6 and 7, Pittsburgh was coming up on March 10 and 11, and then it was back to Minnesota to visit Minneapolis on March 16 and 18, before closing out at Duluth on March 20 and 21.

If Nels Stewart had any remorse for his actions in St. Paul back in February, it was far from apparent in game one. In a contest in which the visitors were badly outplayed despite a close count, the Cleveland star scored all of his team's goals. He gave them an early first-period lead that Quesnelle quickly matched. When Tony Conroy put the AC's ahead early in the second frame, he came back to get two more and a 3–2 victory. Turner had an easy time of it, making only twelve stops.

Cleveland would score three goals the following night, but they were all disallowed for various rule infractions. While the locals argued, there was no mass exit from the ice as in Minnesota, and "the local team displayed sportsmanship on numerous occasions" (*Pioneer Press*, March 8, 1925). St. Paul had cast off its first-game lethargy and beat Turner three times in the first six minutes to effectively put the game away early. Tony Conroy got a fourth goal in the second period, and the visitors were content to lay back and play in a defensive shell, a tactic not uncommon in this era. The home team would be shut out, as Nels Stewart appeared to take the night off, something he was occasionally accused of doing.

"Goheen's Comeback Improves St. Paul for Combats Here" headlined the pregame story in a local Pittsburgh daily on March 10, 1925:

With Frank Goheen, the backbone of the team in shape and ready to play the kind of hockey that stamped him a star and a big favorite here, the St. Paul team is primed

for the games with … the Yellowjackets …
The Saints, fresh from an impressive win
over Cleveland … are determined to keep
the champions from ascending to the top
of the league.

That determination wasn't evident in the series' first game, as Pittsburgh bombarded Elliott
with thirty-eight shots, quite high for the times,
and four got through for a solid victory. The
AC's played far better in the last period, with
Goheen and Abel carrying the puck in deep but
failing to score. It was the kind of essential win
required if the locals were to catch Eveleth.

Pittsburgh desperately needed to follow up
this game with another similar effort, but George
Conroy, now seeing more action and stepping
out of the shadow of his brother, came up with a
big night. According to the *Pioneer Press,* March
12, 1925:

> The Conroy brothers did their stuff, Tony
> carrying the puck after he checked an
> advance in mid ice. They skated the left
> wing lane … As they neared the cage
> they swerved into center ice. Tony made a
> lightning pass to George who made a shot.
> Worters tried to block the shot with his
> skate, but [it] caromed off and trickled in
> for the first goal after 10 minutes and 30
> seconds of play.

George would strike again less than two
minutes later when Abel set him up just like
his brother. Cotton got one for Pittsburgh in
the second canto, but Peltier scored the clincher
midway through the third. Conacher's late goal
closed the gap to 3–2, and St. Paul would return
home on a positive note.

The inability to win the series had sealed
the team's fate after the two losses to Eveleth in
early February. They had played creditably at
times but were simply not consistent enough to
outstrip Pittsburgh or Eveleth. They could, however, with good efforts in their last two series,

finish above .500 in the second half and claim
third place, something they could not do in the
first half because of their horrendous start.

Cy Weidenborner had served as backup
goaltender for the last four years and had not
played a game since the 1920–21 season. In the
first Minneapolis encounter, he would relieve
the injured Elliott and lead the team to victory.
As reported in the *Pioneer Press,* March 17, 1925:

> For several moments the St. Paul delega-
> tion was dumfounded. They were ready to
> quit. Then things started to happen. And
> Weidenborner was right in the midst of
> the excitement. He stopped shot after shot
> with astounding ease. He continued to do
> that very same thing in the second period
> and until twelve minutes of the third period
> when the Millers finally scored their goal.
>
> Weidenborner's work was masterful.

Weidenborner had turned aside twenty-two
shots after relieving Elliott, while his teammates
could get only nine on their opponent's net. Two
of those went in—Peltier and Abel connected in
each of the first two periods—and these were
enough for the win.

Elliott's departure had occurred after a wick-
ed slash by Ade Johnson, but it was not enough
to keep him out of the second game. In a penalty-
filled clash, Goheen got the AC's first goal with a
man advantage, but former teammate Connie
Johannesson tied things up less than two minutes later. The home team scored the game winner when both Abel and Conroy were in the
penalty box.

The game account's reference to the Minneapolis team as the "Millers" again reflects the
custom of the time of using baseball team nick-
names for hockey clubs. Pittsburgh was often referred to as the "Pirates" or "Yellowjackets," and
Cleveland was called the "Indians" or "Blues."
Other unofficial designations were "Hornets"
for Duluth, "Reds" or "Red Rangers" for Eveleth,
and "Rockets" or "Millers" for Minneapolis.

The split was another of the many played by the team during the season, but the trend would finally come to an end in Duluth. St. Paul fell behind 2–0 after the first period but roared back to score four straight goals, two in each period, before the home team managed to make it close at 4–3. It would be Goheen's go-ahead tally in the third session that caused an uproar. In a story in the *Pioneer Press* from March 21, 1925:

> The play which caused the trouble followed a hard shot by Goheen at Thompson. The Duluth goalie stopped the shot, catching it between his legs. He waddled out of the net to drop it and, as he did so Goheen and Garrett made a "center rush" at the Duluth nets crowding Thompson back into the meshes ... Though Referee Nick Kahler's bell had rung, he allowed the score.
>
> A long discussion ... failed to make the official change his decision, and then the crowd took control of the game, hurling cushions, paper bags, and everything they could lay their hands on, out on the ice.

The game was held up for nearly fifteen minutes before the ice was cleared and play could resume. Kahler (former AC player) threatened to forfeit the game but didn't carry through with his threat. It hardly mattered, as the goal stood and Tony Conroy added another. George Conroy and Garrett had scored the earlier markers.

Kahler would have more problems the next night when he sent two Duluth players to the penalty box late in the first period. Sensing that the hostile local crowd might repeat the previous night's spectacle, he withdrew from the game and was succeeded by Helmer Grenner, a local official. Grenner kept things under control by sending a steady stream of players to the penalty box, particularly in the last period, but regulation time ran out without a decision. The teams battled into the second overtime before

Abel beat Thompson when the latter failed to adequately clear the Sault native's first shot.

The long-awaited sweep left St. Paul with a 11–9–0 record and third place in the Western Group, a far cry from the lofty achievements of the past three years but a competitive record nonetheless. The season was over, but there would still be one last game with Minneapolis. St. Paul issued the challenge, and Minneapolis, despite winning the season series, agreed to another game to decide the "city championship." The AC's were enthusiastically eager for the contest, although Abel, Tony Conroy, and Naismith were all nursing injuries of some kind. Naismith had actually sat out the last game in Duluth.

Some five thousand fans turned out for the extra game, which was played at the Minneapolis Arena. The home team led 3–0 early in the third period when St. Paul rallied to make it 3–2 on goals by Goheen and Conroy before the locals got the last two and the right to further confirmation as city champions.

Eveleth's impressive turnaround in the second half gave them the Western Group title by a game over Pittsburgh, eliminating fears that the same team would win both halves of the schedule. Pittsburgh, first-half winner, then swept Eveleth four games to none in the play-offs, setting up an all-Pittsburgh final for the Fellowes Cup. Fort Pitt was a new Pittsburgh-based team that competed in the Eastern Group. They had captured the latter title by defeating the BAA three games to none in that group's play-offs. In the finals they took their neighbors to overtime three times, but lost each while one game ended in a tie. Pittsburgh had their second consecutive Fellowes Cup.

## No Play-Offs, Fewer All-Stars

The *Pioneer Press* named its All-Star team the day after St. Paul's season-ending game in Duluth. The newspaper expanded the team to ten players from nine, but the only AC player named was Goheen at forward. As the newspaper explained on March 22, 1925:

> There could not conscientiously ... be any excuse for keeping Goheen off the team, after his great second half play ... St. Paul fans saw the old Goheen reincarnated, however, and in the final Minneapolis series he was the same backchecking, hard-rushing hockey fool.

The only other American-developed player named to the team was Eveleth's Vic DesJardins, while Nels Stewart made his perennial appearance. Pittsburgh's Lionel Conacher and Minneapolis's "Ching" Johnson were named for the second consecutive year.

Louis Gollop continued naming all-star teams for his new employers at the *Daily News* but split his selections into first and second teams. Goheen was named at wing and Breen on defense for the second squad. Gollop also named DesJardins to the first team, along with Stewart and Johnson. Conacher made the second club.

The team was honored at a season end's banquet at the club's rooms on March 27 and was thanked by President Al Warren for its efforts. As those present listened to his remarks, they may have recalled *Pioneer Press* comments from March 5, 1925:

> Fitzgerald refused to discuss his plans for next season ... it seems almost certain that there will be a shakeup in personnel ... The weakness shown ... make[s] it apparent that ... the first addition to the team must be a center ice man like George Clark. Clark ... always seemed to be around the net at the proper time ...
> A good center ice man ... to work with Quesnelle might have changed the aspect of several games.
>
> Moose Goheen ... didn't regain his old form until the Eveleth series ... Subsequent injuries to Abel, Breen, Tony Conroy, and Garrett left the team weakened perceptively and there were no spares of equal ability to fill in for them.

*A cartoon treatment of the 1925 summer series between St. Paul and Minneapolis at the Kiwanis National Convention*

*The teams face off at the Minneapolis Arena, 1925.*

There was still one more bit of business to take care of before the season could be regarded as over. The Kiwanis International service club held its convention in late June in Minneapolis, and as part of its activities staged a "midsummer ice carnival." This event was primarily a three-game hockey tournament played at the Minneapolis Arena between St. Paul and Minneapolis on June 24, 25, and 26. The AC's were able to bring together most of their regular players supplemented by a few others, most notably George Clark, while Cy Weidenborner played goal. Minneapolis was unable to do quite as well in reassembling their regular roster, so they relied more heavily on others. The greater cohesion of St. Paul showed in the results—they won the series two games to one. Minneapolis won the first game 3–2 before a Kiwanis-only crowd of seven thousand, while St. Paul took games two and three by scores of 4–1 and 1–0. The latter games were open to the general public, and programs of speed and figure skating were also included. While the contests were of questionable quality, the fact that the sport was showcased to a largely unfamiliar audience was a positive indication of how hockey had established itself on the Twin Cities sports scene. A shot from one of the games appears as part of a photo mural recognizing old Minnesota ice arenas that is mounted on the wall of the upper concourse of the Xcel Energy Center.

# 10

# 1925-1926

## *Last Hurrah for the Amateurs*

"For several seasons this league has been amateur in name only. It has had
to spend money liberally to secure players but has found it wise to keep
the amateur label upon which to draw for player talent."

St. Paul Pioneer Press, *February 19, 1926*

The NHL's expansion into the United States a year earlier was followed by the further entry into the league of the New York Americans and Pittsburgh Yellowjackets in September 1925. The pro league essentially took the USAHA's best team, the Yellowjackets, thus effectively ending the amateur group's reign in the sport. It was not a development that was totally unexpected—there were earlier indications that the days of big league amateur hockey were soon to end. Pro scouts had long been coveting the league's best players since at least the time of the earlier approaches to both Goheen and Conroy. It was no secret that Nels Stewart, one of the league's best players, was ready to go pro, and he did so upon signing with the Montreal Maroons on June 25, 1925.

While the Yellowjackets and Fort Pitt were playing off for the Fellowes Cup, the BAA announced its withdrawal from the USAHA, apparently anticipating problems with its players concerning the submission of excessive expense reports. This situation gave rise to a *Christian Science Monitor* article on May 4, 1925, headlined "U.S.A.H.A. About to Disband as Body":

A professional hockey association will be formed to supplant the United States Amateur Hockey Association, and the western group, which has been the backbone of the amateur league, will be included in the organization . . . [T]he move will be the end to the amateur hockey game in the United States. Inability to develop sufficient number of hockey stars to recruit the amateur teams is responsible for the move.

This proposed league may allude to minor pro hockey but in any event the NHL was already in existence and more than willing to pay the players that the amateur league was supposedly having difficulty developing. Salaries in the NHL at the time were in the $1,500 to $2,000 range for journeyman players—upper-end talent could command between $3,000 and $5,000. By the fall of 1925, it was apparent that the USAHA was finished, but the amateurs would have one last hurrah. Meeting in Minneapolis on October 24, the Central Amateur Hockey Association (CAHA) was formed, with St. Paul, Minneapolis, Duluth, Eveleth-Hibbing, Sault Ste. Marie, Ontario, and Winnipeg as members. Al Warren, president of the Athletic Club, was named president of the new group and headed up a board of directors with representatives from the member teams.

The new league adopted three rules designed to speed up play. The ice was divided into three zones with no offsides called when moving into the center zone. As in the NHL, each team was limited to two players and the goaltender on defense (my interpretation of this rule is that the three forwards could not position themselves closely around the net as was frequently the practice when a team wanted to simply protect a lead). Finally, play was extended from fifteen to twenty minutes per period. A ten-minute overtime, split into five-minute segments, would be played, but if a winner was still not determined, no further play would be conducted and the tie would stand.

The schedule called for thirty-eight games for all teams, except Canadian Soo, which would play thirty-two. Each team played each other eight times—four at home and four away. In the case of Canadian Soo, each team was to play two games there and four at home. The plan was for the first-place team to play an Eastern league champion for the national title, but that never happened. The second- and third-place finishers played off against each other, with the winner facing off against the first-place team for the league championship.

The AC's first practice was Friday, November

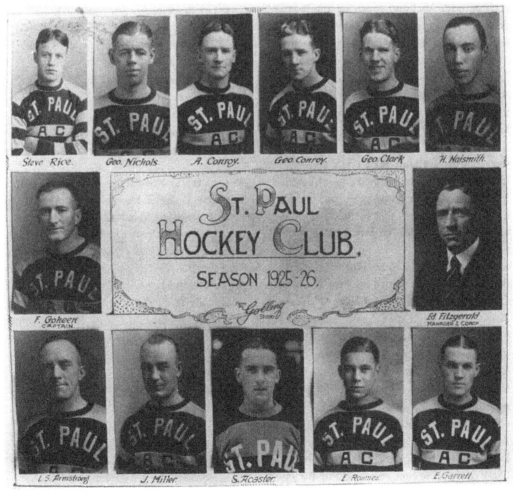

*The 1925–26 AC's*

13, at the Minneapolis Arena, and neither Abel nor Breen was there to begin training. Jeff Quesnelle attended, but he would be gone as well in two weeks. All three had been lured to Minneapolis, and two others, goalie Babe Elliott and forward Wilfred Peltier, had been lured into retirement and Eastern hockey, respectively. Elliott decided to take a position with the Northern Pacific Railroad in Chicago, and Peltier tried out with a team in Springfield, Massachusetts. He later decided to return to Minnesota but failed to make the new roster.

Clearly these were critical losses. Elliott had been with the team four years and had played every game with the exception of part of one. His play was a key factor in the team's past success. Both Abel and Breen were pillars on defense and provided an offensive element as well. Quesnelle had been the club's goal-scoring leader on a low-scoring team, and Peltier performed as an effective, but replaceable, defensive forward. Fitzgerald had key holes to fill if the squad was to build on the prior season's second-half resurgence.

The breakup of the USAHA meant there were players available for CAHA teams, and one of those was Fort Pitt goaltender Joe Miller. Miller would find a home in St. Paul and later have an NHL career that included brief service on the New York Rangers 1927–28 Stanley Cup–winning team. Gus Wilkie, a forward who was involved in the Tony Conroy incident of the previous season, joined from the disbanded Cleveland team, and new imports Syl Acaster, Bonar Larose, and Don Cameron would try to provide some scoring punch up front. But the man most counted on to do that was George Clark, now fully cleared to play in the United States. Clark, producing as he had in his previous time in St. Paul, would go a long way toward solving some of Fitzgerald's problems. If the AC's would have trouble on defense with the loss of Abel, Breen, and Elliott, then perhaps Clark could score enough to make up for a potentially weaker back line.

Fitzgerald planned on using Goheen and George Conroy on defense, with George Nichols slated for duty as a third defenseman. Up front, the coach projected a first line of Tony Conroy, Acaster, and Garrett, with Clark, Cameron, Larose, and Naismith available for a second line. Of all the newcomers, Acaster was viewed as the best, as indicated in the *St. Paul Pioneer Press*, December 5, 1925:

> Those who have seen the Saints practice . . . are unanimous in singing the praises of [Syl] Acaster, the little center ice flash from Regina.
>
> Never in the last few years, has St. Paul gone into another realm for a better looking worker than Ake [Acaster]. His greatest asset is his trickiness in front of the net . . . and his scoring achievements . . . last year for the Canadian Cup . . . had the hockey-hardened fans of Eastern Canada wildly enthusiastic. Lou Marsh, the Toronto referee and hockey critic, proclaimed Acaster the smoothest working amateur of the year.

As soon as ice was available at the Hippodrome, practice was shifted there where the bigger ice surface was viewed as advantageous in getting the players ready for the coming season. Fitzgerald conducted practice there until the team departed for the opening series in Winnipeg on December 5 and 7. The month's schedule would take St. Paul to Duluth on December 17 and 18 and back to the Twin Cities for a home and away set with Minneapolis on December 21 and 22, before Eveleth-Hibbing arrived on December 29 and 30. On the day of the opener, the *Pioneer Press*, December 5, 1925, provided this bit of analysis:

> Never has a St. Paul hockey team started a season with prospects brighter in some respects and more uncertain in others . . . There is not a shadow of a doubt that the

St. Paul forwards will outskate any combination in the league . . . stickhandling, backchecking and shooting ability is included with the speed and the ingredients means sensational offensive hockey . . . Fitzgerald has answered criticism directed at his alleged weak defense . . . there would be no more trouble . . . landing a defense man than a forward . . . it has not been done . . . because the St. Paul director cares to take a chance with Goheen . . . and George Nichols . . . together with George Conroy as a fast-going spare.

The actual pairing would be Goheen and George Conroy, and they would earn the praises of the *Winnipeg Evening Tribune,* December 7, 1925: "Bolstered up by a strong defense that seemed to know what it was doing every time it was attacked, the St. Paul Hockey Club . . . scored a 2–1 victory over the local Maroons." Syl Acaster made those who had projected great things for him feel good when he got the game's first goal just after the midpoint of the first period. Acaster had scored against the soon-to-be-great Charlie Gardiner, who had come to Winnipeg from Selkirk, where the AC's had faced him a year earlier in a preseason game. St. Paul had not played any games before the opener and hardly looked like they needed any. After the home team tied the score early in the second period, Goheen once again proved he could still get it done from any position. The *Winnipeg Evening Tribune,* December 7, 1925, paid a Canadian tribute to the great American star:

He was the outstanding player of the game, and his sensational dashes up the ice were always dangerous as long as he had the puck. The highlight of the evening came from this player, who scored a beautiful goal after a zig-zag rush the length of the rink.

It was the game winner, as Miller turned aside twenty-eight shots and got good protec-

tion from Goheen and George Conroy. Despite the rule against close defensive play, that is exactly what St. Paul did once they had the lead—but apparently not so close as to be penalized. In the practice before the game, Gus Wilkie and George Nichols collided and the latter lost three teeth—keeping him out of the opener. Some series were played back to back, but others would have a day of rest in between. Such was the case with the Winnipeg games, and it was enough time to allow Nichols to make his debut in the second contest. In a penalty-filled affair, the score of the previous game was reversed, and the AC's lost 2–1 as Gus Wilkie got the only goal for the AC's in the middle period. The penalty parade was so extensive in the first period that referee A. B. Cook threatened the players with five-minute calls if things didn't calm down in the second period. They did calm down, but George Conroy still managed to collect seventeen penalty minutes (of two, five, and ten minutes) on the night.

The injuries to Wilkie and Nichols had limited their effectiveness, and the same could be said of Bonar Larose, who had a hip problem. Joe Miller had not come out of the series unscathed, taking a cut after a scramble in front of his net. But these were minor matters compared to the potential loss of Frank Goheen to the pros. The Toronto St. Pats, forerunners to today's Maple Leafs, had made him an attractive offer, as reported in the *Pioneer Press,* December 11, 1925:

The St. Pats club offered Goheen a two-year contract at a reported salary of $3,500 a season but he refused point blank. A boost of $500 in the offer caused Goheen to consider the proposition but he has a good position here and does not care to leave it.

Goheen's decision to remain with the Saints has caused Eddie Fitzgerald to rest easily again. Fitzgerald had a long talk with the star and Goheen assured him that he would stay with the Saints until his playing days are over.

It would appear to be less than coincidental that two days later Goheen was named captain for the third time in his career.

That major problem was solved, and all the other aches and pains were under control—but just before the team got ready to head to Duluth another problem arose. George Clark came up with a mystery illness that put him in the hospital and out of the next series. Duluth had been strengthened by the addition of former Cleveland players Joe Debernardi and "Moose" Jamieson. Also joining from Cleveland was goalie Vern Turner because Tiny Thompson had defected to Minneapolis. Although Thompson was the better goaltender, the acquisition of the other two made Duluth a contender for first-place honors. The AC's would feel Clark's loss in the Zenith City. According to the *Pioneer Press*, December 18, 1925:

> To the Saints' credit, without offering an alibi, Acaster and La Rose [Larose] were not in the best of condition, and minus Clark in center ice there was not the cohesion there will be later.
>
> The Saints had almost an even edge in the play until the third period, when . . . Jamieson . . . poked in two scores in thirty seconds.

Jamieson and Lewis had notched first- and second-period goals to provide a 2–0 lead so that the third-period barrage was more than enough for a 4–0 shutout win. The hosts fired thirty-nine shots on Miller while St. Paul could get only twenty-four on Turner, somewhat disputing the newspaper report of "almost an even edge" in play.

It was far closer in game two when Duluth completed a sweep after Dunfield's shot deflected off of Goheen's glove past Miller late in the second period. That single goal was good enough for the win, and although Turner did not have Thompson's reputation, he did have his second shutout in a row. Fitzgerald had done

some shifting with his two lines, and the result was a much better effort than the night before.

## Home Opener

"Tiny" Thompson of Minneapolis may have been the best goalie in the league, but he was off his game when St. Paul broke out of the scoring drought to put more pucks in the net in one night than they had in the previous four. The 4–0 victory was a great way to open at home against the league-leading club that had three former teammates in the lineup as well as another former Cleveland player, Mickey McQuire, All-Star defenseman "Ching" Johnson, and the top goaltender.

Slightly more than sixty thousand fans had come to the Hippodrome for the twenty home games in 1924–25, and it was hoped that with a good year that number or more might return. Although the 1–3 season start was a downer, the second Duluth game could have gone St. Paul's way and now, followed by the home opening victory, perhaps things were looking up. The locals' goals against Minneapolis had come two each in the last two frames as Garrett, Acaster, Naismith, and Goheen found the range.

The better play carried over to the next night when action shifted to the arena in Minneapolis, causing the *Pioneer Press*, December 23, 1925, to comment:

> Where many expected the St. Paul form of Monday to be a flash in the pan, the Saints kept up the same fire and dash . . . and had an edge on their opponents throughout most of the game . . . This St. Paul hockey team is out for a title and the insinuations that it is not up to standard have fired the players with a vim that bodes ill for the other teams during the remainder of the schedule.

Minneapolis opened the scoring in the second period, but Tony Conroy tied the game with eleven seconds left in the session when George Clark set him up to beat Thompson cleanly. The game went into overtime, and the AC's had their best chance when George Conroy got in close, only to have Abel muscle him off the puck. It would end at 1–1, but the result was good enough to allow the team to share third place with Eveleth-Hibbing and Duluth before the league broke for Christmas.

Fitzgerald held a practice the day after the holiday as the team nursed the usual collection of bumps and bruises that players soldier through while not missing any games. Goheen had taken a slash to his cheek from Abel's stick, Acaster and Larose had lingering hip bruises, Wilkie had a cut on his forehead, Naismith had a leg problem, and Conroy had come down with a severe cold, which excused him from practice. None of these were of any great concern, and there was a sense of optimism expressed by the *Pioneer Press,* December 27, 1925:

> There is a feeling that the Saints, flushed with confidence and back on their feet again, after a series with Minneapolis that proved they had gameness, speed and all-around ability, will filter through the Rangers to score more than the Eveleth-Hibbing Arrowheads will find the net behind Joe Miller.

If only it could have happened. Things started well enough when, after a scoreless first period, Naismith scored off of Acaster's rebound and Goheen's pass to give that most comfortable of hockey leads, 2–0 at the end of two sessions. But within the first minute of the last period, Vic DesJardins, who always seemed to have St. Paul's number, got Eveleth's first goal, to be quickly followed by the tying marker from Hill. Then, with only six minutes to play, "Nobby" Clark got the go-ahead goal, DesJardins the clincher, and Clark the insurance goal. A five-goal period, something quite rare then and not that common today, had dealt a depressing blow

to the team's confidence that would be felt over the next four games.

Things were no better a day later when Pat Byrne shut out the AC's as his teammates got first- and third-period goals. The home team actually had the better of the play for the first two periods, holding a 21–14 edge in shots. Eveleth took control in the last period, but they couldn't breathe easy until the sixteen-minute mark when Lindsey scored for them with Wilkie in the penalty box.

The new year opened with a home and home series with Minneapolis on the first two days of January. The team would then go to Hibbing for January 5 and 6 before returning to host Duluth on January 8 and 9. There would then be a ten-day break before Canadian Soo arrived for games on January 19 and 22, to be followed by Winnipeg on January 26 and 28. The month would close with another Minneapolis series on January 30 and February 2, but both were home games.

The December pre-Christmas series with their Twin Cities neighbors had gone well for St. Paul, but the slide would continue. The New Year's night game in the arena was an even closer affair than the last Eveleth-Hibbing game, but the result would be no better. Minneapolis's second-period goal was all that was needed for victory, but the third-period altercation between Goheen and former teammate Breen was what would make news the next day. The *Pioneer Press,* January 2, 1926, provided the story:

> There is not the best of feeling between the former Saints and the present ones, and more than once body checking exceeded its normal limit as the game wore on … Goheen came down with two mates and started to skate through the defense. He lifted his stick and Breen caught it in the face. Breen retaliated with a wicked club, cutting Goheen's eye, and then Abel tried to get some licks with Goheen lying on the ice. Emmy Garrett … tried to engage Taffy without his stick.

Taffy shoved Emmy back but the slender Saint had halted proceedings until the other players and Grenner [referee] came rushing up to call each other uncomplimentary things . . . Goheen and Breen drew penalties for the rest of the game.

The ice conditions were poor for the game, despite the artificial plant in the new arena, and it cost Garrett a good opportunity. St. Paul had other near misses by Acaster and Wilkie, but Thompson was there to keep his shutout.

The injury to Goheen's eye kept him out of the rematch back at the Hippodrome, and both he and Tony Conroy, whose cold had gotten the best of him, watched the game in street clothes. Conroy had been out since the second Eveleth game, and the team chose not to find an additional player to replace him. Goheen's place on defense was taken by George Nichols though no one could come close to filling in for the Moose. Considering the problems facing the squad, they played their rivals close, but goals by the two now-villainous former AC'ers, Breen and Abel, gave the visitors the 2–1 win. Trailing 2–0 late in the second period, Naismith put St. Paul back in the game when he slid a backhander behind Thompson after beating three defenders. The home team had the better chances in the last period but could draw no closer.

Both Goheen and Conroy would be back in the lineup for the next series with Eveleth-Hibbing as controversy swirled around forward Bonar Larose. Like Smith, Larose was a former Fort Pitt player who had found a place to play in St. Paul but not as much as he would have liked. He let his displeasure be known, and Fitzgerald responded in the *St. Paul Daily News*, January 5, 1926: "I start my men with the strength they show in the practice drills and Larose failed to show me enough to convince me that he would do as a starter in the lineup." Larose would not only not start—he was off the team.

The Eveleth-Hibbing entry in the CAHA split its home games between the two Iron

Range cities, and this series would be played in Hibbing. The AC's would have the honor of helping dedicate the new Hibbing Arena before twenty-five hundred fans from across the Range. They would be treated to some typical Goheen rushes from a man playing with a badly bruised eye, but the visitor's first goal would go to Acaster. That lead held until Rodden prevented what looked like a sure victory by scoring thirteen seconds from the end. The crowd would go home happy when Rodden finished the job by getting the winner in overtime. It was a bitter loss and extended St. Paul's losing streak to four in a row. Things would finally turn around in game two, thanks to Emmy Garrett. The former captain had never been able to regain his goal-scoring prowess of 1921–22, but this night would see some of that old magic return. After the home team scored first in the second period, Garrett came up with two unassisted goals to give the AC's the lead. George Conroy made the final 3–1 when he took Clark's pass and put it past Byrne.

## Home to Some Wins

Fitzgerald must have felt somewhat relieved on the way home. The team had played well enough to have won both games. They were in fifth place, but the club finally seemed to have hit its stride, to use a common contemporary phrase. If they could at least split the coming series with Duluth, they could then enjoy a ten-day-off period to nurse various injuries before Canadian Soo arrived. The Soo had definitely not hit their stride, and two victories over them might put St. Paul back into the play-off hunt.

Goheen had taken a cut to the forehead from Eveleth's Ade Johnson to go along with his previous eye injury, and George Conroy needed some stitches in his leg. Neither situation interfered with their taking the ice against their fourth-place neighbors. The game would mark the debut of Chet Harris, a former Boston Hockey Club player who had been most recently playing in New York as the replacement for Bonar Larose.

It would be a game of "seconds" for the AC's as Gus Wilkie and Tony Conroy got their second goals of the season and Joe Miller got his second shutout. The goals came in the second and third periods, and it was in the latter that Fitzgerald put Harris out in time to effectively block Seaborn's shot. Miller had made twenty-five saves, and the next night he would come up with number thirty-one, but the second game ended in a 1–1 tie. Down by a goal late in the game, Goheen tied it up early in the third frame and Garrett thought he had it won in overtime, but his goal was disallowed when the referee ruled that the puck had entered the net from the side.

Fitzgerald took advantage of the break before the Canadian Soo series to pick up another forward, Steve Rice, formerly of the Toronto Aura Lees, to add some physical presence up front, as reported in the *Pioneer Press*, January 18, 1926:

> The present array of things may call for him at center, with Naismith at left wing and Acaster at right wing . . . light as they are and susceptible to some bumping . . . [they] will show to better advantage flanking a bruising player of the Rice type.
>
> If this arrangement is in effect, Tony Conroy, George Clark and Emmy Garrett will rank as another forward string . . . with Harris also included along with Gus Wilkie . . . The Saints . . . are better fixed with forwards than they have been at any time this year and with Wilkie able to fill a defensive post . . . players and fans now believe the time to rise in the standings has come.

The Soo games would be played on a Tuesday/Friday schedule, with the Canadian entry taking on Minneapolis on a Monday/Thursday basis. Not only was St. Paul rested, but the players would get the visitors a day after they had played a game. That game would be the latest in a season that had produced to date ten losses and two ties for the Soo despite the presence of a number of future NHL players. Most notable among these was forward Bill Phillips, who would play for the Stanley Cup–winning Montreal Maroons before the season was over. On this night they would push the AC's to the limit, rallying from a 3–1 deficit to tie the game with nine minutes left to play. Tony Conroy would get the game winner and second goal of the contest five minutes from the end, when he put in brother George's rebound. Acaster and Clark, who would finally break his goal-scoring drought, had the other goals.

Things were a bit easier three nights later. After George Clark got his second of the year, the team produced a four-goal middle period, with Garrett getting two and Goheen and Clark getting one each, again—bombarding Soo goalie "Flat" Walsh. Miller would lose his shutout before the end of the period when St. Paul native Earl Willey got the visitors' only goal. Willey had just been signed by the Soo and had played briefly for the AC's the previous season. Fitzgerald could take pleasure in Garrett's and Clark's rediscovered scoring touches and Rice's successful insertion into the lineup. The latter move allowed Wilkie to spell George Conroy on defense.

Things could be expected to be somewhat tougher against the league-leading Winnipeg Maroons, and they were, but the results were just as good as against Canadian Soo and far more satisfying. St. Paul held the visitors to only thirteen shots on goal, and Miller did not let one by him while Charlie Gardiner handled thirty-three attempts, but two of those found the back of the net. Naismith's first-period tally was all that was really needed, but Garrett continued on a tear with his team-leading sixth goal in the second frame. The *Pioneer Press*, January 26, 1926, described the game as "as clear cut a victory as ever graced any ice. The inspired St. Paul team beat the Maroons at their favorite game—speed." Two nights later they would prove that the effort was no fluke with another inspired effort, only this time Miller allowed one goal while turning aside eighteen shots. Once again the stepped-up attack of the AC's produced a similar shot total to that of the first game, thirty-five. Two would elude Gardiner, and they were a first-period effort by Rice, his first with the team, and another by Clark, who like Garrett had finally found the range. It had been a bruising, physical game, with the visitors absorbing most of the punishment. Naismith had taken a two-inch cut to the head in the second period but came back to play in the third.

The sweep, which now put the St. Paul winning streak at four, finally got the team to the .500 mark at 8–8–2, but it did not gain them any ground in the standings. They were still in fifth place, but Minneapolis moved ahead of Winnipeg into first place as a result of the Winnipeg losses in St. Paul. Eveleth-Hibbing was third, Duluth fourth, and Canadian Soo sixth. The AC's would have to continue to win to make the play-offs and hope that teams above them would falter.

Winnipeg was new to the large Hippodrome ice surface, and that no doubt contributed to their lack of success. The "A Matter of Opinion" column in the *Pioneer Press*, January 30, 1926, reflected their frustrations:

> "Those skating fools," was the appellation given the St. Paul hockey players by their rivals from Winnipeg ... There is no team that can ... skate with the Saints and keep it up at top speed through an entire game ... on the Hippodrome rink, where one covers a considerable distance in sprinting from one end to the other ... The St. Paul team has been selected and trained to play the game best suited to its home rink and it happens that that expansive surface can best be played by hard and continuous skating.

As good as the team's showing in defeating Winnipeg, their play was somewhat less than that against Minneapolis. Though hampered by slow ice, which hindered the skating skills that the *Pioneer Press* had lauded them for, the AC's nonetheless pressed the attack in the first two periods without success. The visitors then got the better of the play in the last period but couldn't get the win until Bill Boyd beat Miller with two minutes to go in the overtime period. St. Paul was without Goheen for most of the overtime when he got a five-minute penalty for throwing his stick. This game was a winnable game lost, but the home team was outclassed in game two. Minneapolis got two first-period goals, added two more in the third, and won handily 4–0. Once in the lead, the visitors were content to let the AC's come at them, which they did in the second period, but to no avail.

## Slip-Sliding Again

As the team readied for its second trip to the Iron Range, the *Pioneer Press*, February 4, 1926, would observe:

> Somewhat disheartened by the two reverses at the hands of the Millers, the team realizes that it must get started against the Rangers ... The sudden reversal of form in the games with the Millers was surprising to St. Paul fans who watched the Saints make fairly light work of the Canadian Soo and Winnipeg in the previous series.

St. Paul would open at Eveleth on February 4 and then shift to Hibbing for the second contest against the dual-city team. The schedule then called for a return home against Duluth on February 8 and 9 before a trip to Canadian Soo for games on February 11 and 12. Prior to resuming action at the Hippodrome on February 15 and 16, also against Canadian Soo, the squad would play their only non-league game of the year in Marquette, Michigan, against the senior Indians. February would close out against Winnipeg on February 23 and 26.

The goal-scoring drought for the AC's that had started with the last period of the Winnipeg game continued on the Range. Eveleth had also lost their last two games, and there were rumors circulating that Eddie Rodden might soon go pro. That did happen the following season, but the 5-feet 7-inch center would content himself in this game with the game winner at 16:20 of the second period. Five seconds later, "Nobby" Clark made it 2–0, which was all that the home team would need. The AC's had been outshot 42–27, but both Garrett and George Conroy had great opportunities, the latter missing an open net.

The team had now gone seven periods—140 minutes—without a goal, and some veterans probably recalled the play-off round-robin of 1923–24, when goals were even scarcer. Another 37:30 would go by in the next game before Tony Conroy scored a shorthanded goal to tie things at 1–1. The home team went ahead in the third session, but Goheen got that one right back a minute and a half later from a scramble in front of Byrne. The overtime settled nothing, and the AC's had to be content with a point. Minneapolis had now pulled out to a commanding first-place lead that left four of the five other teams with a realistic shot only at the second and third play-off positions. With the team still in fifth place and fourth-place Duluth the next opponent, an optimist might have suggested that with a sweep of that set and the two Canadian Soo series, the AC's could find themselves in third place. Indeed, the optimistic Fitzgerald told the *Pioneer Press,* February 7, 1926:

> There you are. If things work out that way the Saints will stand even with any other team in the race for third place and the team they most likely have to beat, the Rangers [Eveleth-Hibbing] and Winnipeg will still be on the schedule for home and home series which makes it even.

In the second Eveleth game the coach moved Goheen from defense to center between Naismith and Acaster. The other line had Steve Rice centering Tony Conroy and Garrett. Wilkie fell back to take Goheen's defensive post alongside George Conroy. The new combinations produced two long-overdue goals, but Goheen, ever the workhorse, stayed on to play defense even when his line was off the ice.

The new lines worked well in the first Duluth game as the locals carried a two-goal lead well into the third period on soft and sticky ice that made passing difficult. The *Pioneer Press,* February 9, 1926, suggested that the AC's were making a last stand in this game, as far as reaching the play-offs, and sarcastically added: "Apparently they took this last stand business too seriously for at the last they were doing precisely that—standing, while Duluth poked in two goals in 60 seconds." The goals came with 3:15 left to play and allowed an attainable and essential victory to get away as the overtime was scoreless.

Garrett and George Conroy got the St. Paul goals. Neither would figure in the next night's scoring as Goheen counted both, the second tying the game early in the last period. His shot struck the net with such force that it went through and rested against the boards. The visitors protested, but the referee upheld the goal judge. It hardly mattered, as four minutes later Duluth scored the winning marker to take the game 3–2.

The team had now gone 0–4–2 in its last six games, and things would get no better in western Ontario as the lowly Soo got only their third win of the year in game one. George Conroy had drawn the AC's even at 1–1 with his early third-period goal, but Bill Phillips got the game winner on a pass from Sammy Koko with two minutes to go. The slump finally came to an end the next night when the two Georges, Conroy, and Clark, scored three goals among them to get the 3–2 win in a game played on slow ice. Penalties were handed out generously, and St.

Paul was called for thirteen of the nineteen infractions—both Wilkie and Goheen were involved in fighting incidents. The game in Marquette, while producing an easy 6–1 victory, was hardly satisfying. The road to the play-offs outlined in the *Pioneer Press* unfortunately wasn't being followed.

The team arrived back in St. Paul no further along in advancing to the postseason than when they had left. They had not improved beyond fifth place, with the third and last play-off spot looking quite remote. But there were still games on the schedule, and as events played out, the team would rally to make a stirring run at what seemed a long shot at the play-offs. Their recent win against their Canadian hosts was first in line when the locals finally found a way to score some goals.

Canadian Soo arrived in Minnesota minus two key players, including Bill Phillips. Considering how poorly the Soo had played with them, their absence hardly mattered. The last Soo game had been replete with penalties, but this one had only two, and it had five AC goals. Tony Conroy scored in the first period, Clark and Goheen in the second, and George Conroy and Chet Harris closed things out in the last frame. It was Harris's first goal of the year and Miller's fourth shutout.

If that was enjoyable, game two would be almost its equal with the locals skating to a 6–2 triumph, largely on the basis of a five-goal second-period explosion. With the game tied at 1–1 after the first period— Tony Conroy getting the St. Paul goal—Clark opened the scoring at the seven-minute mark by finishing off a rink-length dash. George Conroy would then score three goals, although not the coveted three-consecutive-tallies so treasured by present-day observers. That wouldn't happen because the Soo squeezed in their second goal. Acaster would wrap it up for the home team with a second to go in the period. Like the first game, there were only two penalties, both to the home team.

Winnipeg arrived in the Twin Cities, having

fallen behind Duluth in the struggle for third place in which, amazingly, St. Paul was still a player. The *Pioneer Press,* February 21, 1926, assessed the situation:

> As matters stand now Winnipeg is a strong candidate for third place[;] it can only remain so by playing better hockey in the Twin Cities than it did on the first trip. At that time it played four games and lost that many. If it does the same again St. Paul will find itself well ahead of the Maroons and not far behind the Hornets [Duluth].
>
> The Maroons . . . have a distinct advantage in the schedule which enables them to finish at home.

Winnipeg did not play better hockey than they did the first time, repeating their earlier dismal trip, while the AC's continued to play some of their best hockey of the season. Despite the sweep over Canadian Soo, one of the smallest crowds of the season came out to the Hippodrome for the first game. Another great second period would produce three goals from Clark, Naismith, and Rice. The visitors could collect only one in the third period. The *Pioneer Press,* which had previously dwelt on St. Paul's skating ability, reported with perceptible pleasure on February 24, 1926:

> The Saints choose the strategy of hard skating as best suited to prevail against their travel worn opponents and hard skating won the day . . . From first to last they skated until the Maroons, one by one, wilted under the strain and played through the final period with laborious and lagging strokes.

Three days later, after losing again in Minneapolis, the Canadian visitors were back to, no doubt, play again "with laborious and lagging strokes." Only this time the results were far worse than the first game. The normally goal-deprived AC's would score a season-high nine goals for their most one-sided victory of the season and a resulting one-notch climb in the standings. The home team pressed the attack right from the start—in game one they had waited a period, but the initial frame in this game produced three goals. This was followed by two in the second and four in the third, while Winnipeg could counter with only two in the middle period. Nearly everyone shared in the goal wealth. Garrett had two and Goheen had two. Acaster, Clark, Conroy, Naismith, and Rice had one apiece.

### Renewed Hope

March would bring Eveleth-Hibbing in for the last home series on March 1 and 2, and then the team would end the season on the road with series in Winnipeg on March 4 and 6, Minneapolis on March 15 and 16, and Duluth on March 19 and 20. The *Pioneer Press*, March 1, 1926, laid out how the AC's might see postseason action:

> St. Paul is now three points below Eveleth-Hibbing [third] and four points below the Duluth Hornets [second]. Defeat of the Rangers [Eveleth-Hibbing] would give the Saints a one point advantage over that team, and a Maroon victory over Duluth at the same time would elevate the Saints to a position of equality with that club.

There was renewed concern about ice conditions for the coming series because of a late-winter thaw, so Fitzgerald held no practices—at the time this was presented as a way to avoid "staleness." The coach had no worries in that regard as the adrenaline rush from the Winnipeg games carried over against Eveleth. Steve Rice had yet to exhibit any scoring touch since joining the team in January, but he would finally show an offensive flair in game one with two third-period goals. While there was ample offensive action in the first two periods, neither

team would connect until Goheen's tally late in the second stanza. It was still anyone's game until 9:20 when Rice punched in George Conroy's rebound and then repeated the same action twenty seconds later. Clark made it 4–0 with a late goal.

George Conroy would get some recognition the next night when he set up Garrett for what would be the game's only goal in the middle of the first period. After reviewing earlier concerns about his ability to play adequate defense, the *Pioneer Press*, March 3, 1926, gave him a ringing endorsement:

> It remained for the final series . . . for him to reach his full development. No longer a liability, he was star and savior of the game both offensively and defensively and in another way too, for his fiery spirit held the team to its task when there was good reason for faltering under the dizzy pace in that smoke laden air.

Such extensive tributes in game stories of this period are relatively rare, though, as might be expected, Goheen was virtually always lauded.

The Eveleth wins put the St. Paul winning streak at seven and vaulted them into the coveted third and last play-off spot. Now they needed some success on the road to stay there and extend the season. The prognosis for that was not good—the squad earlier had gone only 3–7–2 away from the Hippodrome, which included a split at Canadian Soo, where most teams were able to sweep.

But the first twelve minutes of game one in Winnipeg gave every indication that the team's road worries were behind them. Goheen set up Tony Conroy at 3:55 when, with the man advantage, he fed him from behind the cage for a 1–0 lead. Close to four minutes later, "the big train of the Saints," as the *Pioneer Press*, March 5, 1926, described Goheen, stickhandled his way from center ice to beat Gardiner. Tony Conroy got his second goal just before the twelve-minute mark when he converted Garrett's pass. Two–0 is always regarded as hockey's worst lead, but in this case 3–0 would prove to be even worse.

Murray Murdoch, who would go on to a fine career with the New York Rangers and then as coach at Yale University, got Winnipeg's first goal twenty seconds before the end of the period. He would get one of two goals in the second, tying the game and forcing overtime. In the middle session Goheen collided with Bill Borland and was knocked unconscious and carried from the ice. He returned in the third period "and got a fine hand from the crowd when he skated on to take his place," according to the *Winnipeg Evening Tribune*, March 5, 1926. It was great that "Moose" was back, but his presence couldn't prevent the home team from winning in overtime with only three seconds to go.

There would be more overtime two days later when the series resumed, but Winnipeg again came out on top and took over possession of third place. Trailing 1–0 after two periods, St. Paul would send the game into overtime when Clark scored with a shot deflected off defenseman Jim Hughes's skate went into the net. That would be the high-water mark for the visitors—Winnipeg collected two overtime goals to complete the sweep. The AC's had certainly played well enough to win both games, but fate ruled otherwise. Now it was back to Minnesota to see if a week of rest could help them make the play-offs by having success in their closing series against Minneapolis and Duluth.

Goheen and Garrett were in particular need of rest and recuperation after the intensity of the games in Manitoba. With that in mind, Fitzgerald conducted light workouts at the Hippodrome, and the *Pioneer Press*, March 15, 1926, assessed their chances:

Winnipeg is the team the Saints must
beat out for third position, and Winnipeg,
which has only two games to play, can only
be tied if the Saints win their remaining
four games . . . Should the Maroons drop

one game to the Soo, then the Saints could
take third place by winning four games
and could tie by winning three.

It didn't happen. The best St. Paul could do was go 0–2–2 against Minneapolis in the first series. What did happen, however, was a renewal of the unpleasantness that had erupted between Goheen and Breen back in January. The teams were tied 1–1 six minutes into the third period when Minneapolis center Vic Ripley boarded Goheen. Lying on the ice, the AC star swung his stick at Ripley, who was also prone, hitting him in the shins. This caused Breen to launch himself on Goheen, landing on his throat and chest and beginning to punch his former teammate. Breen was joined by another Minneapolis player who attacked the Moose's leg and a fan who jumped over the boards to assist him.

As players from both teams and the police attempted to separate the combatants, another fist flew out of somewhere at Goheen, and he attempted to get at the perpetrator while being restrained. This happened again before the St. Paul players finally got to their locker room. Things were still not over, as reported by the *Pioneer Press*, March 16, 1926:

More than 200 Minneapolis fans jammed
the runway in front of the St. Paul dressing
room, the noisy ones threatening harm to
the entire St. Paul club. They were cooled
by the police and ordered back into the
rink. After about 10 minutes, the game was
resumed with Goheen and Denny Breen
barred for the night.

Garrett had scored the AC goal, and neither team would get another in what was left of the third period and in the overtime. There would be a second tie the next night, and Garrett would connect again to send the 3–3 game into overtime, only to have an apparent victory taken away from them. Rice, who along with Tony Conroy had scored the earlier goals, beat

Thompson in the extra session, only to have the Minneapolis goaltender swipe the puck out of the net before the goal judge could rule. It was the ultimate bad break made doubly painful as the home team's third goal was scored when the puck bounced off Goheen's knee and past Miller.

What little play-off hope remained was dashed as the AC's lost game one in Duluth 1–0 when Mike Goodman scored from Peltier late in the first period. Yes, this was the same Wilfred Peltier who had come from Duluth via Winnipeg to play two years in St. Paul before returning to his old team. Miller played quite well in turning aside forty-one shots, while the visitors could put only twenty on Vern Turner.

Miller would not play well at all in the season's finale, giving up a season-high seven goals in the first two periods, as play-off-bound Duluth won 7–1. George Nichols would get his only goal of the year in the second period. Fitzgerald, perhaps anticipating that the play-off hunt would be resolved before the last game, had brought three reserve players along on the trip. They were Don Cameron, Elwyn "Doc" Romnes, and O'Halloran. Cameron had played in two games and would see action in the last, as the coach let Goheen and Tony Conroy have the night off. Romnes, who had played in the Marquette game, and O'Halloran did not play, but Romnes, a White Bear Lake native, went on to a significant hockey career. Ultimately playing for the Chicago Blackhawks, he won the Lady Byng Trophy in 1935–36 and was in the Hawks' lineup when they won the Stanley Cup in 1937–38. After his playing days were over, he coached minor league professional hockey and was John Mariucci's immediate predecessor at the University of Minnesota. He was elected to the United States Hockey Hall of Fame in 1973.

St. Paul's up-and-down season ended with them in fourth place, three points behind third-place Winnipeg. In the ensuing play-offs, second-place Duluth defeated Winnipeg two games to one, and first-place Minneapolis swept Duluth

three games to none in the all-Minnesota finals. The CAHA made plans for another season, but it never took place. The amateur era was over, its demise accurately predicted in the *Pioneer Press* on February 19, 1926:

> The growth of professional hockey in the East and the constant threat of raids by that league [NHL] upon the playing talent here have made it necessary for the Central Association to enter some agreement whereby it can protect itself against the danger of having its teams disrupted in midseason. The only form the agreement can take is a joining of forces in the professional game.

That "professional game" proved to be the minor league American Hockey Association (AHA), which began play in December 1926, with St. Paul as well as CAHA holdovers Duluth, Minneapolis, and Winnipeg as members. They would be joined by Chicago and Detroit. The core of the last AC squad would simply move over to the new pro team, which was named, not surprisingly, the "Saints." St. Paul would be a member of the AHA for most years until 1942, when the league ceased operations because of World War II. The team had its greatest success in 1939–40, when, after finishing second in the regular season, it won the play-off title by defeating Omaha three games to one.

Another St. Paul team playing in the first amateur and then professional Central Hockey League (CHL) in the early 1930s enjoyed a bit of success when it defeated the St. Louis Flyers three games to none in 1935. That St. Paul team, also the Saints, had won the CHL title and played off against the AHA champion Flyers for the mythical midwestern professional hockey championship. The next year, after the CHL folded, St. Paul was back in the AHA that they had dropped out of in 1930. A St. Paul team known as the "Greyhounds" played for six months in the 1932–33 AHA season.

The AHA would be resurrected after World War II as the United States Hockey League, and St. Paul would win that title in 1948–49. The league would fold after the 1950–51 season, and the city would not see professional hockey again until the International Hockey League came to St. Paul in 1959. The Saints would win back-to-back Turner Cup titles in 1959–60 and 1960–61, before moving over to the Central Professional Hockey League in 1963–64. The Saints would be the champions in this league the next season.

The first major league hockey since the days of the AC's arrived in 1972 in the form of the World Hockey Association's Minnesota Fighting Saints, who played their games at the new St. Paul Civic Center. The civic center replaced the auditorium, where St. Paul minor league professional teams started playing in January 1932. Major league hockey would survive in St. Paul until January 1977 and not return until October 2000 when the new NHL Minnesota Wild began play at the state-of-the-art Xcel Energy Center.

The teams that represented St. Paul were rostered largely with Canadian players, as has been true since the beginning of pro hockey. Canada, with its larger pool to draw on, has to this day produced the bulk of professional players. However, St. Paul's teams have had noteworthy Minnesota representation. The 1939–40 AHA Saints had state natives Joe Bretto, Virgil Johnson, Hodge Johnson, Sam LoPresti, and Pete Pleban in their lineup. Bob Dill, a former New York Ranger, was on the 1948–49 USHL team, and Paul Johnson played for the 1960–61 IHL entry. The Fighting Saints featured at various times Mike Antonovich, Henry Boucha, Bill Butters, Jack Carlson, Steve Carlson, Keith Christiansen, Mike Curran, Craig Falkman, Gary Gambucci, Paul Holmgren, Bill Klatt, Len Lillyholm, Jack McCartan, Dick Paradise, Frank Sanders, and Pat Westrum. The Minnesota Wild began their first season with Darby Hendrickson and Jim Nielsen on the squad.

Prior to the Fighting Saints' debut, the NHL had come to Minnesota in 1967 when the new Minnesota North Stars began play at the Metropolitan Sports Center in Bloomington. The franchise would reach the Stanley Cup finals in both 1981 and 1991, losing to the New York Islanders and Pittsburgh Penguins, respectively, before moving to Dallas, Texas, in 1993. Minnesota's sons played a role in the twenty-six-year history of the team, with eighteen natives appearing in more than forty games: Henry Boucha, Neal Broten, Bill Butters, Jack Carlson, Jon Casey, Steve Christoff, Chris Dahlquist, Gary Gambucci, Steve Jensen, Trent Klatt, Dave Langevin, Pete LoPresti, Bill Nyrop, Mike Polich, Gary Sargent, Dean Talafous, Tommy Williams, and Tom Younghans.

The major figures of the AC team would spend their remaining days in Minnesota. The great Goheen continued to play through the 1931–32 season while rejecting NHL offers, preferring to remain in his position with the Northern States Power Company.

He was selected in 1950 as Minnesota's greatest hockey player by a panel consisting of Lyle Wright, longtime Minneapolis hockey promoter; Larry Armstrong, former University of Minnesota coach; and Bob Bebe, *Minneapolis Star* hockey writer. In 1952 Goheen received the ultimate honor of being named to the Hockey Hall of Fame in Toronto. On the occasion of the hundredth anniversary of Minnesota's statehood in 1958, Goheen was selected for the Minnesota Sports Hall of Fame, an institution established by what is now the *Minneapolis Star Tribune* newspaper. When the United States Hockey Hall of Fame was opened in 1973, he was an obvious charter enshrinee. He died on November 13, 1979, at the age of eighty-five.

Tony Conroy retired from hockey in January 1928. While playing, he had worked for the City of St. Paul as deputy purchasing agent and continued in that capacity. He later became involved in politics. Elected to the United States Hockey Hall of Fame in 1975, he died on January 11, 1978. He was eighty-three. Conroy's brother George had passed away much earlier at age sixty. A local restaurateur, he owned establishments in St. Paul and Florida.

The man who anchored the defense and was then behind the bench for the AC's, Ed Fitzgerald, "the raw-boned, rough and ready body checker with the big laugh and great capacity for friendship" (*Minneapolis Tribune*, April 21, 1966), died April 20, 1966, at the age of seventy-three. Poignantly, two days previous he had met Tony Conroy on the street and they had made plans for a reunion once Goheen returned from Florida. Cy Weidenborner, who was in the nets in most of St. Paul's early years and backstopped the team to the shared MacNaughton Cup win in 1920, retired to Northome in northern Minnesota to farm for the rest of his life. He died on November 26, 1983, at age eighty-eight. His brother Frank, who did move out of state and had continued his middle-management insurance career in the New York area, passed away on October 22, 1988, in Montclair, New Jersey, at age ninety-two.

Nick Kahler, the high-scoring center of the early St. Paul teams, spent his post-playing days as a referee and organizer of early Minneapolis senior hockey teams. He was also involved in Golden Gloves boxing and as owner/promoter of the Northwest Sports Show, an event that continues to this day. He was inducted into the United States Hockey Hall of Fame in 1980 and died at age ninety-one in Minneapolis on January 8, 1983.

The St. Paul Athletic Club itself, the organization that gave birth to this historic team, passed into history in 1991 when it ceased operations. The club building at 340 Cedar Street was purchased by the University Club, which now uses it as an adjunct to their regular club rooms on Ramsey Street.

*The jersey and skates of Frank "Moose" Goheen, arguably Minnesota's greatest player and only the second American enshrined in the Hockey Hall of Fame in Toronto.*

In the years following the era of major-league amateur hockey in St. Paul, there would be periodic references in the local print media to reunions and old timers' games involving the principals covered in this book. There was even at one time a St. Paul Hockey Hall of Fame, housed in the former Auditorium, where oversized portraits of both Conroys, Fitzgerald, Garrett, Goheen, and Peltier, as well as others, were hung. Only Goheen's is still known to exist; the fates of the rest are unknown. As recounted in the Introduction, the passage of time has caused these halcyon years to be largely forgotten.

It is the goal of this book to rectify that situation, and, accordingly, I think it appropriate to close with a Halsey Hall poem from Stew Thornley's biography of Hall, *Holy Cow! The Life and Times of Halsey Hall*:

*In Review*

Do you recall in days of old
The Moose's charge when nights were cold;
The threat of Stewart's speed and grace,
Where centers failed to match his pace?
The days when Goodman really flashed,
When Conacher and Seaborn clashed,
When Bonney, of the Pittsburgh clan,
Would make a foe an also ran?
When Drury of the speeding skate
Burned icy paths with blist'ring gait;
Fitzgerald, not a pilot then,
Ranked first among the defense men?
The day when Saintly colors flew;
Far flung to breezes for the view
Of teams that ranked far down the line
From where the A. C. used to shine.
When St. Paul ruled as hockey's best
To lead its rivals from the West?
But grieve not that they triumphed then
When there is a chance to start again.

# League Standings and Play-off Results, 1914–1926

## 1914–15 No league competition.

## 1915–16 American Amateur Hockey Association

|              | W | L | T | GF | GA |
|--------------|---|---|---|----|----|
| ST. PAUL     | 8 | 4 | 0 | 39 | 31 |
| American Soo | 8 | 4 | 1 | 50 | 27 |
| Portage Lake | 3 | 7 | 1 | 30 | 47 |
| Calumet      | 3 | 7 | 0 | 27 | 41 |

ST. PAUL defeats American Soo three games to one for the MacNaughton Cup.

## 1916–17 No league competition.

## 1917–18 No competition.

## 1918–19 No league competition.

## 1919–20 American Amateur Hockey Association

|              | W | L  | T | Pct  |
|--------------|---|----|---|------|
| ST. PAUL     | 9 | 3  | 0 | .750 |
| Canadian Soo | 9 | 3  | 0 | .750 |
| American Soo | 5 | 6  | 1 | .450 |
| Portage Lake | 0 | 11 | 1 | .000 |

ST. PAUL and Canadian Soo share the MacNaughton Cup.

## 1920–21 United States Amateur Hockey Association

### Group One

|                                | W | L | T | Pct   |
|--------------------------------|---|---|---|-------|
| Boston Athletic Association (BAA) | 6 | 0 | 0 | 1.000 |
| Shoe Trades Club (Boston)      | 2 | 2 | 0 | .500  |
| Quaker City (Philadelphia)     | 1 | 4 | 0 | .200  |
| St. Nicholas Club (New York)   | 1 | 4 | 0 | .200  |

### Group Two

|          | W | L | T | Pct   |
|----------|---|---|---|-------|
| Cleveland | 8 | 0 | 0 | 1.000 |
| ST. PAUL | 3 | 5 | 0 | .375  |
| Duluth   | 1 | 7 | 0 | .125  |

### Group Three

|              | W  | L  | T | Pct  |
|--------------|----|----|---|------|
| Eveleth      | 14 | 1  | 1 | .875 |
| Canadian Soo | 13 | 3  | 0 | .813 |
| American Soo | 6  | 9  | 1 | .375 |
| Calumet      | 3  | 13 | 0 | .125 |
| Portage Lake | 3  | 13 | 0 | .125 |

### PLAY-OFFS

#### Semifinals

| March 15, 1921 | Cleveland | 4 | Boston    | 2 ovt | Boston    |
|----------------|-----------|---|-----------|-------|-----------|
| March 16, 1921 | Boston    | 3 | Cleveland | 1     | Boston    |
| March 18, 1921 | Boston    | 3 | Cleveland | 2     | Cleveland |
| March 19, 1921 | Cleveland | 3 | Boston    | 0     | Cleveland |

Cleveland wins on total goals 10–8.

#### Finals

| April 1, 1921 | Cleveland | 6 | Eveleth   | 3 | Cleveland  |
|---------------|-----------|---|-----------|---|------------|
| April 2, 1921 | Cleveland | 6 | Eveleth   | 3 | Cleveland  |
| April 6, 1921 | Eveleth   | 2 | Cleveland | 0 | Pittsburgh |
| April 7, 1921 | Eveleth   | 4 | Cleveland | 2 | Pittsburgh |

Cleveland wins Fellowes Cup on total goals 14–12.

---

| **Appendix Key** |       |     |               |
|-----|-------|-----|---------------|
| w   | win   | ga  | goals against |
| l   | loss  | pct | percentage    |
| t   | tie   | pts | points        |
| gf  | goals for | ovt | overtime  |

## 1921–22  United States Amateur Hockey Association

### Group One

|                              | W  | L  | T | Pct  |
|------------------------------|----|----|---|------|
| Westminsters (Boston)        | 6  | 2  | 0 | .750 |
| BAA                          | 5  | 3  | 0 | .625 |
| Pere Marquette (Boston)      | 3  | 4  | 0 | .429 |
| Quaker City (Philadelphia)   | 3  | 4  | 0 | .429 |
| St. Nicholas Club (New York) | 2  | 6  | 0 | .250 |

### Group Two

|           | W | L | T | Pct  |
|-----------|---|---|---|------|
| ST. PAUL  | 8 | 4 | 0 | .667 |
| Cleveland | 7 | 5 | 0 | .583 |
| Pittsburgh| 5 | 7 | 0 | .416 |
| Duluth    | 4 | 8 | 0 | .333 |

### Group Three

|               | W  | L  | T | Pct  |
|---------------|----|----|---|------|
| Canadian Soo* | 13 | 1  | 0 | .929 |
| Eveleth       | 12 | 4  | 0 | .750 |
| American Soo  | 7  | 6  | 0 | .538 |
| Calumet       | 2  | 9  | 0 | .222 |
| Portage Lake  | 0  | 14 | 0 | .000 |

*Ineligible for Fellowes Cup competition

### PLAY-OFFS

#### Semifinals

| March 3, 1922 | ST. PAUL | 3 | Eveleth  | 1     | Eveleth  |
|---------------|----------|---|----------|-------|----------|
| March 4, 1922 | Eveleth  | 4 | ST. PAUL | 2     | Eveleth  |
| March 6, 1922 | ST. PAUL | 0 | Eveleth  | 0 ovt | St. Paul |
| March 7, 1922 | ST. PAUL | 2 | Eveleth  | 1     | St. Paul |
| March 8, 1922 | ST. PAUL | 0 | Eveleth  | 0     | St. Paul |

ST. PAUL wins on total goals 7–6.

#### Finals

| March 11, 1922 | Westminsters | 3 | ST. PAUL     | 0     | St. Paul |
|----------------|--------------|---|--------------|-------|----------|
| March 12, 1922 | Westminsters | 2 | ST. PAUL     | 1     | St. Paul |
| March 17, 1922 | ST. PAUL     | 0 | Westminsters | 0 ovt | Boston   |
| March 18, 1922 | Westminsters | 2 | ST. PAUL     | 0     | Boston   |

Westminsters win Fellowes Cup 3½ games to ½ game.

## 1922–23  United States Amateur Hockey Association

### Eastern Group

|                              | W | L | T | Pct  |
|------------------------------|---|---|---|------|
| BAA                          | 9 | 1 | 0 | .900 |
| New Haven Westminsters       | 6 | 3 | 0 | .666 |
| Boston Hockey Club           | 6 | 4 | 0 | .600 |
| St. Nicholas Club (New York) | 4 | 6 | 0 | .400 |
| Canadian Club (New York)     | 1 | 8 | 0 | .111 |

### Western Group

|            | W  | L  | T | Pct  |
|------------|----|----|---|------|
| ST. PAUL   | 15 | 5  | 0 | .750 |
| Cleveland  | 12 | 8  | 0 | .600 |
| Eveleth    | 11 | 9  | 0 | .550 |
| Pittsburgh | 10 | 10 | 0 | .500 |
| Duluth     | 8  | 12 | 0 | .400 |
| Milwaukee  | 4  | 16 | 0 | .200 |

### PLAY-OFFS

| March 11, 1923 | BAA      | 2 | ST. PAUL | 1 | St. Paul |
|----------------|----------|---|----------|---|----------|
| March 12, 1923 | BAA      | 1 | ST. PAUL | 0 | St. Paul |
| March 22, 1923 | ST. PAUL | 2 | BAA      | 1 | Boston   |
| March 24, 1923 | BAA      | 2 | ST. PAUL | 1 | Boston   |

Boston Athletic Association wins Fellowes Cup three games to one.

## 1923–24  United States Amateur Hockey Association

### Eastern Group

|                              | W | L | T | Pct  |
|------------------------------|---|---|---|------|
| BAA                          | 9 | 3 | 0 | .750 |
| New Haven Westminsters       | 6 | 6 | 0 | .500 |
| Boston Hockey Club           | 6 | 6 | 0 | .500 |
| Maple Athletic Association (Boston) | 3 | 9 | 0 | .250 |

### Western Group

|             | W  | L  | T | Pct  |
|-------------|----|----|---|------|
| Pittsburgh  | 15 | 5  | 0 | .750 |
| ST. PAUL    | 14 | 6  | 0 | .700 |
| Cleveland   | 10 | 10 | 0 | .500 |
| Eveleth     | 9  | 11 | 0 | .450 |
| Duluth      | 6  | 14 | 0 | .300 |
| Minneapolis | 6  | 14 | 0 | .300 |

### PLAY-OFFS

| March 3, 1924  | Cleveland  | 3 | ST. PAUL   | 2 | St. Paul   |
|----------------|------------|---|------------|---|------------|
| March 5, 1924  | ST. PAUL   | 3 | Cleveland  | 0 | St. Paul   |
| March 7, 1924  | Pittsburgh | 1 | ST. PAUL   | 0 | St. Paul   |
| March 8, 1924  | Pittsburgh | 0 | ST. PAUL   | 0 | St. Paul   |
| March 11, 1924 | Cleveland  | 3 | ST. PAUL   | 0 | Cleveland  |
| March 12, 1924 | Cleveland  | 1 | ST. PAUL   | 0 | Cleveland  |
| March 14, 1924 | Pittsburgh | 5 | ST. PAUL   | 0 | Pittsburgh |
| March 15, 1924 | Pittsburgh | 2 | ST. PAUL   | 1 | Pittsburgh |
| March 18, 1924 | Cleveland  | 1 | Pittsburgh | 0 | Pittsburgh |
| March 20, 1924 | Pittsburgh | 6 | Cleveland  | 0 | Pittsburgh |

Pittsburgh and Cleveland tied with five wins. Pittsburgh advances on total goals 8–3.

#### Finals

| March 26, 1924 | Pittsburgh | 3 | BAA        | 2 | Boston     |
|----------------|------------|---|------------|---|------------|
| March 28, 1924 | Pittsburgh | 1 | BAA        | 0 | Boston     |
| March 29, 1924 | BAA        | 3 | Pittsburgh | 1 | Boston     |
| April 2, 1924  | Pittsburgh | 2 | BAA        | 1 | Pittsburgh |
| April 4, 1924  | Pittsburgh | 6 | BAA        | 1 | Pittsburgh |

Pittsburgh wins Fellowes Cup four games to one.

## 1924–25  United States Amateur Hockey Association

### Eastern Group

| | W | L | T | Pts |
|---|---|---|---|---|
| Fort Pitt | 17 | 7 | 0 | 20 |
| BAA | 16 | 6 | 0 | 20 |
| Maple Athletic Association | 7 | 16 | 0 | -18 |
| Boston Hockey Club | 3 | 14 | 0 | -22 |

### Western Group–First Half

| | W | L | T | Pts |
|---|---|---|---|---|
| Pittsburgh | 15 | 3 | 2 | 26 |
| Duluth | 11 | 8 | 1 | 7 |
| Cleveland | 10 | 8 | 2 | 6 |
| Minneapolis | 8 | 10 | 2 | -2 |
| ST. PAUL | 6 | 12 | 2 | -10 |
| Eveleth | 5 | 14 | 1 | -17 |

### Western Group–Second Half

| | W | L | T | Pts |
|---|---|---|---|---|
| Eveleth | 13 | 6 | 1 | 15 |
| Pittsburgh | 10 | 8 | 2 | 6 |
| ST. PAUL | 11 | 9 | 0 | 4 |
| Minneapolis | 8 | 9 | 3 | 1 |
| Cleveland | 8 | 12 | 0 | -8 |
| Duluth | 6 | 12 | 2 | -10 |

### PLAY-OFFS

#### Semifinals

| March 26, 1925 | Pittsburgh | 4 | Eveleth | 0 | Pittsburgh |
|---|---|---|---|---|---|
| March 27, 1925 | Pittsburgh | 3 | Eveleth | 1 | Pittsburgh |
| March 31, 1925 | Pittsburgh | 2 | Eveleth | 1 | Duluth |
| April 1, 1925 | Pittsburgh | 2 | Eveleth | 1 | Duluth |

#### Finals

| April 3, 1925 | Pittsburgh | 2 | Fort Pitt | 1 ovt | Pittsburgh |
|---|---|---|---|---|---|
| April 4, 1925 | Pittsburgh | 3 | Fort Pitt | 1 | Pittsburgh |
| April 7, 1925 | Pittsburgh | 2 | Fort Pitt | 1 ovt | Pittsburgh |
| April 11, 1925 | Pittsburgh | 2 | Fort Pitt | 1 ovt | Pittsburgh |

Pittsburgh wins Fellowes Cup four games to none.

## 1925–26  Central Amateur Hockey Association

| | W | L | T | Pts |
|---|---|---|---|---|
| Minneapolis | 22 | 10 | 6 | 34 |
| Duluth | 18 | 14 | 8 | 14 |
| Winnipeg | 14 | 15 | 9 | 11 |
| ST. PAUL | 15 | 17 | 6 | 4 |
| Eveleth-Hibbing | 15 | 16 | 7 | 1 |
| Canadian Soo | 8 | 20 | 4 | -20 |

### PLAY-OFFS

#### Semifinals

| March 23, 1926 | Duluth | 2 | Winnipeg | 1 | Duluth |
|---|---|---|---|---|---|
| March 25, 1926 | Winnipeg | 4 | Duluth | 3 | Duluth |
| March 27, 1926 | Winnipeg | 3 | Duluth | 3 | Winnipeg |
| March 29, 1926 | Duluth | 0 | Winnipeg | 0 | Winnipeg |
| April 1, 1926 | Duluth | 2 | Winnipeg | 1 | Duluth |

Duluth wins two games to one.

#### Finals

| April 2, 1926 | Minneapolis | 3 | Duluth | 0 | Minneapolis |
|---|---|---|---|---|---|
| April 3, 1926 | Minneapolis | 4 | Duluth | 0 | Minneapolis |
| April 6, 1926 | Minneapolis | 2 | Duluth | 1 | Duluth |

Minneapolis wins three games to none.

# St. Paul Athletic Club Rosters and Scoring Statistics, 1914–1926

## St. Paul Athletic Club Hockey Team 1914–15

| PLAYERS | POS | HOMETOWN | GM | G | A | PTS | PEN |
|---|---|---|---|---|---|---|---|
| Cy Weidenborner | g (2 shutouts) | St. Paul, MN | 11 | 0 | 0 | 0 | 1 |
| Vern Peterson | p | St. Paul, MN | 9 | 4 | 2 | 6 | 0 |
| Ed Fitzgerald | cp | St. Paul, MN | 11 | 1 | 1 | 2 | 0 |
| Nick Kahler, Captain | c | Dollar Bay, MI | 10 | 13 | 3 | 16 | 2 |
| Frank Goheen | r | White Bear Lake, MN | 8 | 6 | 5 | 11 | 1 |
| Tony Conroy | f | St. Paul, MN | 9 | 5 | 4 | 9 | 0 |
| Larry Brennan | r | Pembroke, ON | 6 | 2 | 1 | 3 | 0 |
| George Henderson | r | Fort William, ON | 4 | 1 | 1 | 2 | 0 |
| Oliver Landirault | f | Pembroke, ON | 3 | 1 | 0 | 1 | 0 |
| Jimmy Owens | f | Duluth, MN | 1 | 1 | 0 | 1 | 0 |
| Leo McCourt | cp | Saskatoon, SK | 1 | 1 | 0 | 1 | 0 |
| Chester Stroud | r | Calumet, MI | 1 | 1 | 0 | 1 | 0 |
| John Dellinger | cp | St. Paul, MN | 1 | 1 | 0 | 1 | 0 |
| Roddie Smith | f | Selkirk, MB | 1 | 0 | 0 | 0 | 0 |
| Joe Simpson | cp | Selkirk, MB | 1 | 0 | 0 | 0 | 0 |
| Brownie Romans | c | St. Paul, MN | 1 | 0 | 0 | 0 | 0 |
| Harold Wessel | p | ? MN | 1 | 0 | 0 | 0 | 0 |
| ? Hickey | f | ? MN | 1 | 0 | 0 | 0 | 0 |

**GAMES**

| | | | | | |
|---|---|---|---|---|---|
| January 1, 1915 | Duluth | 8 | St. Paul | 1 | Duluth |
| January 5, 1915 | St. Paul | 5 | Minneapolis ABC | 0 | St. Paul |
| January 11, 1915 | St. Paul | 3 | Portage Lake | 1 | St. Paul |
| January 19, 1915 | St. Paul | 13 | Grand Forks | 0 | St. Paul |
| January 25, 1915 | St. Paul | 2 | Port Arthur | 1 | St. Paul |
| February 1, 1915 | St. Paul | 5 | Fort William | 3 | St. Paul |
| February 8, 1915 | St. Paul | 2 | Duluth | 1 | St. Paul |
| February 15, 1915 | Ottawa Aberdeens | 4 | St. Paul | 1 | St. Paul |
| February 16, 1915 | Ottawa Aberdeens | 6 | St. Paul | 2 | St. Paul |
| February 23, 1915 | Duluth | 11 | St. Paul | 1 | Duluth |
| March 8, 1915 | University Club | 3 | St. Paul | 2 | St. Paul |

**W 6   L 5**

---

*Appendix Key*

*Pre-1920 positions (7-man game; starting with 1919–20 season, "defense" was used but use of rover was continued)*

| | |
|---|---|
| g | goalie |
| p | point |
| cp | cover point |
| r | rover |
| f | forward (2) |
| c | center |

*Post-1920 positions (6-man play begins in 1920-21 season)*

| | |
|---|---|
| g | goalie |
| d | defense (2) |
| c | center |
| f | forward (2) |

| | |
|---|---|
| POS | Position |
| GM | Games |
| G | Goals |
| A | Assists |
| PTS | Points |
| PEN | Penalties (number of, not minutes) |
| AAHA | American Amateur Hockey Association |
| USAHA | United States Amateur Hockey Association |

## St. Paul Athletic Club Hockey Team 1915–16

| PLAYERS | POS | HOMETOWN | GMS | G | A | PTS | PEN |
|---|---|---|---|---|---|---|---|
| Ray Bonney | g (3 shutouts) | Ottawa, ON | 14 | 0 | 0 | 0 | 0 |
| Cy Weidenborner | g | St. Paul, MN | 5 | 0 | 0 | 0 | 0 |
| Carlos Haug | g | Houghton, MI | 3 | 0 | 0 | 0 | 0 |
| Tony Conroy | f | St. Paul, MN | 14 | 11 | 0 | 11 | 4 |
| Frank Goheen | f | White Bear Lake, MN | 21 | 12 | 0 | 12 | 12 |
| Bill Adams | f | Fort William, ON | 21 | 7 | 1 | 8 | 3 |
| Ed Fitzgerald | cp | St. Paul, MN | 10 | 1 | 0 | 1 | 2 |
| Am Whalen | f | Port Arthur, ON | 12 | 6 | 2 | 8 | 4 |
| Alex Wellington | f | Port Arthur, ON | 16 | 15 | 0 | 15 | 6 |
| Nick Kahler, Captain | c | Dollar Bay, MI | 13 | 6 | 0 | 6 | 2 |
| Bert Mohan | r | Midland, ON | 16 | 22 | 1 | 23 | 7 |
| John Ryan | cp | Port Arthur, ON | 6 | 1 | 0 | 1 | 0 |
| George Henderson | r | Fort William, ON | 5 | 4 | 1 | 5 | 0 |
| Ed Goheen | f | White Bear Lake, MN | 2 | 0 | 0 | 0 | 0 |
| Homer Sweeney | p | St. Paul, MN | 1 | 0 | 0 | 0 | 0 |

### GAMES

| Date | | | | | | |
|---|---|---|---|---|---|---|
| December 27, 1915 | St. Paul | 7 | Duluth | 2 | | St. Paul |
| January 10, 1916 | St. Paul | 4 | Portage Lake | 1 | | St. Paul |
| January 11, 1916 | Portage Lake | 4 | St. Paul | 2 | | St. Paul |
| January 17, 1916 | St. Paul | 7 | Port Arthur | 0 | | St. Paul |
| January 24, 1916 | Calumet | 1 | St. Paul | 0 | | Calumet |
| January 25, 1916 | St. Paul | 2 | Calumet | 1 | | Calumet |
| January 27, 1916 | St. Paul | 4 | American Soo | 2 | | Sault Ste. Marie, MI |
| January 28, 1916 | American Soo | 7 | St. Paul | 2 | | Sault Ste. Marie, MI |
| February 3, 1916 | St. Paul | 1 | American Soo | 0 | | St. Paul |
| February 4, 1916 | St. Paul | 2 | American Soo | 0 | | St. Paul |
| February 7, 1916 | St. Paul | 3 | Portage Lake | 2 | | Houghton |
| February 8, 1916 | Portage Lake | 7 | St. Paul | 6 | | Houghton |
| February 10, 1916 | St. Paul | 8 | Duluth | 4 | | Duluth |
| February 14, 1916 | St. Paul | 10 | Calumet | 3 | | St. Paul |
| February 15, 1916 | St. Paul | 3 | Calumet | 2 | | St. Paul |
| February 21, 1916 | Minneapolis | 5 | St. Paul | 4 ovt | | St. Paul |
| March 6, 1916 | St. Paul | 7 | Minneapolis | 4 | | St. Paul |
| March 16, 1916 | St. Paul (Ross Cup) | 7 | Lachine, PQ | 6 | | Montreal |
| March 20, 1916 | Sons of Ireland of Quebec | 10** | St. Paul | 2 | | Montreal |
| March 24, 1916 | Pittsburgh | 1 | St. Paul | 0 ovt | | Pittsburgh |
| March 25, 1916 | Pittsburgh | 10 | St. Paul | 4 | | Pittsburgh |
| March 27, 1916 | Pittsburgh | 4 | St. Paul | 2 | | Pittsburgh |

**Statistics unavailable

| PLAY-OFFS | GMS | G | A | PTS | PEN |
|---|---|---|---|---|---|
| Bonney | 4 | 0 | 0 | 0 | 0 |
| Conroy, T. | 2 | 1 | 0 | 1 | 0 |
| Goheen, F. | 3 | 2 | 0 | 2 | 2 |
| Adams | 3 | 0 | 0 | 0 | 0 |
| Whalen | 3 | 2 | 0 | 2 | 0 |
| Wellington | 4 | 1 | 0 | 1 | 2 |
| Kahler | 3 | 7 | 0 | 7 | 0 |
| Mohan | 3 | 2 | 0 | 2 | 0 |
| Ryan | 4 | 0 | 0 | 0 | 0 |

### GAMES

| Date | | | | | | |
|---|---|---|---|---|---|---|
| February 28, 1916 | St. Paul | 4 | American Soo | 3 ovt | | St. Paul |
| February 29, 1916 | St. Paul | 4 | American Soo | 3 ovt | | St. Paul |
| March 2, 1916 | American Soo | 4 | St. Paul | 3 ovt | | Sault Ste. Marie, MI |
| March 3, 1916 | St. Paul | 4 | American Soo | 1 | | Sault Ste. Marie, MI |

W 16   L 10   T 0      AAHA   W 8   L 4   T 0      PLAYOFFS   W 3   L 1   T 0

## St. Paul Athletic Club Hockey Team 1916–17

| PLAYERS | POS | HOMETOWN | GMS | G* | A | PTS | PEN |
|---|---|---|---|---|---|---|---|
| Cy Weidenborner | g (3 shutouts) | St. Paul, MN | 11 | 0 | 0 | 0 | 1 |
| ? Hodgeman | g | ? | 1 | 0 | 0 | 0 | 0 |
| Ed Fitzgerald, Captain | p | St. Paul, MN | 12 | 5 | 0 | 5 | 1 |
| Vern Peterson | cp,f | St. Paul, MN | 10 | 7 | 0 | 7 | 5 |
| Herb Drury | r | Midland, ON | 12 | 9 | 2 | 11 | 4 |
| Bert Mohan | c | Midland, ON | 10 | 21 | 0 | 21 | 1 |
| Ransome Tregelone | f | ? | 3 | 1 | 0 | 1 | 0 |
| Tony Conroy | f | St. Paul, MN | 12 | 13 | 1 | 14 | 3 |
| Dick Conway | cp | White Bear Lake, MN | 4 | 0 | 0 | 0 | 0 |
| Frank Goheen | cp | White Bear Lake, MN | 11 | 8 | 0 | 8 | 2 |
| ? McBride | c | ? | 2 | 1 | 0 | 0 | 1 |

*One goal, scorer unknown

**GAMES**

| | | | | | |
|---|---|---|---|---|---|
| January 2, 1917 | St. Paul | 14 | Thief River Falls | 0 | St. Paul |
| January 18, 1917 | St. Paul | 7 | Fort William, ON | 2 | St. Paul |
| January 19, 1917 | St. Paul | 6 | Fort William, ON | 1 | St. Paul |
| January 25, 1917 | American Soo | 3 | St. Paul | 2 | Sault Ste. Marie, MI |
| January 26, 1917 | American Soo | 3 | St. Paul | 2 | Sault Ste. Marie, MI |
| January 30, 1917 | St. Paul | 10 | American Soo | 0 | St. Paul |
| January 31, 1917 | St. Paul | 4 | American Soo | 1 | St. Paul |
| February 6, 1917 | St. Paul | 9 | Minneapolis All-Stars | 2 | St. Paul |
| February 8, 1917 | St. Paul | 9 | Minneapolis All-Stars | 0 | Minneapolis |
| February 13, 1917 | St. Paul | 2 | Duluth | 1 | St. Paul |
| March 23, 1917 | Pittsburgh | 2 | St. Paul | 1 | Pittsburgh |
| March 24, 1917 | Pittsburgh | 4 | St. Paul | 0 | Pittsburgh |

W 8   L 4


## St. Paul Hockey Team 1918–19

| PLAYERS | POS | HOMETOWN | GMS | G* | A | PTS | PEN |
|---|---|---|---|---|---|---|---|
| Forest Henkel | g | White Bear Lake, MN | 6 | 0 | 0 | 0 | 0 |
| Tony Conroy | r | St. Paul, MN | 6 | 6 | 0 | 6 | 1 |
| Emmy Garrett | f | St. Paul, MN | 6 | 11 | 0 | 10 | 0 |
| Vern Peterson | p | St. Paul, MN | 4 | 0 | 0 | 0 | 1 |
| Dick Conway | cp | White Bear Lake, MN | 2 | 0 | 0 | 0 | 0 |
| Al Wilzbacher | f | White Bear Lake, MN | 6 | 8 | 0 | 8 | 0 |
| Everett McGowan | f | St. Paul, MN | 4 | 3 | 0 | 3 | 0 |
| Nick Kahler | c | Dollar Bay, MI | 2 | 1 | 0 | 1 | 1 |
| George Conroy | f | St. Paul, MN | 4 | 2 | 0 | 2 | 0 |
| Al Corboy | p | ? | 2 | 0 | 0 | 0 | 0 |
| ? Rogers | f | ? | 2 | 0 | 0 | 0 | 0 |

One goal, scorer unknown

**GAMES**

| | | | | | |
|---|---|---|---|---|---|
| February 4, 1919 | St. Paul | 7 | Great Lakes Naval Training Station | 1 | St. Paul |
| February 5, 1919 | St. Paul | 10 | Great Lakes Naval Training Station | 1 | St. Paul |
| February 19, 1919 | American Soo | 4 | St. Paul | 0 | Sault Ste. Marie, MI |
| February 20, 1919 | American Soo | 7 | St. Paul | 5 | Sault Ste. Marie, MI |
| March 4, 1919 | Duluth | 7 | St. Paul | 4 | Duluth |
| March 5, 1919 | Duluth | 8 | St. Paul | 5 | Duluth |

W 2   L 4

## St. Paul Athletic Club Hockey Team 1919–20

| PLAYERS | POS | HOMETOWN | GMS | G | A | PTS | PEN |
|---|---|---|---|---|---|---|---|
| Cy Weidenborner | g (5 shutouts) | St. Paul, MN | 22 | 0 | 0 | 0 | 0 |
| Ernie Byers | g | St. Paul, MN | 1 | 0 | 0 | 0 | 0 |
| Ed Fitzgerald, Captain | d | St. Paul, MN | 23 | 1 | 1 | 2 | 2 |
| Frank Goheen | d, r | White Bear Lake, MN | 23 | 22 | 0 | 22 | 3 |
| Tony Conroy | f, r | St. Paul, MN | 23 | 14 | 2 | 16 | 2 |
| Nick Kahler | c | Dollar Bay, MI | 19 | 34 | 0 | 34 | 6 |
| Everett McGowan | f | St. Paul, MN | 2 | 0 | 0 | 0 | 0 |
| Emmy Garrett | f | St. Paul, MN | 21 | 21 | 0 | 21 | 4 |
| Frank McCarthy | f, d | Toronto, ON | 23 | 2 | 0 | 2 | 5 |
| A. C. Gehrke | f | Winnipeg, MB | 3 | 0 | 0 | 0 | 1 |
| George Conroy | d | St. Paul, MN | 2 | 0 | 0 | 0 | 0 |
| Vern Peterson | d | St. Paul, MN | 3 | 1 | 0 | 0 | 0 |
| Gus Olson | d | Duluth, MN | 3 | 1 | 0 | 1 | 0 |

**GAMES**

| | | | | | | |
|---|---|---|---|---|---|---|
| December 30, 1919 | St. Paul | 3 | Duluth | 2 | St. Paul | |
| January 6, 1920 | St. Paul | 4 | American Soo | 2 | St. Paul | |
| January 7, 1920 | St. Paul | 7 | American Soo | 4 | St. Paul | |
| January 12, 1920 | St. Paul | 7 | Duluth | 3 | Duluth | |
| January 13, 1920 | St. Paul | 5 | Duluth | 3 | Duluth | |
| January 14, 1920 | St. Paul | 4 | Eveleth | 0 | Eveleth | |
| January 20, 1920 | St. Paul | 8 | Hibbing | 1 | St. Paul | |
| January 22, 1920 | St. Paul | 7 | Portage Lake | 1 | Houghton | |
| January 23, 1920 | St. Paul | 5 | Portage Lake | 1 | Houghton | |
| January 27, 1920 | St. Paul | 2 | Canadian Soo | 0 | St. Paul | |
| January 28, 1920 | St. Paul | 3 | Canadian Soo | 0 | St. Paul | |
| February 2, 1920 | St. Paul | 3 | Canadian Soo | 2 | Sault Ste. Marie, ON | |
| February 3, 1920 | Canadian Soo | 2 | St. Paul | 1 | Sault Ste. Marie, ON | |
| February 5, 1920 | American Soo | 3 | St. Paul | 0 | Sault Ste. Marie, MI | |
| February 7, 1920 | American Soo | 4 | St. Paul | 2 | Sault Ste. Marie, MI | |
| February 10, 1920 | St. Paul | 12 | Portage Lake | 5 | St. Paul | |
| February 11, 1920 | St. Paul | 6 | Portage Lake | 0 | St. Paul | |
| February 19, 1920 | St. Paul | 10 | Duluth | 6 | St. Paul (Hippodrome) | |
| February 23, 1920 | St. Paul | 2 | Winnipeg Monarchs | 0 | St. Paul (Hippodrome) | |
| February 24, 1920 | Winnipeg Monarchs | 2 | St. Paul | 1 | St. Paul (Hippodrome) | |
| March 12, 1920 | St. Paul | 3 | Pittsburgh | 2 | Pittsburgh* | |
| March 13, 1920 | Pittsburgh | 6 | St. Paul | 1 | Pittsburgh* | |
| March 15, 1920 | Pittsburgh | 4 | St. Paul | 1 | Pittsburgh* | |

*Three periods, six players

W  17   L  6   (AAHA  W  9   L  3)

# St. Paul Athletic Club Hockey Team 1920–21

| PLAYERS | POS | HOMETOWN | GMS | G* | A | PTS | PEN |
|---|---|---|---|---|---|---|---|
| Cy Weidenborner | g (3 shutouts) | St. Paul, MN | 22 | 0 | 0 | 0 | 1 |
| Ernie Byers | g | St. Paul, MN | 3 | 0 | 0 | 0 | 0 |
| Ed Fitzgerald | d | St. Paul, MN | 22 | 1 | 1 | 2 | 1 |
| Jeff Quesnelle | c | Sault Ste. Marie, ON | 23 | 17 | 0 | 17 | 2 |
| Frank Goheen, Captain | d, c | White Bear Lake, MN | 18 | 16 | 2 | 18 | 3 |
| Emmy Garrett | f | St. Paul, MN | 18 | 6 | 0 | 6 | 1 |
| Tony Conroy | f | St. Paul, MN | 23 | 10 | 2 | 12 | 0 |
| Wallie Elmer | d, f | Kingston, ON | 21 | 4 | 0 | 4 | 2 |
| Frank McCarthy | d | Toronto, ON | 6 | 0 | 0 | 0 | 0 |
| Oscar Aubrey | f | Moose Jaw, SK | 5 | 2 | 1 | 3 | 2 |
| Bill Garrett | d | St. Paul, MN | 1 | 0 | 0 | 0 | 0 |
| Blaine Meyers | c | Winnipeg, MB | 10 | 1 | 0 | 1 | 0 |
| George Conroy | f | St. Paul, MN | 4 | 0 | 0 | 0 | 0 |
| Walter Gosweich | f | St. Paul, MN | 1 | 0 | 0 | 0 | 0 |
| ? Lane | ? | ? | 1 | 0 | 0 | 0 | 0 |

*Lineup/statistics unavailable for March 12 game versus Duluth

### GAMES

| | | | | | |
|---|---|---|---|---|---|
| December 27, 1920 | St. Paul | 2 | Winnipeg Wanderers | 2 | St. Paul |
| December 28, 1920 | St. Paul | 1 | Winnipeg Wanderers | 0 | St. Paul |
| January 3, 1921 | St. Paul | 2 | Duluth | 1 | St. Paul |
| January 4, 1921 | St. Paul | 5 | Duluth | 3 | St. Paul |
| January 10, 1921 | St. Paul | 2 | Winnipeg Columbus | 1 ovt | St. Paul |
| January 11, 1921 | St. Paul | 3 | Winnipeg Columbus | 2 | St. Paul |
| January 14, 1921 | Cleveland | 9 | St. Paul | 2 | Cleveland |
| January 15, 1921 | Cleveland | 7 | St. Paul | 1 | Cleveland |
| January 17, 1921 | St. Paul | 2 | Minneapolis | 1 ovt | St. Paul |
| January 19, 1921 | Minneapolis | 4 | St. Paul | 1 | St. Paul* |
| January 24, 1921 | St. Paul | 2 | Fort William, ON | 1 | St. Paul |
| January 25, 1921 | St. Paul | 5 | Fort William, ON | 4 ovt | St. Paul |
| January 31, 1921 | Cleveland | 4 | St. Paul | 2 | St. Paul |
| February 1, 1921 | Cleveland | 6 | St. Paul | 3 ovt | St. Paul |
| February 14, 1921 | St. Paul | 2 | Minneapolis | 0 | St. Paul |
| February 18, 1921 | St. Paul | 5 | Minneapolis | 0 | St. Paul |
| February 21, 1921 | Duluth | 3 | St. Paul | 2 ovt | Duluth |
| February 22, 1921 | St. Paul | 3 | Duluth | 2 ovt | Duluth |
| March 4, 1921 | St. Paul | 6 | Winnipeg Falcons | 1 | St. Paul |
| March 5, 1921 | St. Paul | 2 | Winnipeg Falcons | 1 | St. Paul |
| March 9, 1921 | Eveleth | 11 | St. Paul | 2 | Eveleth |
| March 10, 1921 | Eveleth | 12 | St. Paul | 2 | Eveleth |
| March 12, 1921 | St. Paul | 5 | Duluth | 3 | Duluth |

*Lexington Avenue Rink

**W 15   L 8   USAHA   W 3   L 5**

## St. Paul Athletic Club Hockey Team 1921–22

| PLAYERS | POS | HOMETOWN | GMS | G | A | PTS | PEN |
|---|---|---|---|---|---|---|---|
| Babe Elliott | g (2 shutouts) | Winnipeg, MB | 20 | 0 | 0 | 0 | 0 |
| Frank Goheen | d, c | White Bear Lake, MN | 20 | 17 | 11 | 28 | 8 |
| Wallie Elmer | d | Kingston, ON | 19 | 3 | 3 | 6 | 5 |
| Charles Cassin | f | Winnipeg, MB | 18 | 10 | 1 | 11 | 0 |
| Tony Conroy, Captain | f | St. Paul, MN | 20 | 14 | 6 | 20 | 2 |
| Connie Johannesson | d | Winnipeg, MB | 16 | 0 | 2 | 2 | 2 |
| Emmy Garrett | f | St. Paul, MN | 20 | 22 | 6 | 28 | 2 |
| Russ McCrimmon | c | Windsor, ON | 2 | 3 | 3 | 6 | 0 |
| Jack Chambers | f | Winnipeg, MB | 2 | 1 | 0 | 1 | 0 |
| Bill Garrett | d | St. Paul, MN | 6 | 0 | 0 | 0 | 0 |
| George Conroy | f | St. Paul, MN | 9 | 2 | 0 | 2 | 0 |
| Ryland Rothschild | ? | ? | 1 | 0 | 0 | 0 | 0 |
| Ed Fitzgerald | d | St. Paul, MN | 4 | 0 | 1 | 1 | 0 |

### GAMES

| | | | | | |
|---|---|---|---|---|---|
| December 28, 1921 | St. Paul | 5 | Winnipeg Columbus | 3 | St. Paul |
| December 29, 1921 | St. Paul | 8 | Winnipeg Columbus | 3 | St. Paul |
| January 3, 1922 | St. Paul | 6 | Winnipeg Nationals | 1 | St. Paul |
| January 4, 1922 | St. Paul | 4 | Winnipeg Nationals | 1 | St. Paul |
| January 9, 1922 | St. Paul | 2 | Duluth | 1 ovt | St. Paul |
| January 10, 1922 | St. Paul | 3 | Duluth | 2 ovt | St. Paul |
| January 23, 1922 | St. Paul | 3 | Winnipeg Monarchs | 1 | St. Paul |
| January 24, 1922 | St. Paul | 5 | Winnipeg Monarchs | 1 | St. Paul |
| January 27, 1922 | Cleveland | 6 | St. Paul | 3 | Cleveland |
| January 28, 1922 | St. Paul | 3 | Cleveland | 2 | Cleveland |
| January 30, 1922 | Pittsburgh | 2 | St. Paul | 1 ovt | Pittsburgh |
| January 31, 1922 | St. Paul | 3 | Pittsburgh | 0 | Pittsburgh |
| February 6, 1922 | Pittsburgh | 2 | St. Paul | 1 ovt | St. Paul |
| February 7, 1922 | St. Paul | 1 | Pittsburgh | 0 | St. Paul |
| February 13, 1922 | St. Paul | 3 | Cleveland | 1 | St. Paul |
| February 14, 1922 | St. Paul | 3 | Cleveland | 2 ovt | St. Paul |
| February 27, 1922 | Duluth | 3 | St. Paul | 2 ovt | Duluth |
| February 28,1922 | St. Paul | 7 | Duluth | 1 | Duluth |
| March 21, 1922 | St. Paul | 5 | Pittsburgh | 4 | Pittsburgh |
| March 22, 1922 | Pittsburgh | 6 | St. Paul | 4 | Pittsburgh |

| PLAY-OFFS | GMS | G | A | PTS | PEN | |
|---|---|---|---|---|---|---|
| Elliott | 5 | 0 | 0 | 0 | 1 | 2 shutouts |
| Johannesson | 5 | 1 | 0 | 1 | 1 | |
| Elmer | 5 | 0 | 1 | 1 | 2 | |
| Goheen | 5 | 2 | 0 | 2 | 1 | |
| Garrett | 5 | 3 | 1 | 4 | 0 | |
| Cassin | 4 | 0 | 0 | 0 | 0 | |
| Conroy, T. | 5 | 1 | 1 | 2 | 2 | |
| Conroy, G. | 3 | 0 | 0 | 0 | 0 | |

### GAMES

| | | | | | |
|---|---|---|---|---|---|
| March 3, 1922 | St. Paul | 3 | Eveleth | 1 | Eveleth |
| March 4, 1922 | Eveleth | 4 | St. Paul | 2 | Eveleth |
| March 6, 1922 | St. Paul | 0 | Eveleth | 0 | St. Paul |
| March 7, 1922 | St. Paul | 2 | Eveleth | 1 | St. Paul |
| March 8, 1922 | St. Paul | 0 | Eveleth | 0 | St. Paul |

| FELLOWES CUP | GMS | G | A | PTS | PEN | |
|---|---|---|---|---|---|---|
| Elliott | 4 | 0 | 0 | 0 | 0 | 1 shutout |
| Johannesson | 4 | 0 | 0 | 0 | 3 | |
| Elmer | 4 | 0 | 0 | 0 | 2 | |
| Goheen | 4 | 0 | 0 | 0 | 0 | |
| Garrett | 4 | 0 | 1 | 1 | 0 | |
| Cassin | 3 | 0 | 0 | 0 | 1 | |
| Conroy, T. | 4 | 1 | 0 | 1 | 1 | |
| Conroy, G. | 3 | 0 | 0 | 0 | 0 | |

### GAMES

| | | | | | |
|---|---|---|---|---|---|
| March 11, 1922 | Boston Westminsters | 3 | St. Paul | 0 | St. Paul |
| March 12, 1922 | Boston Westminsters | 2 | St. Paul | 1 | St. Paul |
| March 17, 1922 | Boston Westminsters | 0 | St. Paul | 0 | Boston |
| March 18, 1922 | Boston Westminsters | 2 | St. Paul | 0 | Boston |

**W 17  L 9  T 3      USAHA  W 8  L 4      PLAY-OFFS  W 2  L 1  T 2      FELLOWES CUP  W 0  L 3  T 1**

## St. Paul Athletic Club Hockey Team 1922–23

| PLAYERS | POS | HOMETOWN | GMS | G | A | PTS | PEN |
|---|---|---|---|---|---|---|---|
| Babe Elliott | g (11 shutouts) | Winnipeg, MB | 22 | 0 | 0 | 0 | 0 |
| Clarence Abel | d | American Soo | 20 | 4 | 3 | 7 | 8 |
| Frank Goheen | d, f | White Bear Lake, MN | 22 | 13 | 10 | 23 | 11 |
| Emmy Garrett, Captain | f | St. Paul, MN | 22 | 7 | 2 | 9 | 4 |
| Tony Conroy | f | St. Paul, MN | 22 | 4 | 3 | 7 | 6 |
| Joe McCormick | f | Buckingham, PQ | 19 | 6 | 5 | 11 | 0 |
| George Conroy | f | St. Paul, MN | 8 | 1 | 0 | 1 | 4 |
| George Clark | c | Winnipeg, MB | 22 | 20 | 7 | 27 | 3 |
| Dennis Breen | d | Owen Sound, ON | 22 | 3 | 4 | 7 | 10 |
| Charles Cassin | f | Winnipeg, MB | 3 | 1 | 1 | 2 | 0 |
| George Nichols | f | St. Paul, MN | 1 | 0 | 0 | 0 | 0 |
| Bill Garrett | f | St. Paul, MN | 2 | 0 | 0 | 0 | 0 |

**GAMES**

| Date | | | | | |
|---|---|---|---|---|---|
| December 18, 1922 | St. Paul | 2 | Niagara Falls, ON | 2 | St. Paul |
| December 19, 1922 | St. Paul | 11 | Niagara Falls, ON | 0 | St. Paul |
| December 21, 1922 | Milwaukee | 1 | St. Paul | 0 | Milwaukee |
| December 22, 1922 | St. Paul | 2 | Milwaukee | 0 | Milwaukee |
| December 26, 1922 | Duluth | 2 | St. Paul | 0 | St. Paul |
| December 27, 1922 | St. Paul | 3 | Duluth | 0 | St. Paul |
| January 2, 1923 | St. Paul | 1 | Eveleth | 0 | St. Paul |
| January 3, 1923 | St. Paul | 1 | Eveleth | 0 | St. Paul |
| January 15, 1923 | St. Paul | 3 | Pittsburgh | 0 | St. Paul |
| January 16, 1923 | Pittsburgh | 1 | St. Paul | 0 ovt | St. Paul |
| January 22, 1923 | St. Paul | 3 | Milwaukee | 2 | St. Paul |
| January 23, 1923 | St. Paul | 5 | Milwaukee | 0 | St. Paul |
| January 25, 1923 | Duluth | 5 | St. Paul | 0 | Duluth |
| January 26, 1923 | St. Paul | 4 | Duluth | 2 | Duluth |
| February 9, 1923 | St. Paul | 3 | Eveleth | 0 | Eveleth |
| February 10, 1923 | St. Paul | 3 | Eveleth | 1 ovt | Eveleth |
| February 19, 1923 | St. Paul | 7 | Cleveland | 0 | St. Paul |
| February 20, 1923 | St. Paul | 3 | Cleveland | 1 | St. Paul |
| March 2, 1923 | St. Paul | 1 | Pittsburgh | 0 | Pittsburgh |
| March 3, 1923 | St. Paul | 2 | Pittsburgh | 1 | Pittsburgh |
| March 9, 1923 | St. Paul | 3 | Cleveland | 0 | Cleveland |
| March 10, 1923 | Cleveland | 4 | St. Paul | 2 | Cleveland |

| FELLOWES CUP | GMS | G | A | PTS | PEN |
|---|---|---|---|---|---|
| Elliott | 4 | 0 | 0 | 0 | 0 |
| Abel | 4 | 0 | 0 | 0 | 7 |
| Breen | 4 | 1 | 0 | 1 | 1 |
| Clark | 4 | 0 | 0 | 0 | 1 |
| Garrett | 4 | 0 | 0 | 0 | 0 |
| McCormick | 4 | 0 | 0 | 0 | 0 |
| Goheen | 4 | 3 | 0 | 3 | 3 |
| Conroy, T. | 4 | 0 | 0 | 0 | 0 |

**GAMES**

| Date | | | | | |
|---|---|---|---|---|---|
| March 13, 1923 | Boston Athletic Association (BAA) | 2 | St. Paul | 1 | St. Paul |
| March 14, 1923 | BAA | 1 | St. Paul | 0 | St. Paul |
| March 22, 1923 | St. Paul | 2 | BAA | 1 | Boston |
| March 24, 1923 | BAA | 2 | St. Paul | 1 | Boston |

**W 18   L 8     USAHA W 15   L 5     FELLOWES CUP   W 1   L 3**

## St. Paul Athletic Club Hockey Team 1923–24

| PLAYERS | POS | HOMETOWN | GMS | G | A | PTS | PEN |
|---|---|---|---|---|---|---|---|
| Babe Elliott | g (5 shutouts) | Winnipeg, MB | 22 | 0 | 0 | 0 | 0 |
| Dennis Breen | d | Owen Sound, ON | 22 | 6 | 2 | 8 | 9 |
| George Conroy | d, f | St. Paul, MN | 14 | 2 | 0 | 2 | 2 |
| George Clark | c | Winnipeg, MB | 22 | 13 | 5 | 18 | 5 |
| Frank Goheen, Captain | f | White Bear Lake, MN | 22 | 10 | 6 | 16 | 17 |
| Tony Conroy | f, d | St. Paul, MN | 22 | 6 | 4 | 10 | 6 |
| Bill Broadfoot | f | Regina, SK | 18 | 3 | 1 | 4 | 4 |
| Wilfred Peltier | f | Winnipeg, MB | 22 | 12 | 2 | 14 | 4 |
| Emmy Garrett | f | St. Paul, MN | 22 | 3 | 4 | 7 | 2 |
| George Nichols | f | St. Paul, MN | 3 | 0 | 0 | 0 | 0 |
| Clarence Abel | d | American Soo | 3 | 1 | 0 | 1 | 0 |

**GAMES**

| | | | | | |
|---|---|---|---|---|---|
| January 2, 1924 | Eveleth | 2 | St. Paul | 1 | Eveleth |
| January 3, 1924 | St. Paul | 2 | Eveleth | 1 | Eveleth |
| January 9, 1924 | Pittsburgh | 1 | St. Paul | 0 ovt | St. Paul |
| January 10, 1924 | St. Paul | 3 | Pittsburgh | 2 | St. Paul |
| January 15, 1924 | St. Paul | 2 | Cleveland | 1 ovt | St. Paul |
| January 17, 1924 | St. Paul | 2 | Cleveland | 1 | St. Paul |
| January 21, 1924 | St. Paul | 2 | Minneapolis | 1 | St. Paul |
| January 28, 1924 | St. Paul | 5 | Minneapolis | 0 | St. Paul |
| January 29, 1924 | St. Paul | 1 | Minneapolis | 0 | St. Paul |
| February 1, 1924 | Cleveland | 4 | St. Paul | 2 | Cleveland |
| February 2, 1924 | St. Paul | 3 | Cleveland | 1 ovt | Cleveland |
| February 5, 1924 | St. Paul | 1 | Boston Hockey Club | 0 | Boston |
| February 6, 1924 | BAA | 2 | St. Paul | 1 ovt | Boston |
| February 8, 1924 | Pittsburgh | 5 | St. Paul | 3 | Pittsburgh |
| February 9, 1924 | Pittsburgh | 4 | St. Paul | 0 | Pittsburgh |
| February 12, 1924 | St. Paul | 4 | Duluth | 1 | St. Paul |
| February 13, 1924 | St. Paul | 2 | Duluth | 1 | St. Paul |
| February 15, 1924 | St. Paul | 3 | Minneapolis | 0 | St. Paul |
| February 18, 1924 | St. Paul | 4 | Eveleth | 0 | St. Paul |
| February 19, 1924 | St. Paul | 5 | Eveleth | 2 | St. Paul |
| February 22, 1924 | Duluth | 4 | St. Paul | 3 | Duluth |
| February 23, 1924 | St. Paul | 7 | Duluth | 3 | Duluth |

| PLAY-OFFS | GMS | G | A | PTS | PEN | |
|---|---|---|---|---|---|---|
| Elliott | 8 | 0 | 0 | 0 | 0 | 2 shutouts |
| Breen | 8 | 0 | 0 | 0 | 4 | |
| Conroy, G. | 2 | 0 | 0 | 0 | 0 | |
| Clark | 8 | 2 | 0 | 2 | 2 | |
| Goheen | 8 | 1 | 1 | 2 | 4 | |
| Conroy, T. | 8 | 1 | 0 | 1 | 4 | |
| Broadfoot | 1 | 0 | 0 | 0 | 0 | |
| Peltier | 8 | 2 | 0 | 2 | 2 | |
| Garrett | 8 | 0 | 0 | 0 | 1 | |
| Abel | 8 | 0 | 0 | 0 | 5 | |

**GAMES**

| | | | | | |
|---|---|---|---|---|---|
| March 3, 1924 | Cleveland | 3 | St. Paul | 2 | St. Paul |
| March 5, 1924 | St. Paul | 3 | Cleveland | 0 | St. Paul |
| March 7, 1924 | Pittsburgh | 1 | St. Paul | 0 | St. Paul |
| March 8, 1924 | St. Paul | 0 | Pittsburgh | 0 ovt | St. Paul |
| March 10, 1924 | Cleveland | 3 | St. Paul | 0 | Cleveland |
| March 12, 1924 | Cleveland | 1 | St. Paul | 0 ovt | Cleveland |
| March 14, 1924 | Pittsburgh | 5 | St. Paul | 0 | Pittsburgh |
| March 15, 1924 | Pittsburgh | 2 | St. Paul | 1 | Pittsburgh |

**W 16　L 13　T 1　USAHA W 14　L 6　T 0　PLAY-OFFS　W 1　L 6　T 1**

## St. Paul Athletic Club Hockey Team 1924–25

| PLAYERS | POS | HOMETOWN | GMS | G | A | PTS | PEN |
|---|---|---|---|---|---|---|---|
| Babe Elliott, Captain | g (9 shutouts) | Winnipeg, MB | 43 | 1 | 0 | 1 | 2 |
| Cy Weidenborner | g | St. Paul, MN | 1 | 0 | 0 | 0 | 0 |
| Clarence Abel | d | American Soo | 42 | 8 | 3 | 11 | 27 |
| Dennis Breen | d, g | Owen Sound, ON | 43 | 2 | 3 | 5 | 22 |
| Jeff Quesnelle | c | Sault Ste. Marie, ON | 43 | 11 | 2 | 13 | 5 |
| Emmy Garrett | f | St. Paul, MN | 42 | 8 | 4 | 12 | 11 |
| Tony Conroy | f | St. Paul, MN | 36 | 10 | 3 | 13 | 10 |
| Frank Goheen | f, c | White Bear Lake, MN | 34 | 8 | 4 | 12 | 9 |
| George Conroy | d | St. Paul, MN | 19 | 6 | 1 | 7 | 3 |
| George Nichols | d | St. Paul, MN | 4 | 0 | 0 | 0 | 0 |
| Wilfred Peltier | f | Winnipeg, MB | 41 | 4 | 3 | 7 | 6 |
| Harvey Naismith | f | Regina, SK | 41 | 4 | 2 | 6 | 7 |
| Earl Willey | f | St. Paul, MN | 2 | 0 | 0 | 0 | 0 |

### GAMES

| | | | | | |
|---|---|---|---|---|---|
| November 21, 1924 | St. Paul | 2 | Winnipeg Tiger-Falcons | 2 | Winnipeg |
| November 22, 1924 | St. Paul | 4 | Selkirk, MB | 3 | Winnipeg |
| December 5, 1924 | Cleveland | 2 | St. Paul | 1 | Cleveland |
| December 6, 1924 | Cleveland | 4 | St. Paul | 0 | Cleveland |
| December 12, 1924 | Pittsburgh | 3 | St. Paul | 1 | Pittsburgh |
| December 13, 1924 | Pittsburgh | 3 | St. Paul | 1 | Pittsburgh |
| December 19, 1924 | St. Paul | 1 | Minneapolis | 1 ovt | Minneapolis |
| December 20, 1924 | Minneapolis | 2 | St. Paul | 1 | Minneapolis |
| December 22, 1924 | Duluth | 2 | St. Paul | 1 | Duluth |
| December 23, 1924 | Duluth | 3 | St. Paul | 1 | Duluth |
| December 29, 1924 | St. Paul | 2 | Eveleth | 1 | St. Paul |
| December 30, 1924 | Eveleth | 3 | St. Paul | 0 | St. Paul |
| January 2, 1925 | Minneapolis | 2 | St. Paul | 1 | St. Paul |
| January 3, 1925 | St. Paul | 1 | Minneapolis | 1 ovt | St. Paul |
| January 6, 1925 | St. Paul | 2 | Eveleth | 1 ovt | Eveleth |
| January 7, 1925 | St. Paul | 1 | Eveleth | 0 | Eveleth |
| January 9, 1925 | St. Paul | 2 | Duluth | 1 | St. Paul |
| January 10, 1925 | Duluth | 1 | St. Paul | 0 ovt | St. Paul |
| January 19, 1925 | Pittsburgh | 2 | St. Paul | 0 | St. Paul |
| January 20, 1925 | St. Paul | 2 | Pittsburgh | 0 | St. Paul |
| January 26, 1925 | St. Paul | 4 | Cleveland | 0 | St. Paul |
| January 27, 1925 | Cleveland | 1 | St. Paul | 0 ovt | St. Paul |
| February 2, 1925 | St. Paul | 2 | Minneapolis | 0 | St. Paul |
| February 3, 1925 | Minneapolis | 1 | St. Paul | 0 | St. Paul |
| February 5, 1925 | Eveleth | 1 | St. Paul | 0 | Eveleth |
| February 6, 1925 | Eveleth | 3 | St. Paul | 2 ovt | Eveleth |
| February 9, 1925 | St. Paul | 2 | Duluth | 1 | St. Paul |
| February 10, 1925 | St. Paul | 1 | Duluth | 0 | St. Paul |
| February 16, 1925 | St. Paul | 1 | Pittsburgh | 0 | St. Paul |
| February 20, 1925 | Pittsburgh | 2 | St. Paul | 1 | St. Paul |
| February 23, 1925 | St. Paul | 3 | Cleveland | 2 | St. Paul |
| February 24, 1925 | St. Paul | 2 | Cleveland | 0 * | St. Paul |
| March 2, 1925 | Eveleth | 3 | St. Paul | 1 | St. Paul |
| March 3, 1925 | Eveleth | 1 | St. Paul | 0 | St. Paul |
| March 6, 1925 | Cleveland | 3 | St. Paul | 2 | Cleveland |
| March 7, 1925 | St. Paul | 4 | Cleveland | 0 | Cleveland |
| March 10, 1925 | Pittsburgh | 4 | St. Paul | 0 | Pittsburgh |
| March 11, 1925 | St. Paul | 3 | Pittsburgh | 2 | Pittsburgh |
| March 16, 1925 | St. Paul | 2 | Minneapolis | 1 | Minneapolis |
| March 18, 1925 | Minneapolis | 2 | St. Paul | 1 | Minneapolis |
| March 20, 1925 | St. Paul | 4 | Duluth | 3 | Duluth |
| March 21, 1925 | St. Paul | 1 | Duluth | 0 ovt | Duluth |
| March 24, 1925 | Minneapolis | 5 | St. Paul | 2 ** | Minneapolis |

*Play halted at 6:19 third period
**non-league game

**W 18   L 23   T 2        USAHA   W 17   L 21   T 2**

## St. Paul Athletic Club Hockey Team 1925–26

| PLAYERS | POS | HOMETOWN | GMS | G | A | PTS | PEN |
|---|---|---|---|---|---|---|---|
| Joe Miller | g (6 shutouts) | Ottawa, ON | 39 | 0 | 0 | 0 | 0 |
| George Conroy | d | St. Paul, MN | 39 | 6 | 7 | 13 | 30 |
| Frank Goheen, Captain | d | White Bear Lake, MN | 36 | 9 | 10 | 19 | 37 |
| George Clark | c | Winnipeg, MB | 35 | 14 | 2 | 16 | 11 |
| Syl Acaster | c | Regina, SK | 37 | 6 | 3 | 9 | 7 |
| Gus Wilkie | f | Sydney, NS | 33 | 2 | 1 | 3 | 27 |
| Emmy Garrett | f | St. Paul, MN | 39 | 12 | 4 | 16 | 24 |
| Tony Conroy | f | St. Paul, MN | 34 | 11 | 5 | 16 | 24 |
| Harvey Naismith | f | Regina, SK | 39 | 7 | 0 | 7 | 11 |
| Steve Rice | c | Niagara Falls, ON | 24 | 6 | 4 | 10 | 2 |
| George Nichols | d | St. Paul, MN | 19 | 1 | 0 | 1 | 2 |
| Bonar Larose | f | Ottawa, ON | 11 | 0 | 0 | 0 | 0 |
| Don Cameron | f | Ottawa, ON | 4 | 0 | 0 | 0 | 0 |
| Chet Harris | f | Saskatoon, SK | 8 | 1 | 0 | 1 | 0 |
| Elwyn Rommes | f | White Bear Lake, MN | 1 | 0 | 0 | 0 | 1 |

GAMES

| | | | | | |
|---|---|---|---|---|---|
| December 5, 1925 | St. Paul | 2 | Winnipeg | 1 | Winnipeg |
| December 7, 1925 | Winnipeg | 2 | St. Paul | 1 | Winnipeg |
| December 17, 1925 | Duluth | 4 | St. Paul | 0 | Duluth |
| December 18, 1925 | Duluth | 1 | St. Paul | 0 | Duluth |
| December 21, 1925 | St. Paul | 4 | Minneapolis | 0 | St. Paul |
| December 22, 1925 | St. Paul | 1 | Minneapolis | 1 ovt | Minneapolis |
| December 28, 1925 | Eveleth-Hibbing | 5 | St. Paul | 2 | St. Paul |
| December 29, 1925 | Eveleth-Hibbing | 2 | St. Paul | 0 | St. Paul |
| January 1, 1926 | Minneapolis | 1 | St. Paul | 0 | Minneapolis |
| January 2, 1926 | Minneapolis | 2 | St. Paul | 1 | St. Paul |
| January 5, 1926 | Eveleth-Hibbing | 2 | St. Paul | 1 ovt | Hibbing |
| January 6, 1926 | St. Paul | 3 | Eveleth-Hibbing | 1 | Hibbing |
| January 8, 1926 | St. Paul | 2 | Duluth | 0 | St. Paul |
| January 9, 1926 | St. Paul | 1 | Duluth | 1 ovt | St. Paul |
| January 19, 1926 | St. Paul | 4 | Canadian Soo | 3 | St. Paul |
| January 22, 1926 | St. Paul | 5 | Canadian Soo | 1 | St. Paul |
| January 26, 1926 | St. Paul | 2 | Winnipeg | 0 | St. Paul |
| January 28, 1926 | St. Paul | 2 | Winnipeg | 1 | St. Paul |
| January 30, 1926 | Minneapolis | 1 | St. Paul | 0 ovt | St. Paul |
| February 2, 1926 | Minneapolis | 4 | St. Paul | 0 | St. Paul |
| February 4, 1926 | Eveleth-Hibbing | 2 | St. Paul | 0 | Eveleth |
| February 5, 1926 | St. Paul | 2 | Eveleth-Hibbing | 2 ovt | Hibbing |
| February 8, 1926 | St. Paul | 2 | Duluth | 2 ovt | St. Paul |
| February 9, 1926 | Duluth | 3 | St. Paul | 2 | St. Paul |
| February 11, 1926 | Canadian Soo | 2 | St. Paul | 1 | Sault Ste. Marie, ON |
| February 12, 1926 | St. Paul | 3 | Canadian Soo | 2 | Sault Ste. Marie, ON |
| February 13, 1926 | St. Paul | 6 | Marquette, MI | 1 | Marquette |
| February 15, 1926 | St. Paul | 5 | Canadian Soo | 0 | St. Paul |
| February 16, 1926 | St. Paul | 6 | Canadian Soo | 2 | St. Paul |
| February 23, 1926 | St. Paul | 3 | Winnipeg | 1 | St. Paul |
| February 26, 1926 | St. Paul | 9 | Winnipeg | 2 | St. Paul |
| March 1, 1926 | St. Paul | 4 | Eveleth-Hibbing | 0 | St. Paul |
| March 2, 1926 | St. Paul | 1 | Eveleth-Hibbing | 0 | St. Paul |
| March 4, 1926 | Winnipeg | 4 | St. Paul | 3 ovt | Winnipeg |
| March 6, 1926 | Winnipeg | 2 | St. Paul | 1 ovt | Winnipeg |
| March 15, 1926 | St. Paul | 1 | Minneapolis | 1 ovt | Minneapolis |
| March 16, 1926 | St. Paul | 3 | Minneapolis | 3 ovt | Minneapolis |
| March 19, 1926 | Duluth | 1 | St. Paul | 0 | Duluth |
| March 20, 1926 | Duluth | 7 | St. Paul | 0 | Duluth |

W 16　L 17　T 6　　　CAHA　W 15　L 17　T 6

# BIBLIOGRAPHY

## Articles

Clark, Donald M. "Early St. Paul, 1896–1942." Unpublished manuscript (c. 1985).

___. "Early Minneapolis Hockey, 1895–1942." Unpublished manuscript (c. 1985).

___. Thomas Clark, and Roger A. Godin. "United States Amateur Hockey Association, 1920–1926." Unpublished manuscript (1998).

Godin, Roger A. "Facing the Falcons: The 1920 United States Olympic Team." *Hockey Research Journal* 6, no. 1 (2002).

___. "On the Trail of the McNaughton (sic) Cup: The 1915–16 St. Paul Athletic Club Team." *Hockey Research Journal* 5, no. 1 (2001).

Unattributed. "The Husky Hockey Home." Northeastern University, Hockey Game Program (2002–3).

## Books

Coleman, Charles L. *The Trail of the Stanley Cup.* Vol. 1, 1893–1926. Montreal: National Hockey League, 1966.

Duplacy, James. *The Rules of Hockey.* Toronto: Dan Diamond and Associates, 1996.

Eskenazi, Gerald. *The Fastest Sport.* Chicago: Rutledge Publishing Company, 1974.

Fischler, Stan and Shirley Walton Fischler. *The Hockey Encyclopedia.* New York: Macmillan Publishing Company, 1983.

Godin, Roger A. *Enshrinee Biographies.* Eveleth, Minn.: United States Hockey Hall of Fame, 1984.

Hubbard, Kevin, and Stan Fischler. *Hockey America.* Indianapolis: Masters Press, 1997.

Kenney, Dave. *Northern Lights: The Stories of Minnesota's Past.* St. Paul: Minnesota Historical Society, 2003.

Klein, Jeff, and Karl-Eric Reif. *The Hockey Compendium: NHL Facts, Stats, and Stories.* Toronto: McClelland and Stewart, 2001.

Meier, Peg. *Bring Warm Clothes: Letters and Photos from Minnesota's Past.* Minneapolis: Minneapolis Star and Tribune, 1981.

Menke, Frank G. *The All Sports Record Book.* New York: A. S. Barnes & Company, 1950.

Podnieks, Andrew. *Canada's Olympic Hockey Teams: The Complete History, 1920–1998.* Toronto: Doubleday Canada, 1997.

Thornley, Stew. *Holy Cow! The Life and Times of Halsey Hall.* Minneapolis: Nodin Press, 1991.

*Total Hockey*, 2d ed. Kingston, NY: Total Sports Publishing (Dan Diamond Associates), 2000.

Wingerd, Mary Lethert. *Claiming the City: Politics, Faith, and the Power of Place in St. Paul.* Ithaca, NY: Cornell University Press, 2001.

## Guides

*Official Ice Hockey Guide and Winter Sports Almanac.* Charles Provencher, Editor. Montreal: Canadian Sports Publishing. 1924.

*National Hockey League Official Guide and Record Book 2003.* Chicago: Triumph Books, 2002.

*Official Ice Hockey Guide and Winter Sports Almanac.* Edited by Charles Provencher. Montreal: Canadian Sports Publishing, 1924.

United States Amateur Hockey Association. *Constitution, Rules of Competition and Laws of the Game, Grouping of Clubs, and Schedule of Matches, Season 1922–23.* Publisher unknown.

## Internet

ESPN.com

## Newspapers

*Boston Evening Transcript*

*Boston Globe*

*Christian Science Monitor*, Boston

*Daily Mining Gazette*, Houghton, MI

*Eveleth* (MN) *News*

*Evening News*, Sault Ste. Marie, MI

*Minneapolis Star*

*Minneapolis Tribune*

*New York Times*

*Pittsburgh Post*

*St. Paul Daily News*

*St. Paul Dispatch*

*St. Paul Pioneer Press*

*White Bear Lake* (MN) *Press*

# INDEX

# PHOTO CREDITS

For institutional listings, the name of the photographer, when known, is given in parentheses, as is additional information about the source of the item.

DONALD CLARK COLLECTION
Pages iii, 8 (*St. Paul Dispatch*), 11, 20, 23, 33, 50, 65, 74, 80, 104, 134

ROGER GODIN
Pages 61, 69, 108, 129, 167

BEVERLY GOHEEN
Pages 9, 10, 58, 67 (photo by Eric Mortensen/ MHS), 84

MARY JO MURRAY
Page 29

MINNESOTA HISTORICAL SOCIETY COLLECTIONS
Pages vi; 5; 6; 7, 70, 92 (Charles P. Gibson); 13; 19; 21; 22 (Juul-Ingersoll Company); 24 (Brown's Photo Studio); 25; 26 (St. Paul Athletic Club Scrapbook); 38; 41 (both); 47 (all); 76; 77; 81; 83 (both); 89 150, 164 (*St. Paul Pioneer Press*); 95 (*Minneapolis Star-Journal*); 144; 146 (Paul W. Hamilton); 165

MINNESOTA WILD
Page 109

NEW YORK TIMES / TIMES WIDE WORLD PHOTOS
Page 64

THE NORTHEAST MINNESOTA HISTORICAL CENTER AT THE UNIVERSITY OF MINNESOTA-DULUTH.
Page 52 (Photo by Hugh McKenzie. Used with permission.)

NORTHEASTERN UNIVERSITY, BOSTON
Page 102

THE ST. PAUL ATHLETIC CLUB
Pages 32, 34, 43 (1915–16 AC Scrapbook); 63 (*The ACE*); 125 (*Boston Globe*)

U.S. HOCKEY HALL OF FAME
(all photos by Eric Mortensen/MHS)
Pages 91, 97, 181

WESTERN COLLEGIATE HOCKEY ASSOCIATION
(WCHA)
Page 35

*Before the Stars* was set in Minion, a typeface designed
by Robert Slimbach and issued by Adobe in 1989.

Book design and composition by Wendy Holdman
at Stanton Publication Services, St. Paul.

Printed by Maple-Vail, Binghamton, New York.

CPSIA information can be obtained
at www.ICGtesting.com
Printed in the USA
BVOW04s1004111017
497379BV00003B/9/P